ORNAMENTALISM

Ornamentalism

Anne Anlin Cheng

Oxford University Press is a department of the University of Oxford. It furthers the University's objective of excellence in research, scholarship, and education by publishing worldwide. Oxford is a registered trade mark of Oxford University Press in the UK and in certain other countries

Published in the United States of America by Oxford University Press
198 Madison Avenue, New York, NY 10016, United States of America

First issued as an Oxford University Press paperback, 2021.

This publication is made possible in part from the Barr Ferree Foundation Fund for Publications, Department of Art and Archaeology, Princeton University.

Library of Congress Cataloging-in-Publication Data
Names: Cheng, Anne Anlin, author.
Title: Ornamentalism / Anne Anlin Cheng.
Description: New York : Oxford University Press, 2019. | Includes bibliographical references and index.
Identifiers: LCCN 2018027099

Hardback ISBN: 9780190604615
Paperback ISBN: 9780197599778

Cloth ISBN: 9780190604615
UPDF ISBN: 9780190604622
EPUB ISBN: 9780190604639

Subjects: LCSH: Femininity. | Asians.
Classification: LCC BF175.5.F45 C485 2019 | DDC 155.3/33089951—dc23 LC record available at https://lccn.loc.gov/2018027099

The manufacturer's authorised representative in the EU for product safety is Oxford University Press España S.A. of El Parque Empresarial San Fernando de Henares, Avenida de Castilla, 2 – 28830 Madrid (www.oup.es/en or product.safety@oup.com). OUP España S.A. also acts as importer into Spain of products made by the manufacturer.

For my mother and my daughter

Contents

Preface ix
Acknowledgments xv

Introduction 1

1. Borders and Embroidery 26

2. Gleaming Things 61

3. Blue Willow 86

4. Edible Pets 107

5. Dolls 127

Coda: Chokecherry 152

NOTES 159
WORKS CITED 187
INDEX 197

Preface: A Feminist Theory of the Yellow Woman

WE SAY *BLACK women, brown women, white women*, but not *yellow women.* Is it because this last category is no longer relevant? Or is it because this outdated locution, rooted in nineteenth-century racial nomenclature, names something inadmissible, what is very much a mute but live animus in our world today? From museums to movies, fashion houses to science fiction, the boardroom to the bedroom, this highly fabricated figure and the particular kind of designed femininity that she evokes haunt and fuel American imaginations about persons and nonpersons. Even as the label of the "yellow woman" fades from contemporary parlance, the Asiatic figure that it denotes still stimulates passion and derision in multiple sectors of everyday life. How is it that a figure so encrusted with racist and sexist meaning, so ubiquitously deployed to this day and so readily recognized as a symptom, should at the same time be a theoretical black hole, a residue of critical fatigue?

In *The Erotic Life of Racism*, Sharon Patricia Holland speaks of the "woman of color," specifically the queer black body, as a "dead zone," by which she gestures to the impasse between recognition and reification.[1] Amber Jamilla Musser, too, has noted that the "woman of color"—primarily represented for Musser by the black woman and the crisis of "black flesh"—is a stalled category that marks "historical wrongs [that are] not assimilated into a political future."[2] But when it comes to the community of racialized women, some zones are deader than others and in different ways. With a rich array of groundbreaking theoretical ventures from Hortense

Spillers, Alex Weheliye, Jayna Brown, Kimberly Juanita Brown, and Musser, just to name a few key figures among many others, the "black woman" and "black female flesh" are far from critically lifeless, while the broader category of "woman of color" teeters dangerously close to the tiresome, a category of critical exhaustion that in fact has never come to full life.

The racialized logic of feminism itself has always been a thorny issue for feminists dedicated to the ideals of coalition and collaboration.[3] In critiquing the racialized logic of the politics of intersectionality, Jasbir Puar observes:

> [*Women of color*] has now become . . . simultaneously emptied of specific meaning in its ubiquitous application and yet overdetermined in its deployment. In this usage, intersectionality always produces an Other, and that Other is always a Woman of Color (now on referred to as WOC, to underscore the overdetermined emptiness of its gratuitousness), who must invariably be shown to be resistant, subversive, or articulating grievance. More pointedly, it is the difference of African American Women that dominates the genealogy of the term *women of color*. Indeed, [Kimberlé Crenshaw] . . . makes it clear that she centralizes "black women's experience." . . . Thus, the insistent consolidation of intersectionality as a dominant heuristic may well be driven by anxieties about maintaining the "integrity" of a black feminist genealogy.[4]

I suggest that the critical impoverishment surrounding the WOC is particularly concentrated for the yellow woman, whose fraught access to the complicated "privilege" of injury demands a different kind of attention and whose peculiar form of corporeality and synthetic personhood—so historically, materially, and imaginatively distinct—demands that we think differently.

In the invidious history of race and gender, we have spoken much about how people have been turned into things, but we should also attend to how things have been turned into people and how that conflation impacts our very understanding of what constitutes things and persons. This project draws on feminist theory, race studies, aesthetic philosophy, and new materialism, but it also aims to attend to the aporias that have been created in their wake. Given the extensive, historic discrimination leveled at the yellow woman, it is startling how the bulk of feminist theory—French feminism, white feminism, black feminism—has overlooked this figure beyond granting it its nominal pathology. I use the term y*ellow woman*, rather than *Asian woman in the West* or *Asian American woman*, because these more ameliorative, politically acceptable terms do not conjure the queasiness of this inescapably racialized and gendered figure. I am not so much interested in recuperating "yellowness" as a gesture of political defiance as I am intent on grasping the genuine dilemma of its political exception. What does it mean to survive as someone too aestheticized to suffer injury but so aestheticized that she invites injury?

What makes the yellow woman the exception in the larger category of WOC is precisely the precariousness of her injury, a fact at once taken for granted and questionable. This figure is so suffused with representation that she is invisible, so encrusted by aesthetic expectations that she need not be present to generate affect, and so well known that she has vanished from the zone of contact. Given that the reality of the woman of color has long been reduced to the volume of her *ressentiment*—and even there—the yellow woman remains mute and absent. In our contemporary culture of grievance, itself gendered (women "complain" while men "identify problems"), anger seems to be the one emotion that grants the woman of color visibility on the sociopolitical stage. Yet while many people might say that they are familiar with or have met the "angry black woman" or the "angry brown woman," they rarely speak of the angry yellow woman. This is not because she does not exist, but because jagged rage has not been in keeping with the style of her aesthetic congealment. At most, Asian female anger exists on the American public stage in a peripheral, miniaturized, and cutified cartoon version (consider Lela Lee's *Angry Little Girls*), or only seems to register in public consciousness when it appears in the form of internalized rage (consider the Tiger Mom).[5] Insofar as American culture has always been more at ease with grievance than grief, as I have long argued, racial identity in this country seems to garner recognition only when it can marshal sufficient indignation.[6] We accept *black* and *brown*, these brutish categories of color, as denominating categories of injury, but *yellowness* feels too ugly and crude to use. Such perverse delicateness seems to speak directly to the particular problem of yellow womanhood as a condition of denigration and violence that peculiarly and insistently speaks through the language of aesthetic privilege.

Is the yellow woman injured—or is she injured enough? The fact that such a question can be and is constantly being asked signals something of her exceptionality. To answer no is to ignore the past and the present, to exercise what Toni Morrison would call willful blindness ("It requires hard work *not* to see").[7] To answer yes is to consign this figure to what Wendy Brown in *States of Injury* has identified as the numbing quarantine of perpetual, political *ressentiment*. More than exemplifying the double-edged sword of racial damage in American politics, the yellow woman also makes visible another unspeakable aspect of injury: its unnerving capacity to be seen as a quality of beauty and to incite appreciation. There are few figures who exemplify the beauty of abjectness more than the yellow woman, whose condition of objectification is often the very hope for any claims she might have to value or personhood. We thus cannot talk about yellow female flesh without also engaging a history of material-aesthetic productions. The yellow woman's history is entwined with the production and fates of silk, ceramics, celluloid, machinery, and other forms of animated objectness.

This project accounts for the yellow woman *as hybrid*: present/absent, organic/synthetic, a figure of civilizational value and a disposable object of decadence. Her corporeality raises issues of mattering more than enfleshment. From Donaldina Cameron and other white missionaries during the Progressive Era to Julia Kristeva to Zhang Yimou, there has been no shortage of rescue missions aimed at the yellow woman. Yet as a wise friend said in response to this observation, it is as if none of these saviors, including the real Chinese man above, has ever met a real Chinese woman.[8] At the same time, it seems to me that the answer is not to insist on the realness of this figure. As we know, claims of the "real" and the "authentic" can impose coercions of their own. Critics from Peggy Pascoe to Rey Chow have long demonstrated how the progressive agenda—past and present, moralistic and political—has re-essentialized and reconscripted the Asian woman in the name of liberation.[9]

I propose that we come at the problem from a different angle and focus not on the real Asian or Asian American woman but instead on the very real formation of her ghost in Euro-American culture: the yellow woman. I want to blow up into large relief and distill the aesthetic schemas, both invidious and recuperative, that have come to incorporate, precondition, and structure yellow femininity in order to understand and acknowledge the conditions and consequences of living as an *aesthetic being*. Let us then encounter this figure *as* figure, a composite, with all its uncanny components. This figure generates a set of oppositions with lingering consequences that continue to live but are rarely confronted. For me, these consequences produce a series of substantive, corrosive, and ineffable afterlives, but they also carry the potential to direct us toward reconceptualizing alternative modes of ontology and personhood altogether. Indeed, the larger gambit of this project is to position this figure not only as a blind spot in feminist and race studies but also as a vital and transformative figure, rather than merely "the other," in the genealogy of modern, Western personhood.

I do not wish to sidestep the concerns of the real. I hope that it is not necessary for me to rehearse the authenticity controversy, galvanized by the famous debate between Maxine Hong Kingston and Frank Chin, that earmarked the identity politics of Asian American studies in the eighties. Approaching the real or the experiential requires thoughtfulness and nuance. In writing about the yellow woman, I recognize that I invariably raise the issue of "real women" and "real lived experiences." On the one hand, I am wary of this focus's ability to slip facilely into assumptions or claims of authenticity, especially when traces of many of the nonfictional female subjects under analysis in this book are missing from archives: women whose biographies cannot be retrieved, whose lived presences in history exist only as representations. On the other hand, I think that this absence—this "undocumentedness"—is a critical and constitutive part of Asiatic women's lived experiences. Thus while it is important to not forget lived experiences, I want to tread cautiously with regard to addressing them, just as I think the hegemony of representation is profoundly bound up with, not independent from, real lives.

Moreover, behind the question of the real is often a larger, implicit anxiety about the political efficacy of critical analysis, that is, whether theory helps real women. Yet insofar as feminist theory can be said to have affected the lived experiences of women, to generate serious theorization about Asiatic feminism is surely important. At the same time, I strongly resist the divide between "theory" and "politics." Much of my work has been occupied by the uneasy meeting place between aesthetics and politics. What happens in seemingly immaterial realms of imaginative cultural production not only is a reflection of material culture and history but also may provide important vocabularies or perspectives not accommodated by standard political stances. I am more interested in understanding *the political* than in prescribing politics. This, then, is not a manual that teaches Asian and Asian American women how to act. But by tracing the complex dynamics between subjecthood and objecthood, we might begin to shake loose some of our most fundamental assumptions about what kind of person, what kind of injury, or, indeed, what kind of life can count.

This project is about wounds that the indifferent public, the impatient legal system, the well-intentioned liberal, and sometimes even our loved ones tell us are no longer wounds. I aim to theorize a condition of denigration so profound and expansive that it could go unsaid or unnoted even as it lives, produces a great deal of beauty, and enacts violence. This book presents a willful encounter with yellow femininity as persistent, brutal, exquisite style. This is a fight song that wishes to take head on, not simply deny or decry, the object conditions on which yellow womanhood has been built.

Acknowledgments

IT FEELS LIKE my whole adult life has been a series of negotiations leading to this book. The last couple of years have brought challenges that shook my belief in my ability to finish this very personal project. But a group of big-hearted interlocutors have kept me buoyed with their warmth and insights: Elizabeth Anker, Greg Blatman, Hazel Carby, Allison Carruth, the Honorable Judge Denny Chin, Michelle Coghlan, Zahid Chaudhary, Mo Chen, Jill Dolan, Michele Elam, Judith Hamera, William Gleason, Eric Hayot, Regina Kunzel, Rachel Lee, David Miller, Tim Murray, Sianne Ngai, Kinohi Nishikawa, Jeff Nunakawa, Carolyn Rouse, Kyla Tompkins, Sarah Wasserman, and Henry Yu. Each of these individuals has given me flashes of light and delight that I treasure. Deborah Prentice, Provost of Princeton University, gave me time and space when I desperately needed it. The editors at *Critical Inquiry*, *The Los Angeles Review of Books*, *PMLA*, and *Resilience*, which published sections of this project in earlier incarnations, were extremely helpful; I am especially grateful to Lauren Berlant and Anna Shechtman for their generous and wise editorial hand in refining not just my argument but my thinking. I thank my family in the Program in American Studies: Dirk Hartog, whose wisdom I lean on almost every day, has taught me much about how to be a teacher and a force for good; Judith Ferszt and Candice Kessel have enabled me in countless ways. Kim Bain supplied superlative research skills and valued camaraderie.

Several friends read sections of the manuscript and, in some cases, the entire manuscript: Jason Friedman, Bob Hass, Sharon Marcus, and Valentina Vavasis. I have been relying on them for years for their brilliant, expansive, and unique insights, and I am more grateful for their enduring friendships that I can ever say. Saidiya Hartman continues to be a source of inspiration and strength in work and in life: thank you for giving me the courage to say the thing that needed to be said and for pushing me beyond my curmudgeon tendencies.

This book is dedicated to my mother, Mei-Yin Cheng, and my daughter, Anlin Samantha Kopf. I hope what I have written here pays tribute to the former and helps the latter in negotiating this world. And, to the two Georges in my life, all my love always.

ORNAMENTALISM

Introduction

IS THERE ROOM in the dehumanizing history of race to talk about a figure whose survival is secured through crushing objecthood?

This study argues there is a distinct kind of human figure whose endurance and enchantment entail a fusion between synthetic objecthood and organic personhood in ways that demand a fundamental reconceptualization of what Frantz Fanon has named the "racial epidermal schema."[1] Our principal, though not exclusive, case study for this human formation—ornamental, at once abstract and material, embodied and disembodied—will be the yellow woman. This designation is not meant to essentialize but to name the processes of racialization, with all their historic and living force, that adhere to the Asian/Asian American woman in American culture. The term *yellow woman* denotes a person but connotes a style, promising yet supplanting skin and flesh, an insistently aesthetic presence that is prized and despoiled. The particularity of this kind of object-person who is radically undone yet luminously constructed—that is, meticulously and aesthetically composed yet degraded and disposable—troubles some of our deeply held, politically cherished notions of agency, racial embodiment, subjecthood, and ontology.

While widely acknowledged as one of the oldest and most commonplace figures of sexist and racist denigration, the yellow woman remains largely absent from critical theory. As Maitreye Chaudhuri laments, when it comes to Asian American feminist scholarship, there is "a rich body of writing on women's activism on the one hand and a sparseness of *theoretical* writing on the other."[2] This is not to say that there has not been vibrant, if not widely recognized, Asian American feminist activism, a social and political movement accompanied by groundbreaking works from writers, scholars, and artists, especially in the 1980s and 90s. But Asian American critical feminism remains hampered by the divide between practice and theory. If Asian American feminist theory feels stuck in the first wave, and if the mere mention of the Asian woman these days invokes critical fatigue, it is partially due to this stubborn gulf, not to mention the ongoing suspicion of so-called Western, universalizing theory, even though, when it comes to an other who has been deeply woven into and out of the history of Western aesthetic history, it is misleading and unproductive to continue to think in terms of Western abstraction versus Eastern reality. Indeed, decades of symptomatic and redemptive readings have reproduced this figure as always and only a subject of *ressentiment* with all the limits of this critique, as Wendy Brown has diagnosed for women's studies in general over two decades ago.[3] Unlike the shattered "fact of blackness," which has been recomposed for the mournful black subject through a rich body of theoretical gambits (Fanon, Spillers, Weheliye, Musser, and more), the "fact of yellowness" remains an active myth that enjoys no critical stature and whose cultural capital, if we can call it that, remains the source of its dismissal.[4]

We have yet to look closely at the strange figuration of the yellow woman because she/it stirs up a set of embattled issues that have always haunted feminism: the distressing affinity that can exist between agency and complicity, antiessentialism and authenticity, and affirmation and reification.[5] Exemplifying a symptom that is neglected by being all-too-known, she stands to the side of a prevalent contemporary feminist and racial discourse centered on the "injured flesh," which has not been as attentive to a racial and gendered figure whose fleshliness survives through abstract and synthetic rather than organic means, and whose personhood is animated through, rather than eviscerated by, aesthetic congealment.

Simultaneously consecrated and desecrated as an inherently aesthetic object, the yellow woman calls for a theorization of persons and things that considers a human ontology inextricable from synthetic extensions, art, and commodity. Instead of being pure capture or representing fugitive flight from the nominative biological or anatomical raced body, the yellow woman emerges as a "body ornament" whose perihumanity demands that we approach ontology, fleshliness, and aliveness differently. By perihumanity, I mean to identify the peculiar in-and-out position, the peripherality and the proximity of the Asiatic woman to the ideals of the human and the feminine. At once closely linked to ideas of ancient civilizational values and yet far removed from the core of Western humanist considerations, she circles but is excluded from humanity. She represents feminine values but is often not considered a woman at all. In *Ariel's Ecology: Plantations, Personhood, and Colonialism in the American Tropics*, Monique Allewaert offers us an evocative account of another kind of interstitial being, what she calls the "parahumanity" of Africans and Afro-Americans, who were also not considered human beings while not being precisely inhuman. Allewaert explains, "I put animals, parahumans, and humans in horizontal relation (that is to say, *para* or beside each other) without conflating them.... Afro-Americans drew on the brutal colonial circumstance of dismemberment and bodily disaggregation to produce models of personhood that developed from the experience of parahumanity and in relation to animal bodies."[6] I am interested in thinking about the yellow woman as a comparable form of interstitial life, but in intimate relation more to objects than to animal life, and with a body that is not so much disaggregated as thickly encrusted. If black parahumanity by way of Allewaert offers us a way to consider the potential of "a condition of fragmentation between the human and the animal," then seeing the perihumanity of yellow womanhood enables us to theorize an ontological condition produced out of synthetic accretions that challenge the very division between the living and the nonliving.[7]

If we are willing to confront the life of a subject who lives as an object, then we will arrive not at an easy politics, but rather at an alternative track within the making of modern Western personhood, one that is not traceable to the ideal of a biological, organized, and masculine body bequeathed from a long line of Enlightenment thinkers, but is instead peculiarly synthetic, aggregated, feminine, and non-European. I trace this alternative figure and its spectral archaeology across a wide range of domains: law, politics, art, theater, literature, and popular culture. And I offer a theoretical frame that I call *ornamentalism* in order to turn our focus to the peripheral and the supplemental and to explore the transitive properties of persons and things. I want to track the incarnations of Asiatic femininity in Western modernity and its expansive embroilment with the ornamental and the Oriental. This figure embodies what Achille Mbembe calls the "aesthetics of superfluity": that fragile mediation between indispensability and expendability that informs labor and life, especially at the height of imperialism and the subsequent global movements of bodies and things.[8] This book is a story about what I am calling *ornamental personhood* and how it brings into view a much broader, often unseen, genealogy within the making of modern Western personhood. This is also a story about a different kind of flesh in the history of race making.

In order to lay out this alternative lineage, I braid two discursive histories: on the one hand, the vast material and representational history that is the "yellow woman"; on the other, the long, expansive Western philosophic debate about moral and social value engendered by the ornament.

THE YELLOW WOMAN

She goes by many names: Celestial Lady, Lotus Blossom, Dragon Lady, Yellow Fever, Slave Girl, Geisha, Concubine, Butterfly, China Doll, Prostitute. She is carnal and delicate, hot and cold, corporeal and abstract, a full and empty signifier. Here I echo and depart from Hortense Spillers's memorable opening to "Mama's Baby, Papa's Maybe: An American Grammar Book" in order to suggest that, in addition to black female flesh, we should also attend to yellow objecthood as alternative American racial logic.[9] Instead of seeing the overnaming of the yellow woman as confounding identity or authenticity, I offer a different grammar as a provocation about the hybrid that is ornamental Asiatic femininity. What if we were to take the collusion between abstraction and racial embodiment as the given condition of Asiatic femininity? And what if, instead of seeing this amalgamation as eccentric to the conceptualization of a modern personhood, we were to see this peculiar figure as its constitutive double? That is, philosophically speaking, Western modern personhood as inherited from the Enlightenment is generally understood to be organic, individualistic, masculine, and white. Yet in the everyday practice of the courtroom, the boardroom, the bedroom, and the cutting room, that ideal has always been deeply embroiled with, not just opposed to, a history of nonpersons. Scholars of American slavery have long pointed out the legal and philosophic challenges posed by the enslaved person, for instance. Here I suggest that synthetic Asiatic femininity is another such constitutive strand in the making of modern personhood and that, alongside the black enslaved body, we must also consider the synthetic Asiatic woman as a ghost in the machine.

What happens when we consider ornamental forms and fungible surfaces, rather than organic flesh, as foundational terms in the process of race making? For a long time now, there have been two primary frameworks through which many of us conceptualize racial embodiment: Frantz Fanon's "epidermal racial schema" and Spillers's "hieroglyphics of the flesh."[10] The former denaturalizes black skin as the product of a shattering white gaze; the latter has been particularly powerful in training our gaze on the black female body and the ineluctable matter of ungendered, jeopardized flesh. Yet in the years since its revolutionary impact, has the "epidermal racial schema" hardened for us into a thing of untroubled legibility? To what extent have the "hieroglyphics of the flesh" prevented us from seeing an alternative materialism of the body?

Saidean Orientalism and the Foucauldian critique that it entails have not been able to focus on the peculiar materiality of Asiatic, female flesh, its impossibilities and possibilities. Encrusted by representations, abstracted and reified, the yellow woman is persistently sexualized yet barred from sexuality, simultaneously made and unmade by the aesthetic project. Like the proverbial Ming vase, she is at once ethereal and base, an object of value and a hackneyed trope. Like the black woman, she has suffered a long history of painful denigration; she, too, has been enslaved, abused, mummified, spectacularized, and sold. Yet her discursive construct is qualitatively different. Consider the two iconic nineteenth-century images of racialized femininity in plates 1 and 2. On the one hand, Sarah "Saartjie" Baartman, the so-called Hottentot Venus (plate 1),[11] was reduced to bare flesh, what Spillers calls "the zero degree of social conceptualization"; on the other hand, Afong Moy, a young Chinese woman imported by the Carne Brothers and later taken over by P. T. Barnum to tour major U.S. cities in the 1830s–1850s as a living museum tableau and known simply as the Chinese Lady (plate 2), offered a scopic pleasure that centered on her textual thickness: her material, synthetic affinities.[12] The latter's appeal does not derive from her naked flesh but from her decorative (and projected ontological) sameness to the silk, damask, mahogany, and ceramics alongside which she sits. While primitivism rehearses the rhetoric of ineluctable flesh, Orientalism, by contrast, relies on a decorative grammar, a phantasmic corporeal syntax that is artificial

PLATE 1: *Love and Beauty—Sartjee the Venus Hottentot* (1811). Hand-colored etching. Christopher Crupper Rumford, Courtesy of Library of Congress, Prints and Photographs Division.

PLATE 2: Afong Moy, *The Chinese Lady* (1835). The Miriam and Ira D. Wallach Division of Art, Prints and Photographs. Courtesy of New York Public Library Digital Collection.

and layered. If black femininity has been viciously erased by a cultural logic that has reduced it to, in Spillers's words, "transitional mere flesh," then yellow femininity has been persistently presented as something more like portable supraflesh.[13] Spillers famously observed that, since the black female is barred from crossing the symbolic threshold into personification, she is stuck on the threshold dividing the human and the not human, rendering her "vestibular to culture."[14] Where black femininity is *vestibular*, Asiatic femininity is *ornamental*.

To put it crudely, our models for understanding racialized gender have been predominantly influenced by a particular view of bodies of African origins that has led us to think in a certain way about raced female bodies, when there has been in fact something of a bifurcation within the racial imaginary between bare flesh and artificial ornament. These two aesthetic vocabularies are clearly both racialized, but they do *not* necessarily or even primarily index racial identities. In fact, the predominant trope of "black female flesh" has at times kept us from seeing those black female bodies that have thrived through *un*fleshliness. (Josephine Baker, a figure I have studied elsewhere, in *Second Skin*, provides an example of how the dominant trope of black female flesh has prevented us from seeing the complex fabrication that is her "skin.") Thus while critical race theory and black feminism have done the vital work of reminding us that the black woman has been reduced to bare flesh, those insights have not been as helpful in theorizing the figure of the racialized woman who is assiduously assembled.

The point here is not to posit a naturalized difference between Africanist and Asiatic femininities. Indeed, my argument will insist on the promiscuousness of these modes of racialized representations, as well as ultimately suggesting that both Orientalism and primitivism draw from technologies of ornamentalism. But in order to follow these intricate turns, however, we must first specify a racial imaginary that has been at once pervasive and taken for granted. The tying of ornamental artifice to Asiatic femininity in Euro-American visual and literary cultures is ancient and persistent, reaching as far back as Plato, through the writings of Marco Polo in the thirteenth century, the novels of Joris-Karl Huysmans and Oscar Wilde, the visual expressions of art nouveau, French symbolism, American rococo, and all the way up to wide-ranging iterations in the twentieth and twenty-first centuries (plates 3–15). Throughout this study, we will continue to revisit, revise, and extend this visual repertoire, but for now let us allow this vast archive to sink in.

PLATE 3: Gustav Klimt, *Woman with Fan* (1917–1918). Wikimedia Commons.

PLATE 4: Aubrey Beardsley, *The Peacock Skirt, or John the Baptizer and Salomé* (1894). Created for Oscar Wilde's *Salome* by the artist. Line black print on Japanese vellum, the Victoria and Albert Museum.

PLATE 5: Henri Privat-Livemont, *Bitter Oriental* (1897). Public domain.

PLATE 6: Claude Monet, *La Japonaise/Camille Monet in Japanese Costume* (1876). Public domain.

PLATE 7: Georges Barbier, *Chez la Marchande de Pavots/At the Poppy Merchants* (1921). Courtesy of British Library.

PLATE 8: James McNeill Whistler, *Purple and Rose: The Lange Leizen of the Six Marks* (detail, 1864). Courtesy of the John G. Johnson Collection, Philadelphia Museum of Art.

PLATE 9: Arnold Genthe, *Little Tea Rose* (1896–1906). Arnold Genthe Collection. Courtesy of Library of Congress, Prints and Photographs Division.

PLATE 10: Arnold Genthe, *A Slave Girl in Holiday Attire* (1896–1906). Arnold Genthe Collection. Courtesy of Library of Congress, Prints and Photographs Division.

PLATE 11: Anna May Wong in *Limehouse Blues* (1934, dir. Alexander Hall). Courtesy of Paramount Pictures.

PLATE 12: Photograph of Anna May Wong taken by Otto Dyer (1921). Courtesy of Kobal/Rex/Shutterstock.

PLATE 13: Li Gong in *The Curse of the Golden Flower* (2006, dir. Zhang Yimou). Beijing New Picture Film Co./Sony Pictures Classics. Screenshot capture by author.

PLATE 14: Maggie Cheung in *In the Mood for Love* (2000, dir. Wong Kar-wai). Universal Pictures, Paradise Film. Screenshot capture by author.

PLATE 15: Yves Saint Laurent and Tom Ford. Evening dress, autumn–winter 2004–2005. Yellow silk satin embroidered with polychrome plastic sequins. *China: Through the Looking Glass,* 2015, Metropolitan Museum of New York. Courtesy of Platon Images.

This extensive, racial-aesthetic, and ornamental project is both world-creating and world-erasing, making persons and undoing them. Most of all, it suggests that Asiatic femininity in the Western racial imagination does not need to pass through the biological or the natural in order to acquire its most palpable, fully sensorial, supple, and vibrant presence. It is astounding that so little has been done to consider the production of this particular form of synthetic personhood. Oppositional concepts such as authenticity versus illusion, interiority versus surface, and real person versus synthetic construct cannot adequately address this kind of figure. We have marshalled this vast and tenacious history under a broad heuristic that we might roughly label "Oriental female objectification," refracted through the lenses of commodity and sexual fetishism. Yet we barely know how to process the political, racial, and ontic complications of confronting a human figure that emerges *as* and *through* ornament.

To speak of Asiatic femininity, then, is to speak of a style, which claims specificity but lends itself to promiscuous transferability. It designates a specific racial category but can be applied to different racial subjects. It can be enlisted by those wielding power and, more disturbing, by those deprived of it. *It is an abstraction that materializes*. To recognize racial difference and ontology as style does not trivialize either but instead acknowledges that formalist abstraction can be a precondition for, not just a side effect or obfuscation of, the perception of embodiment. Race is a dream of embodiment that speaks, paradoxically, through abstract forms. As Galen Johnson, speaking of Maurice Merleau-Ponty and the insights of phenomenology, elegantly sums up, "all perception stylizes because embodiment is a style of the world."[15] And one consequence of this insight for our understanding of racial embodiment is that we must reconceive the ontological terms of human fleshliness.

Neither mere flesh nor mere thing, the yellow woman, straddling the person-thing divide, applies tremendous pressures on politically treasured notions of agency, feminist enfleshment, and human ontology. What we need, then, is not just an account of how Asiatic people have been used as things, or how Oriental things have influenced our uses of them, but instead a conceptual paradigm that can accommodate the deeper, stranger, more intricate, and more ineffable (con)fusion between thingness and personness instantiated by Asiatic femininity and its unpredictable object life.

THE ORNAMENT

The history and discourse of racialized femininity are deeply embroiled with the larger philosophic history of the ornament, its complicated relation to modernity, and its enduring entanglement with the Asiatic. Like the yellow woman, the ornament is a category that, for all its glamour, has suffered a long history of denigration. In everyday usage, *ornament* refers to the insignificant, the superfluous, the merely decorative, the shallow, and the excessive. In aesthetic-philosophic history, the ornament triggers heated debates about the differences between excrescence and essence, surface and interiority, the peripheral and the central, femininity and masculinity. From Plato's critique of bad mimesis to Immanuel Kant's Third Critique and beyond, the ornament in Western philosophy, while signaling material worth, has for the most part been seen as a distraction, leading us astray from true moral value and genuine beauty. Kant famously claimed that ornamentation/adornment/*parerga* is a form of inessential augmentation that "takes away from the genuine beauty." E. H. Gombrich warned against the ornament's dazzling effects to persuade "the mind to submit without reflection." Siegfried Kracauer and Walter Benjamin worried over the disenchantment produced by the mass ornament. Walt Whitman argued that "[m]ost works are most beautiful without ornament." And who could forget modernism's most terse denouncement, Adolf Loos's dictum that ornament is crime?[16] In this light, modernism's minimalist revolution, with its ardent de-ornamentation, is but a continuation of this ancient apprehension about the seduction of the ornament.

At the same time, this famous modernist rejection of the ornament is also something of a myth. As Theo Davis, Alina Payne, and I in different contexts have argued, the ornament and especially its spectral, racial demarcations, far from being exiled, continue to thrive in modern aesthetic practices even, or especially, for those most seemingly allergic to it.[17] In *Second Skin: Josephine Baker and the Modern Surface*, I traced the ways in which the so-called naked modern surface, instead of being an erasure of regressive racial markings, in fact actively recalls and re-materializes some of the most profound racial fantasies of the twentieth century, in particular, the fantasy of black skin. It was while researching that project that I first gleaned the much bigger picture triggered by the history of the ornament: its articulation of not only the "primitive" but also the "Oriental," and how it informs the way we think about the denuded modern surface and modern personhood itself.

While scholars (Naomi Schor, Mark Wigley) have observed how gendered the discourse of the ornament is from Plato to Kracauer, less attention has been paid to how deeply racialized and specifically Orientalized this history has been as well.[18] Since antiquity, the ornament has almost always been associated, even downright identified, with the Oriental and the Asiatic. In both *The Republic* and *The Laws*, Plato labeled excessive ornamentation as Oriental and despotic.[19] In the eighteenth century, William Warburton, bishop of Gloucester, in speaking of theatrical gestures, describes Oriental character as unduly dramatic.[20] And one can find musings about the monstrous ornamentality of the Chinese from eighteenth-century aesthetic debates about Protestant purity to Friedrich Schiller and Gottfried Semper. It is hardly surprising that by the nineteenth and twentieth centuries, men as diverse as Henry David Thoreau, Adolf Loos, and William Morris will come to predicate modern, masculinist, and nationalist Euro-American aesthetic character on the very rejection of the Oriental and the ornamental.

Thus even as pronouncements from J. C. Flügel's Great Masculine Renunciation to Le Corbusier's Law of Ripolin celebrate de-ornamentation, the ornament and especially the ornamentality of the Asiatic continue to provide a charged site for the modernists, precisely because the ornament triggers the fluctuation between essence and supplement, depth and surface, utility and decoration, interiority and exteriority, organicity and the inorganic, femininity and masculinity, and finally, Western discipline and Oriental excess. Far from dismissed, the Asiatic ornament and its impulse blossomed in the early twentieth century in the realms of culture, art, literature, law, philosophy, and even economic theory (think of Thorstein Veblen's notions of excess). In each realm, the glimmering appeal of the ornament encompasses an expansive discourse of racial difference that animates major strains of modernist thinking about gender, nationhood, the human, and the inhuman, in the senses of racial difference as well as synthetic fabrication.

The minor aesthetic category, to follow Sianne Ngai's lead, of Asiatic feminine ornamentality is therefore far from minor; it bears the traces of some of the deepest and broadest philosophic debates underpinning modernity.[21] It is nothing less than the very battleground on which struggles over beauty, racial and gender difference, and the boundary of the human are played. For me, then, the ornament resonates on multiple registers: as racialized material artifacts, as a linchpin in modernism's primal aesthetic crisis (itself also raced and gendered), as a struggle over the superfluity of persons and things, and as a problem about prosthetic humanness.

While the Western philosophic discourse surrounding the ornament, especially at the height of modernism, is expressly one of debasement,[22] it is nonetheless deeply drawn to the ornament, a paradox that reveals a tenacious and genuine struggle with the problem of beauty, its radiant debt to horror and defilement. We might say that the history of Western art from Titian's *Tarquin and Lucretia* to Pablo Picasso's *Guernica* has been endlessly preoccupied with how to come to terms with the meeting of beauty and brutality. But for the yellow woman, this *is* her (im)material condition. As a figure of artistic investment and racial denigration, the yellow woman bears the privileges as well as the penalties for being an aesthetic being.

Contrary to their promises otherwise, aesthetics and violence both enact experiences that distort the borders between subject and object, consumer and consumed. What kind of life subsists along those porous edges? What can action or agency look like for someone who emerges out of that unmaking? How does an economy of trivial things alter how we think about the indispensability and expendability that inform labor and life, people and things? For the yellow woman, politically treasured notions such as agency, consent, and embodiment take on complications that we have yet to really confront. When it comes to the defiled (raced and gendered) subject, caught in the haunting convergence between aesthetic experience and material abuse, it is not enough to say that she serves as a tool for power or its sublimation, or that she offers nothing but the congealment of commodification. Both statements are undoubtedly true, but neither is sufficient to address the profound, intrinsic, and often unspeakable ways in which the subjugator and the subjugated find themselves or meet each other in and through aesthetic forms.

When we attend to the critical labor of ornament, we will repeatedly find the intersection of beauty and terror, immateriality and corporeality, life and privation across a wide range of domains. Scars blossoming into the shocking beauty of chokecherry. Bare flesh growing like jewel shards. The law adjudicating legal persons through the sartorial. It is at the site of the unexpected entanglement with, or the inconvenient animation of, the ornament during moments of intense pain and privation that we begin to discern how the ornament as aesthetic decoration marks a political problematic about personhood.

The resistance against objectification almost always returns to the reconstitution of the person, just as the reparation for injuries to the body invariably seeks to re-privilege the flesh. I am interested in pursuing a different line of inquiry. I want to inquire after bodies that refuse the ontology or embodiment imputed to them, as well as those bodies that never get these options. This book is about a defiance of objectification that results in more objectness, a consequence that alters the very logic of racial embodiment as we know it and leads to much messier and more uncanny modes of materialization. It also shakes our assumptions about personhood and its often unacknowledged indebtedness to objecthood.

Let us think through, rather than shy away from, that intractable intimacy between being a person and being a thing. Let us try to build a different historiography of raced bodies: one constructed through fabrics, ornaments, and "skins" that never enjoyed the fantasy of organicity; one populated by nonsubjects who endure as ornamental appendages. Let us substitute *ornament* for *flesh* as the germinal matter for the making of racialized gender. Let us, in short, formulate a feminist theory of and for the yellow woman.

ORNAMENTALISM

I propose *ornamentalism* as a conceptual framework for approaching a history of racialized person-making, not through biology but through synthetic inventions and ornamentations. First, ornamentalism names the critically conjoined presences of the *Oriental* and the *ornamental*. Second and more importantly, ornamentalism describes the peculiar processes (legally, materially, imaginatively) whereby *personhood is named or conceived through ornamental gestures*, which speak through the minute, the sartorial, the prosthetic, and the decorative. We can find various examples of subject-as-object enchantment through the nineteenth and twentieth centuries, but Asiatic female ornamentality provides one of the richest, broadest, and most intense sources of power for this alchemy.

Since the mid-nineteenth century, art historians have used the term "ornamentalism" to refer to the deployment of ornament for decorative purposes, especially when done in excess.[23] I, however, wish to resuscitate what seems to have gone completely unheard so far in the term's evocation: its almost homophonic resonance with Orientalism. As noted above, the intertwining of the Orient in the history of the ornament has largely gone critically unnoted even as it has always exerted its force. Recently the term *ornamentalism* enjoyed a revival thanks to historian David Cannadine's intriguing study *Ornamentalism: How the British Saw Their Empire*. Yet even there, the sonic and semiotic residue of Orientalism behind the term remains mute. This is because Cannadine argues that class, more than race, provided the lens through which Britain imagined its empire hierarchically. His project is thus not interested in the racial imaginary or even in the ornament per se, since ornamentalism for Cannadine refers broadly to a set of social rituals.[24] But I believe that retrieving the Oriental logic of ornamentation and, conversely, the ornamental technologies of Orientalism will open up important conversations about some of the most basic terms structuring our notions of race, persons, and the human, as well as the categories of modernism and Orientalism.

Orientalism is a critique, ornamentalism a theory of being. The latter, for me, names the perihumanity of Asiatic femininity, a peculiar state of being produced out of the fusion between "thingliness" and "personness." As such, ornamentalism often describes a condition of subjective coercion, reduction, and discipline, but it can *also* provoke considerations of alternative modes of being and of action for subjects who have not been considered subjects, or subjects who have come to know themselves through objects. The making of personhood through synthetic assemblage or accretion can be impoverishing and additive. It can produce a person-assemblage that destroys autonomy but one that disrupts the privileged notion of natural bodies as well. It encapsulates a history of dehumanization, but it also speaks to a desire for objectness in the dream of the human. Ornamentalism thus offers us a capacious theoretical rubric by which to attend to the afterlife of a racialized and aestheticized subject that remains very much an object, even as the human stakes remain chillingly high.

The political stakes of "ornamentalist personhood" emerge beyond the dichotomies that normally inform our discussions about race, social justice, and the primacy of the human for both: dichotomies such as subject/object, interiority/exteriority, agency/oppression. To attend to ornamentalism is to ask how racial personhood can be assembled not through organic flesh but instead through synthetic inventions and designs, not through corporeal embodiment but rather through attachments that are metonymic and hence superficial, detachable, and migratory. Parsing the transformative magic of ornamentalism will allow us to address those bodies that, even as they are being deprived of it, do not seek humanity; to acknowledge those bodies that repel rather than instantiate the attempts to equip them with psychic or corporeal interiority. Ornamentalism thus serves as a critical framework through which I track this haunting alchemy between persons and things and its strange products.

This account of ornamentalism differs conceptually from an existing body of scholarship on sartorial performance or self-decoration as intentional or redemptive acts of self-affirmation. In lieu of traditional notions of agency, ornamentalism helps us address the unexpected, perhaps even unspeakable, forms and residues of ontology and survival. It is easy to identify the wrongness of treating someone like a thing for one's own invidious gains, but it is much harder to understand or to judge when one treats oneself like a thing. In making room for stranger forms of less-than-human agency that might erupt out of these moments of ornamentalist transformation, I hope to clear some new ground beyond the political cul-de-sacs of feminist and race studies: the impasse between victimization and agency, antiessentialism and authenticity, and so on. Ornamentalism for me poses less a dilemma of identity than a problematic about the imbrication of personhood and materialization. *Ornamentalism* is therefore an admittedly inelegant word that names an elegant—that is to say, seamless—alchemy between things and persons. Those of us invested in the critique of power have long been alert to the crisis of persons who have been turned into things, but we should also attend to the ways in which things have been taken for persons and how this impacts our ideas about human ontology and aliveness. If, on the one hand, race studies have, understandably, been overinvested in the redemption of the flesh, and if, on the other, new materialism has too quickly abandoned or neglected the human stakes, this study hopes to open a conversation in that lacuna.

The goals of taking this insidious elision between the Oriental and the ornamental as the foundation for a yellow feminist theory are, therefore: (1) to detach us from the ideal of a natural and an agential personhood that invariably accompanies critiques of power and from which the Asiatic woman is already always foreclosed; (2) to take seriously what it means to live as an object, an aesthetic supplement; (3) to attend to peripheral and alternative modes of ontology and survival; (4) and finally, to contend that the discourse of Asiatic femininity—at once pervasive and marginal, enhancing and disparaging, dated and yet contemporary—is part of a much larger debate about beauty and violence, as well as about life and artificiality, nestled in the making of modern Euro-American personhood.

So what does ornamentalism allow us to see that an understanding of Orientalism alone does not? Let us return in plate 16 to the iconic Victorian image of "the Chinese Lady." Little is known about her; even the accuracy of her Chinese name is dubious.[25] At the level of fact, there is no rescuing her; she is lost to history. At the level of theory, she remains reified. Psychoanalytic fetishism, for one, would tell us that this is a scene of lack and compensation: Moy's racial and sexual lack has been displaced onto her sartorial splendor even as it is iterated through her bound feet, which are neatly and conspicuously displayed on a little stool. Marxist fetishism would train our gaze on the proliferation of commodified objects. Indeed, every object in this room—the chintz, the silk, the mahogany or rosewood implied by the furniture, the tea, the sugar, the porcelain, and of course the Asian woman herself—is saturated with colonial and imperial history.

PLATE 16: Afong Moy, *The Chinese Lady* (1835). The Miriam and Ira D. Wallach Division of Art, Prints and Photographs. Courtesy of New York Public Library Digital Collection.

Historians of American Orientalism (John Kuo Wei Tchen, Lisa Lowe, Teemu Ruskola, Colleen Lye, Josephine Park, among others) have well documented the instrumental role that the uses of people and things from Asia in real and imagined forms have played in the formation of American modern politics, economy, cityscapes, cultural identity, and citizenship; the construction of notions of class and taste since the early colonials; the so-called China Trade's foundational role during the American Revolution in inaugurating the birth of "American free trade" and supplying the rationale for the articulation of American liberation and manifest destiny; the great wealth that built great modern American cities like New York and Boston (or famous East Coast universities like my own home institution); the exploitation of Asian labor in the construction of American agriculture and landscape; the segregation and discipline of Asian bodies in America providing the crucible for the formation of modern U.S. citizenship; the formative role of so-called Asian aesthetics in modern American arts and letters; and, finally, the enormous contemporary American appetite for "Asian styles" from the cute to the erotic. Against this extensive backdrop, it should not surprise us that the staging of Afong Moy in the nineteenth century presents an instantiation of the ghostlier demarcations that lie behind much more mainstream Victorian representations of white femininity, especially when the latter becomes conflated with commodity culture. Think, for example, of Becky Sharp posed for sale in the drawing room with her silk shawl and damasked cotton and her notable "small feet" on display.[26] Or consider Lily Bart's intense spiritual materialism in the face of an exquisite tea service.[27]

At the same time, this expansive history of commodification—and the extensive critical attention is has received—has nonetheless *not* been able to accommodate the more unwieldy interface between consumer and consumed. The paradigm of "Oriental fetishism," while accurate enough, cannot address the strange life and the unpredictable encounters bred by this history of global exchange. What if, instead of seeing this scene as the petrification of Orientalism, we were to attend to the animation of ornamentalism?

The lady in question here is part of a composition of objects revolving around a dynamic exchange between foreground and background, skin and fabric, persons and things. This still tableau is very much alive. The immobile lady's ontological promise, her imagined interiority, is not just framed but also deeply infused by the built environment. Even as her "interiority" has presumably been displaced by flat surfaces—indeed, textiles—there is nonetheless an affective, sensorial, and semiotic reciprocity at work in this scene. She accessorizes the furnishings, while the furnishings accessorize her; she lends the human element to this theater even as the props lend her a human domesticity. The sitting woman repeats the two "Chinese" figures behind her, themselves European replicas of Chinese paintings.[28] This "human" triptych is in turn echoed by the teapot and lone cup, both surely empty, on the table, reminding us that a woman's close proximity to "china" allows her to be read as a particular kind of surface: perfectly contained, perfectly empty, but also perfectly coextensive.[29] I will say more, especially in the chapter on blue willow (chapter 3), about the semiotic conductivity of china; for now I simply wish to underscore how this highly recursive scene offers a fantasy about the interchangeability of persons and things. The subject here *is* tableau vivant: the art of transforming life into the paradox of still life. And the pleasure afforded by this scene—the piquant insistence of nonliving live things—is not fleshly indulgence but rather the naughty porousness between persons and things, the alluring satisfaction of ontological shallowness. It makes us wonder whether we enjoy still life because it imitates or eschews life.

Ornament becomes—*is*—flesh for Asian American female personhood. Commodification and fetishization, the dominant critical paradigms we have for understanding representations of racialized femininity, simply do not ask the harder question of what constitutes being at the interface of ontology and objectness. We need to find new ways to think about the entanglement of organic corporeality and aesthetic abstraction exemplified by yellow womanhood. How do we begin to think about racialized bodies that remain insistently synthetic and artificial? What about bodies not undone by objectness but enduring *as* objects?

The peculiar materialism and materiality of "yellow decorativeness" press us to reconsider the facticity of racialized presence. Simultaneously consecrated and desecrated, materialized and displaced, the yellow woman challenges us to formulate a humane politics that accommodates artifice and objectness. The history that I invite us to consider here delivers a particular production of personhood that calls for a different kind of reading and a new account of race making. The imbrication or transference between things and bodies—commodified, yes, but also always asked to act and emit "beingness"—demands that we understand commodities in transit as neither simply cargo nor easily translatable back into cherished human subjects.

This book aims to bring to light those mercurial moments when ornaments become skin and flesh; when superfluous details provide the conditions under which personhood is negotiated; when artificial matter animates the human. These moments relocate the cherished notion of life to a different juncture and open up opportunities for us to discern alternative modes of existence—sites of peripheral or interstitial being. We will witness the disciplinary and damaging effects of the willful conflation of persons and things, but we will also begin to see how the resulting "ornamental personhood" invokes unspoken and still unexplored possibilities about the fungibility of objects and subjects that reshape how we understand the imaginative trajectories of modern freedom.

Ultimately at stake is not just the objectification of people but how that very objectification opens up a constitutive estrangement within the articulation of proper personhood and life. Ornamental personhood points us to a different genealogy of modern personhood. This synthetic being, relegated to the margins of modernity and discounted as a nonperson, holds the key to understanding the inorganic animating the heart of the modern organic subject. She/it brings into view an alternative form of life, not at the site of the free modern subject and his celebrated autonomy, but on the contrary, at the encrusted edges and crevices of defiled, feminine, ornamented bodies.

Throughout this project I do not attempt to secure redemptive, subversive agency as acts of self-will or intention, because the subjects that haunt this study are those for whom will and intention have been severely compromised. Nor am I offering up the real or the authentic as antidotes to a thick sediment of misrepresentations. On the contrary, the very premise of this project takes seriously, rather than simply decries, the intractable imbrication among femininity, the ornamental, and the Oriental, in order to explore the entanglement of living and living-as-thing. Certainly the center (the white, masculine, organic personhood of Western modernity) uses the marginal (the racial and gendered other) oppositionally in order to fortify its borders, but more important, the so-called marginal (that artificial, ornamental, Oriental femininity) is more integral to the historic, philosophic, cultural, and even legal making of modern personhood than suspected. What follows attempts to track the traces of this critical component in the constitution of Western personhood from nineteenth-century legal concepts of proper personhood to twenty-first-century scientific imaginings about the future of persons.

AN ARCHAEOLOGY OF RADIANT THINGS

The subjects and objects that fuse and come into view in this project are, for the most parts, American. But since the Asiatic/Asian American femininity under consideration is itself a century-long product that grew out of what Gordon Chang calls the "fateful ties" among America, Asia, and imperial Britain, this study speaks more properly to what some Asian American scholars have come to call transnational American racial modernity.[30] In many ways, this project assumes that American studies is itself a profoundly global critical venture and thereby understands the trope of "Asiatic femininity" as a global product circulating within American culture.

Although the racialization of Asians in America has been legally, phenotypically, and culturally fraught, as well as subject to historical contingencies and political expediency, the trope of Asiatic femininity circulating in mainstream American culture that is the focus of this study makes no such distinctions and remains remarkably fixed.[31] When I speak of ornamental yellow womanhood or Asiatic femininity, I do not intend to essentialize or reify this category but instead to track the endurance of a miniaturizing yet expansive motif and aesthetic practice. I am less concerned here with the question of racial identity than in the processes of racialization and identification and the surprisingly profound role that style plays in their making. I offer the yellow woman here not as the real but rather as a conceptual category and a critical agent, with the clear understanding that the origin of this term derives from a racist framework that is indifferent to ethnic and national specificities and to diasporic realities.

The chapters that follow move historically and additively, building on one another, rather than simply offering different examples of the same. I track the varied and developing manifestations of ornamentalism from the mid-nineteenth century to the twenty-first, especially as they respond to changing contexts and technologies of personhood. Each chapter is devoted to a particular modality of Asiatic ornamentality and its critical labor in the construction of Western personhood in a variety of registers: in the arenas of law (legal personhood), cinema (celebrity), fashion (sartorial personhood), food (consuming persons), and technology (artificial intelligence and other synthetic persons). In each of these cases, ornamentalism is at times a method of controlling definitions of personhood, but at other times, it opens up radical new modes of ontology that undo our certitude about the human. Ornamentalism thus operates in this project less as a prescription than a critical lens for tracing the fluctuations between subjects and objects, persons and things that have been activated by the evocation and construction of Asiatic femininity. Each chapter is devoted to an ornamental artifact or category of artifacts and a corresponding instance of Asiatic female ornamentality, with a coda that explores the potential of ornamentalism to speak to black feminism.

This study thus begins with the adjudication of legal personhood in the Supreme Court in the mid-nineteenth century; moves to the rise of fabricated personhood in the form of modern celebrity in the early twentieth century; travels to a contemporary exhibit of extravagantly embodied objects in a great American museum; visits the transformation of persons, things, and animals through the rituals of ornamental eating in a sushi restaurant; and finally, arrives at futuristic and technological visions of posthuman persons. In all these instances, Asiatic femininity bridges personhood and thingness. One reason for moving chronologically is to follow the historic development of ornamentalism. Moreover, I hope that by the end of the book, it will become clear that the seemingly atavistic, trivial, and disposable eruptions of Asiatic femininity in American law and culture powerfully enable the imagining of the inorganic as ontologically durable, and that Asiatic femininity is fundamentally important to ideas of futurity in modernity. Similarly, ornamentalism applies tremendous pressure on the temporality of known categories such as Orientalism, primitivism, and modernism, and on their accepted subjects and objects. I hope the archaeology I am building here will reveal ornamental personhood to be not an exception to modern personhood, but its intimate sister.

1

Borders and Embroidery

PLATE 17: Arnold Genthe, *Dressed for the Feast* (1896–1906). Arnold Genthe Collection. Courtesy of Library of Congress, Prints and Photographs Division.

> Yes, sir; that is what distinguishes them from the virtuous female—that style.
>
> —DR. OTIS GIBSON, CLERGYMAN, 1874

> [A]ll perception stylizes because embodiment is a style of the world.
>
> —GALEN JOHNSON ON MERLEAU-PONTY

WHAT DO CHINESE women have to do with American conceptualization of legal personhood? As it turns out, quite a lot, especially at the critical juncture of formulating legal personhood as it emerges out of the making of modern American citizenship on the cusp of nineteenth-century immigration reform. To examine this unexpected relationship, this chapter excavates a little-known case that was arguably one of the most important, and certainly most colorful, habeas corpus cases in the latter half of the nineteenth century. Impacting immigration and citizenship laws in the decades to follow, the case turns on the surprising drama of Asiatic femininity and its ornamentality.[1]

A sensation at the time, the "Case of the Twenty-Two Lewd Chinese Women," as it was popularly known, went through the San Francisco District Court, the California Supreme Circuit Court, the Circuit Court for the District of California, and finally the U.S. Supreme Court, marking the first time that a Chinese litigant ever appeared before America's highest court. The unexpected and dramatic eruption of Asiatic female ornamentality during the course of the trial, set in a nineteenth-century courtroom packed with white men, offers us more than an instance of Orientalist blindness and racist projection. The episode also provides a fascinating view into how a raced and gendered body comes to be legible to the law through its supplementarity. This case demonstrates not only the Orientalist imagination of nineteenth-century American law but also what I am calling the logic of *ornamentalism*—the displacement of biological "personness" through the fabrication of synthetic "personness"—at work within the logic of legal personhood.

In this case, we will see the workings of ornamentalism abetting the assumptions of Orientalism and functioning in a highly disciplinary, punishing way; at the same time, however, the process of conflating things with persons also unveils the fragile, sartorial, and synthetic foundation supporting the erection of proper legal personhood. Questions of who is considered eligible to be a person and who can be seen by the law take on surprising and sharp turns throughout the litigation. The display of extravagant Asiatic ornamentality (see, e.g., plate 17) generates a vertiginous drama toggling between visible and the invisible, the present and the imagined. As we will see, the moment the yellow woman materializes as a recognizable legal category is also the very moment when she becomes unassimilable and disappears into the thingness that defines her. What follows then is a series of propositions: (1) The law contributes to the making of Asiatic female visuality in ways that conflate race not with biological epidermis, as is often assumed, but rather with synthetic adornment, thereby revealing the abstraction and artifice fundamental to the logic of race. (2) The forensic use of visual evidence started not with the introduction of modern technologies like photography, but instead with the phantasmic construction of "illegible" and "foreign" bodies. (3) Finally, nineteenth-century Orientalism's impact on the legal imaginary altered the assumptions of eighteenth-century natural laws and continues to impact contemporary conceptualizations of legal personhood in fascinating and complex ways.

AT THE HARBOR

On August 24, 1874, an American steamer named the SS *Japan*, carrying almost six hundred Chinese passengers traveling from Hong Kong to America, docked in San Francisco's harbor after over thirty days at sea (plates 18 and 19). According to the National Climatic Data Center, it was a sunny balmy day, and for those with cabin fever, the sight of the sprawling city beyond the harbor must have offered a welcoming, though unfamiliar, sight. That afternoon, Rudolph Piotrowski, the California commissioner of immigration and himself an immigrant from Poland, went aboard the ship and after a brief inspection allowed everyone to disembark except a group of twenty-two young women ranging in ages from seventeen to twenty-three. "They were lewd," he said (plate 20). [2]

PLATE 18: Isadore-Laurent Deroy. Hand-colored lithograph of San Francisco Harbor, circa 1860. Courtesy of Library of Congress, Prints and Photographs Division.

PLATE 19: W. Endicott & Co, Pacific Mail Steam Ship Company's steamer S.S. *Japan* (New York, ca. 1868). Lithograph. John Haskell Kemble Collections. Courtesy of Huntington Library.

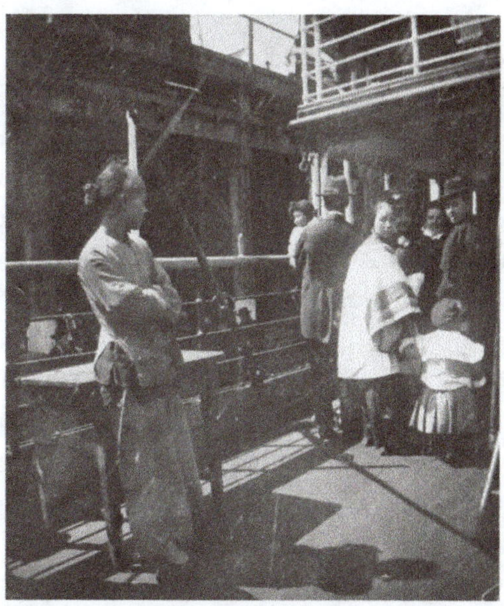

PLATE 20: Photographer unknown, Chinese passengers on ferry in San Francisco Bay (ca. 1900). Burckhalter Family Collection. Courtesy of UC Berkeley, Bancroft Library.

Piotrowski thought the women were prostitutes because he found them traveling alone (we might say, *un*decorated by husbands or children). And based on a cursory visual inspection and brief interrogation through translators, he judged their appearances to be "perfectly unsatisfactory." Moral delicacy did not prevent the commissioner from asking the ship's master, Captain John Freeman, to pay a bond of $500 in gold coins (roughly equivalent to $10,204 today) for each woman to disembark.[3] When the Pacific Mail Ship Company for which Freeman worked refused to pay, Piotrowski ordered the women detained on board and forcibly returned to Hong Kong on the ship's return.

No one came forward to claim the women, but someone did obtain legal counsel for them.[4] In the four-day (August 26–29, 1874) trial that followed in the Fourth District Court of San Francisco, Judge Robert F. Morrison agreed with Piotrowski's assessment and reaffirmed the state's right to protect itself from "immoral, pestilential visitation."[5] This decision is then echoed on September 7, 1874, by the Supreme Court of California which affirmed Judge Morrison's decision (*Ex Parte Ah Fook*, 49 Cal. 420 [1874]). The Supreme Court of California invoked the 1874 California State Political Codes granting the commissioner of immigration the right to "satisfy himself whether or not any passenger who shall arrive in this State by vessel from any foreign port ... is lunatic, idiotic, deaf, dumb, blind, crippled, or infirm ... or is a convicted criminal, or a lewd or debauched woman."[6] Apparently, as historian Paul Kramer dryly observes, "for California officials and in the eyes of the law, there is little difference between disability, immorality, and Chinese femininity."[7]

The women in question actually did possess proper papers. As Judge Leander Quint, the women's counsel, pointed out during the trial, these women had the right to enter the country under the sixth article of the 1868 Burlingame Treaty between China and the United States. They carried signed documents and had been interviewed several times by both Chinese and U.S. officials in Hong Kong before their departure. Captain Freeman also testified that he did not see any untoward behavior on the part of the women during the voyage. Yet the women were detained and treated like criminals anyway.[8]

A few weeks later, on September 21, the case went before the Circuit Court for the District of California, where Justice Stephen Field (in *In re Ah Fong*, 1F. Cas. 213 [1874]), to the surprise and distress of many, ruled in favor of the women. Field, however, did not see this as a case about the women's personal or immigrant rights, nor was he concerned about their future. Instead he saw the case as a dangerous instance of the state overstepping its power, so he recommended that the government take the case to the U.S. Supreme Court. The women were released except for one young woman named Chy Lung, who stayed to represent the others. The case, now named *Chy Lung v. Freeman* (1875), subsequently went before the U.S. Supreme Court, where Field's ruling was upheld and Lung finally released.

What freedom meant for these young women is uncertain. Although the Case of the Twenty-two Lewd Chinese Women generated a media storm during its time, soliciting almost daily reporting by the local press for months, that attention fell away overnight after the case was finally decided.[9] We have no further information about any of the women after their trial. No follow-up news stories, no census records, no memoirs—they seemed to have disappeared into the streets of Chinatown.[10] It was wholly possible that these women came, as they all testified, to find their spouses and/or to work. At the same time, the situation of Chinese women in America at the time was precarious, haunted on one side by the specter of human trafficking and on the other by the fracturing impact of Chinese male trans-Pacific labor migration on Chinese familial structure.[11] Many of the Chinese men living in the United States at that time had for all practical purposes abandoned their wives back in China and started new lives here, at times taking up new, common-law wives. This may explain why the women in this case were not claimed by doting spouses or seemed not to know the exact whereabouts of their partners. In short, little was known about these women, yet much was presumed.

What this final legal outcome meant for the future of Chinese immigration is much clearer and darker. Later in the same year that *Chy Lung* was playing out its drama, we will see the passing of the Page Act (named after Horace Page, a politician representing California in the House of Representatives), which prohibited the entry of immigrants considered "undesirable" and imposed a steep fine and maximum jail sentence of a year upon anyone who tried to bring a person from China, Japan, or any Asian country to the United States "without their free and voluntary consent, for the purpose of holding them to a term of service." Ostensibly about protecting laborers and women, the goal was in fact to, in Horace Page's words, "end the danger of cheap Chinese labor and immoral Chinese women," making it quite clear that gender and race were significant factors in immigration policy and that there was tremendous anxiety over and backlash against the Supreme Court's decision in *Chy Lung*. The Page Act serves as the first restrictive federal immigration law, prefiguring the better-known and more draconian 1882 Chinese Exclusion Act. The Page Act also anticipates the racial-sexual panic to follow during the Progressive Era. Hence the liberation of these twenty-two young women was bittersweet in hindsight and a Pyrrhic victory on many levels.

Of course, at first glance, this case of discrimination against a little group of Chinese women is hardly surprising. The discourse of the Yellow Peril was about to consolidate and intensify within less than a decade of this case. California had already spent the previous decades passing laws to get rid of the Chinese after having solicited their labor: the Foreign Miners' Tax Act of 1850 had siphoned off roughly half of the already low wages of Chinese miners; the Chinese Police Tax had been charged to persons of the so-called Mongolian race; Chinese adults were prohibited from testifying against whites in criminal or civil cases; Chinese children were denied access to the public school system.[12] However, *Chy Lung*, especially the proceedings at the District Court, invokes a series of dilemmas about gendered and racial corporeality that will continue to trouble all the legal attempts to categorize and contain it and also, as the end of this chapter will demonstrate, to influence our contemporary conceptions of civil rights and the bodies that bear them.

Surprising and noteworthy, to begin with, was the unexpectedly intense visual component in the deliberations in the California state courts and the complication that this monomaniacal focus produced at the intersection of ornament, raced bodies, visual evidence, and the making of legal personhood. Amid a burgeoning tension between state anxiety about Chinese immigration and American diplomacy in China, the prosecution decided to pursue an apparently eccentric line of inquiry: the question of what the twenty-two young women were wearing and, in particular, the ornaments said to adorn them. During the course of the trial, much if not *most* of the attention was paid to the question of decoration: detailed discussions about forms of costume; the colors, patterns, and feel of fabrics; the cuts of sleeves; and even hairstyles. Thus although this case invoked serious concerns about immigration policy and even thornier arguments about state versus federal power, these issues appear to have been sidelined by the trial court's exceptional interest not in actual biological components or in the interpretation of the law but instead in the question of superficial feminine style.

Since the case apparently turned on whether the women were "lewd," an elaborate effort was undertaken to determine the difference between respectable Chinese wives and debauched Chinese prostitutes. The young women were displayed in court, and several expert witnesses were called to provide accounts of Chinese courtesan sartorial style. Most of these witnesses were white men who did not know the women, did not speak Chinese, and were not on board the steamer, and whose sole qualification appeared to be that they had resided in China at one point or another or, as was the case with our first witness below who happened to have come to port to see, in his words, the curious sight of "a hundred or eighty Chinese women arriving in a ship."[13] According to these testimonies, sartorial practices offered telltale signs. One particularly animated witness, a Dr. Otis Gibson, who had been a missionary in China, reassured the court that he had "no familiarity with prostitutes in any country" but nonetheless offered the following detailed analysis:

> [C]courtesans are in the habit of wearing a kind of flowered garment generally—not always, but generally. You will find silk; you will find silk yellow & figured,

> & things of that kind, which are not worn so much by the wives; the wives wear plain colors, except on gala days, when there is a great deal of dressing up for company.[14]

Gibson also made observations about specific hairstyles and decorative accessories:

> There is a certain class of prostitutes, boat-women, that wear handkerchiefs on their heads; the same women here do not always do it; the same class in every other respect do not always wear the handkerchiefs on their head....
>
> [T]he manner of dressing the hair is somewhat different, though I could not well explain it. They have many modes of doing the hair in different places.[15]

A Mr. Ira M. Condit concurred that a penchant for festive and bright colors (especially the color yellow) indicates dissolute character. Prostitutes, he testified, wear:

> gayer style of dress, a dress with yellow in it, & brighter colors. There is no definite dress which distinguishes them as such from the others more than that general feature of dress... [and again, later] they wear a great deal of bright yellow.... On occasion they ["the wives"] dress up very gayly; that is, when they go to the theatre, or to the burying-ground to feed the dead, and Josh days.[16]

These testimonies are strikingly incoherent and contradictory. For example, only prostitutes wear certain things, styles, and colors, but then so do respectable and wealthy Chinese wives.[17] Indeed, as the trial proceeds, the boundary between "respectable Chinese wives" and "pestilential prostitutes" becomes increasingly hard to determine. The local police officer, Delos Woodruff (who will reappear later in our story), in charge of Chinatown testified that he rarely saw anything untoward in Chinese familial relations, though he also thought that the uncommon living arrangements in Chinatown (that is, crowded tenements) made it very difficult to ascertain "proper" familial relations, suggesting that the non-Christian (that is, "heathen") Chinese may not in fact have understood the notion of a proper marriage at all.

The incoherence of the testimonies did not loosen the association between Asian femininity and debauchery, nor at any point did anyone try to ascertain whether these women were in fact prostitutes. And while the women eventually won their case, they were never explicitly exonerated of the claims made about them. But regardless of whether the women were or were not "debauched," as per the discourse of the State Political Code, the presumptions about their character, which were directly linked to their eligibility for legal personhood, rest on the seemingly frivolous category of ornaments.[18]

At a time when the increasing influx of Chinese laborers into the United States was causing labor competition and Euro-American views of China had started to shift from acquisitive fascination with Chinese things and "quaint" Chinese people in the previous century to suspicion and contempt, this association between ornamentation and debauched femininity came to condense around—indeed, became synonymous with—the Chinese female body. Unlike African Americans, whose legal racialization was based on something beyond visibility alone—the infamous one-sixteenth "blood" rule, intended to bypass the potentially deceptive visible, as in the cases of passing—the racialization of the Chinese was intractably tied to their physical appearances and their nonpassable, inescapably "foreign-looking" bodies.

If the story ended here, we might still find the connection between sartorial practice and moral assessment not so remarkable. After all, Britain has been passing sumptuary laws since the Elizabethan period, and early America did as well. Yet the most visually telling evidence in this case—the women's ornamentality—turns out to be also the most spectral. A close reading of the trial transcript shows that the ornamental objects under much debate throughout the trial were in fact speculative rather than factual. The state had something of an evidential challenge on its hands, for the much-cited ornaments were rather elusive. Our good clergyman, Dr. Gibson, for example, had to reach for what is not readily available to the eye:

> They are accustomed to wear flowered gaudy kind of clothing—clothing that is not worn by respectable wives. There is no indelicacy in seeing or examining them; those women will show it if the' [*sic*] exposed there [*sic*] arms; & you will find . . . under their outside clothing in 9 out of 10 cases some of this variegated silk or imitation of silk, some fancy clothes that has [*sic*] a bright color. . . .
>
> They have a black one on the outside, but just under that you will see the kind of cloth I was describing.[19]

This then led Mr. Ryan the prosecutor to call several of the women forward, in order to raise and peek into their sleeves. More eyeballing ensued, with the men inspecting the hems of the women's gowns and examining their hair; there was even a heated debate about just how wide a sleeve could be before tipping into licentiousness.

Yet according to court recording and press coverage at the time, the women in question mostly wore uninteresting, black, loose-fitting clothes. (Let us remember that these women had been aboard a cramped ship for over a month.) Thus all the categories that the California court took to be visually and hence materially evident in this case—corporeality as evidence of racialized subjectivity, feminine decoration, the relations between skin and what rests on it—turn out to be *not* evident. The invocation of ostentatious female ornamentation—that most visible and material of categories—pivoted between imagined presence and projected absence. The women were thus simultaneously dressed up and stripped down. The evidence of an overmaterialized and scopically available body emerges not out of bare flesh or real ornaments, but instead from their phantasmic conflation, an overlapping of surfaces located in teasing peripheries: the borders of a collar, the peep of a hem, the gleaming edge of a sleeve.

To dismiss this scene as yet another regrettable example of racist prurience or Puritanical conservatism is to miss the extraordinary negotiation of the visible and the invisible at play here. The California court took the Chinese female body to be self-evident. But how that body evidences the invisible in its visibility or vice versa has yet to be fully examined. What happens when we consider the ideas of body, skin, cloth, and ornament as interrelated metaphors for thinking about personhood in American social and legal realms in the nineteenth century, and what are the legacies of these entwined ideas for us today?

ORNAMENTAL PERSONHOOD

The eminent English legal historian Frederic William Maitland once ascertained that "[t]he only natural persons are men. The only artificial persons are corporations."[20] While the concept of legal personhood, especially of abstract corporate personhood, has long been a subject of study for legal historians, and more recently for scholars in the humanities interested in notions of persona or artificial persons, less attention has been paid to race and sexuality in the making of this artifice.[21] Almost every term of Maitland's assertion comes into question when we introduce these two supposedly most biological of categories. Who constitutes a "natural person," and how do we move from a biological to a legal standing? What legal alchemy enables the transformation from singularity to collectivity, from embodiment to abstraction? What does the "feminine"—simultaneously erased by Maitland's calculus and implicitly relegated to the realm of the artificial—do to this equation? And how do racialized individuals, often exempted from personhood, fit into this postulation? The exclusion of women, and in particular women of color, from the discourse about legal personhood may not seem surprising, but the peculiar critical agency that their absent presences lent to the adjudication of what counts as a person in U.S. legal history demands much further consideration.

The case of *Chy Lung* allows us to view a visual-legal culture during the critical decades when anti-Chinese sentiment and modern American citizenship intertwine and are forged. *Chy Lung* dramatizes how the judicial making of the "Oriental body," a moment of making racial difference highly visible, is also paradoxically the moment when that body disappears into ornamentality, and the idea of what is visible, of what can be seen in the courtroom, becomes *de*naturalized. Indeed, one of the most fascinating aspects of this case must be the question of what constitutes "visual evidence" and how racialized femininity impacts and alters that assumption.

In the nineteenth-century courtroom, "race" turns out to be a drama of re-codable surfaces and metaphoric displacements. The epidermal schema, often thought today to be the very *visible matter* of racial difference, in fact posed an epistemic dilemma. In the trial of the women, we find the male prosecution team laboring hard to stage its evidence and knowledge. Indeed, "visual evidence" poses a challenging concept in *Chy Lung*, because the invocation of ostentatious female ornamentation—that most visible and objective of categories—pivots on an elaborate negotiation between imagined presence and projected absence. What constitutes *visual* evidence and what does it mean to *produce* evidence? What does it mean to bear witness to and participate in the "reality" of bodies that are produced at the margins between imagined interiority and equally imagined exteriority?[22]

When it comes to discussions of visual material in the courtroom, photographic evidence usually takes a central role. Legal scholar Jennifer L. Mnookin observes that the use of photography as evidence in courtrooms in the late 1880s triggered an unprecedented groundswell of visual representations—maps, charts, models, and so on—in the courtroom.[23] She also argues that the entrance of photography into courtrooms brought into existence that category of proof we now call "demonstrative" or "constructed" evidence and initiated broader changes in courtroom practice and the conceptualization of evidence. As Mnookin explains, a significant consequence of this new judicial, epistemic category has to do with how evidence is gathered and presented:

> Witnesses, attorneys, plaintiffs, and defendants actually went out and *made* evidence themselves. Preparing for a case no longer involved merely *locating* appropriate people and objects; it was now likely to involve actively *creating* a representation. Evidence was something to be *constructed* as well as collected.... [T]hese forms of [new visual] evidence turned jurors themselves into *virtual witnesses*, able to see the evidence... directly with their own eyes.... The late nineteenth century thus witnessed the birth and development of a new way of establishing truth: the emergence of a "culture of construction."[24]

With the introduction of this new culture of visual and constructed evidence, new and entangled questions about its reliability—that is, evidentiary dilemmas—also emerged, in spite of the photograph's promise of objectivity and indexicality.

The heavily visualized and intensely spectralized Asiatic female body in that California courtroom offers something of a protophotographic forensic dilemma, with all its material promises and accompanying evidentiary crisis. On the one hand, a case like *Chy Lung*, a decade prior to the technical developments that Mnookin documents, tells us that external, synthetic visual aids are not necessary when there are twenty-two real bodies on the ground, ready for inspection. On the other hand, the trial demonstrates that those real bodies in fact had to be marshaled, created, and constructed in order to be "evident." The women's *virtual* bodies allowed the judges and lawyers to plunge into the experience of being *virtual witnesses*. This was never a case about the politics of self-presentation; it was about how the legal system affirms and expands its own epistemic jurisdiction.

Just as photographs are never merely indexical, as Roland Barthes famously observes, the so-called materiality of the Asiatic female body does not function indicatively even if its figuration hinges on a language that is persistently indicative.[25] More than registering the anxiety of what style signifies, *Chy Lung* instantiates a dilemma of legal presencing: how to make bodies evident in the eyes of the law. Legally, it's the body that seems to tell all, when in fact it's the body's surface that speaks. The drama of *Chy Lung* reveals that the ineluctable corporeality of the Asian female body (tied to the anxiety about prostitution and presumed a body for sale) depends, counterintuitively, on that body's fundamental spectrality.[26] The Asiatic female visuality is thus a figure whose materiality is acquired through the imagined projection of the real that in turn relies on an ongoing fluctuation between presumption and facticity. This is why what is at stake here is a question of Asiatic female *visuality* rather than visibility.

The trial offers us an interesting view into the phenomenology of what Alan Hyde calls "a jurisprudence of human presence."[27] Hyde tells us that the law relies on a distinction between the physical and the discursive body. I suggest there is a third term—the ornamental—at play. Indeed, the seemingly peripheral and trivial presence of the ornament offers the very mediating agent that enables the law to make the necessary slippage between the biological and discursive body. We can now address the larger relationship between ornament and the conceptualization of rights and natural personhood in the law. In *Chy Lung*, Asiatic feminine ornamentality plays a vital function in the legal adjudication of racialized personhood that sanctions categories and hierarchies of oppression. If we understand modern legal personhood to have its roots in an Enlightenment ideal of masculinized, natural persons, then the artificial, criminalized figure of Asiatic femininity—conflated with the imagined-and-real bodies of Asian women themselves, relegated to the margins of modernity, and discounted as nonpersons—may provide the key to a different but equally constitutive Western personhood.

The questions of *what is a natural body* and *what is on a body* have a long, troubled, entangled, and formative history in U.S. legislation, especially when it comes to adjudicating which body counts and which does not. Yet what are the terms of this body? This question is, of course, quite fraught when it comes to a racialized or gendered body. In *Roberts v. The City of Boston* (1849), the desegregation case that served as a precedent for the "separate but equal" doctrine of *Plessy v. Ferguson* (1896), Justice Lemuel Shaw states:

> The great principle, advanced by the . . . advocate of the plaintiff, is that . . . all persons without distinction of age or sex, birth or color, origin or condition, are equal before the law. This, as a broad general principle . . . is perfectly sound. . . . *But,* when this great principle comes to be applied to the actual and various conditions of persons in society, it will not warrant the assertion, that men and women are *legally clothed* in the same civil and political powers. [emphasis added][28]

All bodies may be considered equal, but their civil covering is not.

With *Roberts*, the court appears to be confirming equality before the law based on the commonality of naked bodies, but it immediately delimits that universality by subsuming the biological body in the social body—or, more accurately, social ornamentation. Moreover, that social ornament is itself subject to difference: male versus female and, implicitly in *Roberts*, white versus racial otherness. Thus what starts out as potentially an admission that all are equal before the law turns out to deny equality and reconstitute the very powers and privileges enabled by those constructions.

The sartorial logic here is specifically a decorative one: the "cloth" adorns and hence attaches meaning to an otherwise abstract and unseen body. Here "legal cloth" signals more than a rhetorical flourish and articulates the very logic of civil rights as a form of extra adornment. What makes a theoretically blank body come to emit meaning and visibility (whether the visibility of legitimacy or otherwise) turns on this external overlay. In *Dress, Law and Naked Truth: A Cultural Study of Fashion and Form*, Gary Watt traces the long etymological connection between law and dress; we often speak of "the cloak of justice," "vested interests," "to pin a crime on someone," and so forth.[29] But where Watt posits law and dress as cultural equivalents (in that both the judicial and the sartorial aim to regulate and order the body, which is why his study focuses on the regulation of uniforms, judicial robes, etc.), I suggest that the relationship is not simply analogous but structural. I want to pinpoint the ornamental function of the sartorial in order to consider the act of "dressing" or "putting something on" as a dynamic and judicial process. I also want to underscore how this logic of the ornament bears a philosophic relation to Oriental sartorialism.

Dress designates civility and quotidian order, as Watt insightfully observes, but *ornament* designates a category of dress that is marginal, excessive, and nonutilitarian (that is, unlike dress that is required by civil society). It is precisely this philosophic distinction that allows the law to adjudicate what kind of sartorial coverings counts or not. So what does it mean to recognize that racialized corporeality, like legal subjecthood, is always already an effect of a sartorial—and, in fact, an ornamental—logic? In proclaiming that rights and legal personhood are decorative rather than biological or essential, *Roberts* reminds us that personhood is a function of legal ornaments. The contiguity of skin and cloth that I have been tracing implicates skin as well: a distinguishing mantle that confers or rescinds rights. Indeed, skin—that most biological and racialized of surfaces—is shown to be wholly subject to refabrication in the history of citizen making, what I call the drama of skin surfaces.

Ozawa v. U.S. (1922) and *U.S. v. Thind* (1923) are instances where the determining evidence of "skin color" reveals all its dizzying contingencies and mutabilities.[30] In 1922 Takao Ozawa appealed for citizenship based on his allegiance to America, exemplified through his daily practices and family life. The Court denied his appeal on the biological and scientific ground that he is "Asian/Japanese" and hence not "white." (Ironically, photographs show that Ozawa was rather Caucasian-looking and could probably have passed as white, reminding us yet again that what is at stake is not epidermal visibility but racial visuality.) Ozawa asked the law to recognize the habits of his life (where he works, where he goes to church, what he wears, and more), but the Court resorts to a language of biology to deny the meaning of such quotidian adornment.

This language of biology, however, will itself turn out to be subjected to ornamental overlays. A year after the Ozawa trial, Bhagat Singh Thind fought against the repeal of his citizenship by claiming not only that he, too, has been an exemplary citizen (having even served in the U.S. military) but also that he is from the Caucasus and hence scientifically and biologically Caucasian. The Court denied his appeal, but this time, going against its stance just a year before in *Ozawa*, asserted that "whiteness," rather than being a biological category, must be understood by what the Court called "common understanding," and by that measure, Thind clearly did not quality. This time, the scientific discourse of biology is itself subject to resignification through, we might say, the attachment of cultural perceptions.[31]

Legal personhood is thus constructed along a series of delicate slippages between bodies and their surfaces, essences, and attributes. The marking of an unmarked (or, in the case of *Chy Lung*, unaccompanied) body into a visible state of idealization or denigration relies on these conflations that the law both instigates and represses. This sartorial cladding of a person to render him or her visible in the eyes of the law suggests that legal personhood has very little to do with "natural" bodies even as this legal fiction has real effects on real bodies.

Thus it is not only the material history of immigration policy that polices and hence racializes bodies, as historians have documented, but also, entwined with it, a history of legislating visuality that produces a curious and dizzying archive of imagined material bodies.[32] The case against the Chinese women unfolds multiple layers of covering and absences. Let us remember that those (unadorned yet overadorned) female bodies have already been subjected to other forms of erasure. Imprisoned and stripped of rights—consider the duration of these women's ordeal in uncertain detention and even imprisonment, after already having been trapped in cramped quarters for a long voyage[33]—these bodies have been profoundly dislocated as products of trans-Pacific labor migration. The ghosting of these women's bodies—through both physical custody and the cloaking logic of Orientalist female visuality—veils the profound crisis of mobility that in fact conditions these women's lives. In addition to the question of what is presumably shown on the surfaces or edges of these women's bodies as indexes for imagined character and interiority, there was also a long line of inquiry during the trial on whether Chinese women (both in China and in Chinatown) had "permission" to be walking on the streets at all. The quotidian constraint of female movement speaks to more than gender inequality; it also reminds us that these women, who have exiled themselves to embark on this daunting journey, have had to place themselves in the new global economy as both agents *and* commodities. Some of these women came in search of husbands they barely knew and whose whereabouts they could only ascertain through hearsay. Others came alone in a wild gambit for work and a better life, just like the men, who put themselves in the maelstrom of what Zygmunt Bauman calls "liquid modernity."[34] Yet others most likely were sold, with or without their knowledge and perhaps even by their own families.

Caught between a dream of self-fashioning and a legal system that cloaked them in racialized transparency, these women had to weave their way through difficult, if not impossible, layers of constraints conditioning the personal, cultural, social, and legal fabrications of their personhood. It is more than a little ironic, then, that when it finally came time for the women to speak on their own behalf, as the *Transcript* records, almost all of them, wives or not, stated that they came to America to become "seamstresses."

AT THE EDGES OF OUR CIVIL BODIES

In March 1876, Justice Samuel Miller of the U.S. Supreme Court articulated three reasons for overturning the original California District ruling. First, the California state immigration law allows petty state officials such as Piotrowski to extort money.

Second, that law produces shallow profiling. Third, the state does not have the power to determine immigration policy and U.S. foreign relations. As historian Paul Kramer puts it, "A legislative recipe for extortion; a capricious exercise of perception and power; a dangerous usurpation of federal law: What was *not* wrong with California's immigration law?"[35] Yet the lucidity of Miller's 1876 decision would seem to bear repeating, given, for example, California's Proposition 187 in 1994 and Arizona's infamous immigration law in 2000—as well as our current moment. Both Proposition 187 and Arizona sought to allow state laws to intervene in federal immigration policy, and both profiled "illegal aliens" in ways that were finally found to be unconstitutional. Indeed, we might see the 1876 Supreme Court case as an ongoing rebuke to the practice of racial profiling to this day.

Finally, this 1876 case raises a larger, theoretical concern about our present conceptualization of constitutional rights. What does it mean that the legal language about our civil rights is tied to and relies on an ideal about "natural personhood" when legal personhood is anything but natural? The Anglophone, Enlightenment conception of philosophic and hence legal personhood, from Thomas Hobbes to John Locke to William Blackstone, is indebted to a dominant fiction of the person as a living, organic, and organized human body "such as the God of nature formed us."[36] Obviously, the practice of slavery poses a challenge to this ideal. The recent works of scholars including Stephen Best and Monique Allewaert focus on how the enslaved black body challenges this philosophic or legal construction of personhood.[37] Best contends that the conceptions of slave property are indebted to abstract rather than biological aspects of personhood, while Allewaert argues that plantation labor practices and ecological peculiarities contest the ideal of a person as a discrete, purely biological agent. Here I suggest that the Asiatic body—especially the feminine, ornamental body—also sheds light on the particularly synthetic and sartorial roots of legal personhood, with profound implications for the contemporary conceptualization of the "natural" person and "natural" rights.

In the Orientalism of the nineteenth-century California court, it is the *virtual* (alternately projected and unseen) ornamentality of the women's bodies that allows the judges and lawyers to plunge into the "real" possibility of bearing witness to material Asiatic femininity, to make the necessary slippage between the biological and discursive body. But these "exceptional" bodies must also compel us to reconsider the extent to which this slippage is always already the condition of legal personhood. The questions of what is a natural body and what are its natural rights have a long and troubled history in U.S. legislation, especially when it comes to adjudicating which body counts and which does not. The writ of habeas corpus, for example, as noted earlier, means literally in Latin "may you have the body." Yet what are the terms of this "body"?[38] Indeed, which "natural" bodies have which rights has been a constant problem for the courts when it comes to racialized or gendered bodies. In proclaiming that personhood is decorative rather than biological or essential, *Roberts* reminds us that *constitutional personhood is a function of legal ornaments*. Racialized skin, that most biological of surfaces, is here implicated by the ornamental logic and subject to refabrication in the history of citizen making. Historian Mae M. Ngai has pointed out that before the Johnson-Reed Act of 1924, racial categories in the United States were far from rigid, and that it took a great deal of juridical wrangling to make them so.[39]

Chy Lung registers a delicate moment. Before the full denial of legal personhood that we see in the Exclusion Act of 1882 and on the cusp of the solidification of racial categories through increasing restriction of race-based immigration, the issue is not yet so much legal personhood per se as what *kind* of person is or is not acceptable, that is, the *preconditions* for legal personhood. This case thus signals the beginning of a legal process of categorizing people that will become the foundation for solidifying modern racial categories, which will in turn justify more stringent constitutional denials to come. Thus while the Chinese women in this case were not denied legal personhood per se—they were in no position to ask for anything beyond legal entry—their story shows that they were already being excluded from the narrative and idea of modern personhood, insofar as the latter implies property, family, civil society, and state.

Today, the language of the sartorial resurfaces in both critical legal studies and colloquial conversations. But this language is mostly invoked symptomatically to refer to the mourned divide between individual authenticity and social coercion. *Chy Lung* compels us to see that the sartorial as a function of the ornamental is more than rhetorical and speaks to something structural about the law's imagination; and that, more important, the relation between personhood and its external covers or decorations must be understood as vitally, even if disturbingly, imbricated.

Oriental sartorialism, transitioning into ornamentalism, survives in our contemporary legal imagination in strange and convoluted ways. In his enormously popular study *Covering: The Hidden Assault on Our Civil Rights*, critical race theorist and constitutional scholar Kenji Yoshino astutely reminds us that contemporary antidiscrimination laws are based on what are understood to be so-called natural and immutable traits (such as blood, chromosomes, and skin color). They do not protect what are thought to be "superficial" characteristics: behaviors, style, cultural practice, and other, more ornamental practices.[40] Thus an individual might not be able to get fired for being black or gay, but that same person can be fired for wearing cornrows or "flaunting" his or her gay marriage—in short, for style. For Yoshino, one of the tasks of formulating the new civil rights must be the freedom to exercise one's vision of one's sense of authenticity, the right to self-fashioning.

This call for social visibility and self-making is, of course, enormously appealing for anyone who has enjoyed neither. But the history of the delineation of racialized bodies that we have been studying suggests that something more fraught is at stake than authenticity, or suppressed or ineluctable visibility for that matter. Covers and ornaments can indeed enact a "hidden assault on our civil rights," but as we have seen (via the "clothing" of race), they also form the basis for anchoring our rights—and perhaps even our embodied sense of ourselves. It is beyond the scope of this chapter, but this discussion bears relevance for other "ornamental" practices such as wearing the veil. Some feminists have decried the practice, but others have pointed out that the relationship between institutional demand and self-performance may be much more complex than simply an issue of external disciplinary covering versus an oppressed true self.[41] The ideal of a naked or unornamented self, seductive as it may be, cannot be the solution to the problem of racism, oppression, or discrimination, for that ideal denies how the (racialized) "self" is always already an effect of the ornament worn.

This is not simply an academic insight. This understanding goes straight to the heart of the complex reality of our everyday senses of our own embodiment. Clothing and ornaments can offer the performance, the *habitus*, through which we acquire our sense of selfhood. The separation of essence from performance, assumed in the contemporary formulation of our civil rights, elides the insight that our experiences of our own racial, sexual, and ontic identities arise most acutely precisely at the intersection of *being* and the *doing* that supposedly decorates it. Our sense of our racial and sexual ontologies emerges most intensely as and through performances in a social context. We are thus effectively legally protected exactly where our racial and sexual identities do *not* live.

In an odd twist, the intervention of nineteenth-century Orientalism into our legal imaginary about natural personhood has morphed into the peculiar (double-layered?) discourse of our "authentic" civil rights. Under the cover of Yoshino's call for authenticity lies an intricate narrative that suggests a much more fraught picture of our relations to our sartorial selves. The most haunting and stirring aspects of *Covering* arise out of those moments when the author helps us to see not the opposition between authenticity and false covers, but indeed the active negotiation between the experience of subjectivity and acts of social performance. Almost every personal account in this poignant book suggests that authenticity is not an integral or a priori entity but instead a palimpsest of identifications, layered and riddled with internal contradictions. If anything, Yoshino demonstrates the psychoanalytic insight that we are every one of us the sum of the history of the ghosts we have taken in. When, for example, the author realizes that after years of Japanese school training, his sister "is no longer passing as Japanese, but that she was Japanese," he has located a highly imbricated dynamic between essence and performance, body and discipline.[42] What it means to be at home in your own skin turns out to signal the necessary distance between ontology and its ornaments.

Even more tellingly, when Yoshino describes the critical moment of his coming out, he gives us a rather Lacanian mirror scene with sartorial roots:

> One Saturday, [my friend Maureen] and I wandered into a haberdashery.... I found a vest—gold lions ramping through a cobalt brocade.... [A]s I ran the brittle fabric between my thumb and finger, I experienced a jackdaw craving for it. I slipped it on.... "It becomes you," the shop keeper said gruffly through his waxed mustache. I realized it did become me, and that I could become it. It did the work of... [driving] my invisible difference to the surface and held it there.... The shop did not take checks, so Maureen put the vest on her credit card, and I signed away an alarming portion of my living stipend to her. By next mail, she sent back my pale green check cut in half and folded into two origami cranes.[43]

The challenge to the limits of personal liberty is being articulated here by an Asian American legal subject confronting his sexual orientation, mediated through a mirror image (at once personal and social) and a series of recognizable Orientalist tropes (gold brocade, jackdaw, origami). Synthetic and natural personhood collide in this scene; both bring productive as well as limiting capabilities. We cannot fail to note that this scene of coming out is taking place in a literal closet (that is, the dressing room) and that this scene of discovery is facilitated by covers and ornaments. What enables the narrator to come out to himself is not nakedness, literally or otherwise, but the agential work of a piece of clothing, a highly decorated and racialized one at that.[44] Moreover, we might remember that the word *vesture* is linked to the notion of legal power as something that can be "invested"; we speak, for example, of "vested interests."[45] Here the vested interests of personal liberty and selfhood acknowledge the very logic of ornamentation that the discourse of covering had set out to redress. Finally, this moment of self-possession and self-investment is, significantly, also a moment of debt, of becoming indebted to another. This is why the "gift of selfhood" is such a paradoxical and revealing phrase, for self-possession is often made possible through the layers and mediations of "otherness."

In this extraordinarily layered scene of revelation, mediation, recognition, projection, self-owning, and self-giveaway, we are presented with covers that uncover. Psychoanalytic insights tell us that fantasy occupies a constitutive place in the imaginary act of self-recognition. The legal imaginary teaches us that what allows the subject to emerge from the closet is not liberating nakedness, but instead social ornamentation. And that ornament is never "just" a costume. As Yoshino tells us, "it did become me, and.... *I could become it*" (emphasis added).

All of this is not to deny the importance of authenticity as an ideal or as a necessary fiction in our lives. But like all ruling or originary fantasies we have about ourselves, these fictions are at once tenacious and fragile, insistent and susceptible. This is why "subjective agency" is at once so valuable yet so deceptive a notion for an individual who is already suffering under the violence of a compromised individuality. I want to underscore the disquieting insight that personhood—on ontological, social, and legal levels—has always been implicated by its external vestment. Ornament is never mere ornament. It is an add-on that allows us, retroactively, to fantasize about natural personhood. Can our civil rights law accommodate the profundity and the dilemmas of our sartorial personhood?

The Orientalism that fueled *Chy Lung* blinded the men in power into making categorical mistakes; but the ornamental logic reveals something deeper about the illogic of how a person comes to be legible to the law. What are the conditions under which a (raced and gendered) body becomes visible? This question drives at the psychological, social, and even legal basis for forging identity and its concomitant rights. To think about law and the ornament is therefore to confront a set of political dilemmas that structure personhood and, by implication, racial materiality. The Case of the Twenty-two Lewd Chinese Women reminds us that being seen is not a condition of the visible but of the law and that how a body matters is a less a function of flesh than of ornament.

We leave *Chy Lung* with yet another twist in the fiction of the visible. In a detail of the trial that has gone unnoted, the men not only had to contort themselves and their female subjects to see what was not there, they also had to labor to not see what was there. Here I am referring not to the legality of the Burlingame Treaty that granted these women the right to come to America, or to the certified, legal papers that the women possessed and displayed in their defense, but instead to what turned out to be under (or up) their sleeves. During the trial, Captain Freeman described the manifold procedures the women underwent before boarding the steamer:

> [In Hong Kong] the women are all obliged to go to the counsel's, and are there interviewed by him and his interpreters. He satisfies himself that they are respectable women, & he gives them a permit to buy a ticket. At that time, *he stamps them upon their arm*; from there they are obliged to go to the harbor-master, and [there] he satisfies himself on the same grounds *& he stamps them [again]*, then they go to the office and buy their tickets. The day the ship leaves Hong Kong the harbor master... & the counsel himself come on board and see that the women... are the same; they are again interviewed... *& the stamps are still upon their arm.* (Emphasis added)[46]

The women's bodies were in fact "ornamented" after all. Their skin was literally imprinted by legal ornaments that the law both imparts and erases. Retrieving this last, lost ornamental detail compels us to confront the invisibility of the visible on the one hand and the visibility of the invisible on the other. This parable for the modern visuality of race is based not on the visible or the corporeal, but instead on the invisible markings that stand in for the flesh.

AFTER IMAGES

A little than less than two decades after the SS *Japan* docked in San Francisco, another steamer, this time the much more luxuriously appointed SS *Normannia*, landed in New York Harbor, carrying on board a young German doctor of philosophy serving as tutor to a wealthy German family. This young man, Arnold Genthe, made his way to San Francisco in 1895, took up photography as a hobby, and became one of the most celebrated photographic portraitists of the early twentieth century, with a clientele that included Sarah Bernhardt, Jack London, Gertrude Stein, Theodore Roosevelt, Woodrow Wilson, John D. Rockefeller, Greta Garbo, Anna Pavlova, Isadora Duncan, and Ruth St. Denis. What sparked Genthe's interest in glamour photography and launched his professional career were, as it turned out, the slums of Chinatown.

Enticed by a travel guide that admonished "'[i]t is not advisable to visit the Chinese quarter unless one is accompanied by a guide,'" the young Genthe found himelf a regular roamer in the cramped eight blocks that made up San Francisco's Chinatown.[47] He soon bought his first camera in order to capture the less than glamorous sights that fascinated him. Contrary to the elite social subjects who would occupy the rest of his career, Genthe was irresistibly drawn to what he saw as the grimy denizens in the underbelly of civilized San Francisco. In his memoir, he recounted what repeatedly drew him to this marginalized neighborhood in the heart of the city:

> In the dark alleys and courtyards rickety staircases led up to tenement hovels where the derelicts of the underworld found cover. The most sinister was the "Devil's Kitchen," an evil-smelling courtyard where drug addicts and suspicious characters of all sorts cooked on charcoal burners the scraps of food they had picked up in the streets, and came out only at night to squat on doorsills or to pursue their insidious ways.[48]

With his first camera fitted with a Zeiss lens, Genthe captured some of the most memorable images of San Francisco's Chinatown before the 1906 earthquake. In

1908 he published a series of images from over two hundred glass plates that offered his contemporary, white Victorian audience the terrible beauty of Chinatown: images that were alternately picturesque, sinister, absorbing, and cautionary (plates 21–24).[49] Valued as an exceptional archive of rare historic images, Genthe's photographs were celebrated in their day for their candid portrayals of quotidian street life and its less than "celestial" inhabitants. The success of these images of Old Chinatown allowed Genthe to quit his job as a tutor and set himself up in a studio on Nob Hill, achieving, in short, the American Dream.[50]

If several years earlier, the SS *Japan* gave the locals the extraordinary sight of a bunch of "lewd Chinese women," then Genthe gave the world the first sustained "insider" view of the "foreign" terrain of Chinatown and its grim "bachelors" within.[51] We might think of Genthe's work as an aesthetic residue of the legal criminalization of the Chinese in America. Scholars of photography have well documented the link between race and criminality in the early history of photography,

PLATE 21: Arnold Genthe, *The Devil's Kitchen (by night)* (1896–1906). Arnold Genthe Collection. Library of Congress, Prints and Photographs Division.

PLATE 22: Arnold Genthe, *The Morning Market* (1896–1906). Arnold Genthe Collection. Library of Congress, Prints and Photographs Division.

PLATE 23: Arnold Genthe, *The Opium Fiend* (1896–1906). Arnold Genthe Collection. Library of Congress, Prints and Photographs Division.

PLATE 24: Arnold Genthe, *The Street of the Gamblers (by day)* (1896–1906). Arnold Genthe Collection. Library of Congress, Prints and Photographs Division.

but there is also a direct link connecting photography and criminality to the Chinese in America.[52] Anna Pegler-Gordon, for instance, traces the origin of our passport photos today to the anxious need to identify and discipline "indistinguishable" and illegal Asian bodies in the nineteenth century.[53] To this formal emergence of visual regulation in immigration policy, we can now add a parallel development of the use of art photography in criminalizing the Chinese.

We can consider Genthe's Chinatown album next to another one, belonging to the annals of forensic photography. A comprehensive source of images of Chinese immigrants in San Francisco's Chinatown from that period comes to us not from another commercial photographer but from an amateur one: Delos Woodruff, the very same officer who had testified in the *Chy Lung* case. Woodruff was a police officer assigned to the "Chinatown beat" in the years between 1871 and 1875 who had "distinguished himself as an expert in the apprehension of Chinese thieves."[54] In addition to being an "expert" on the Chinese in Chinatown, he was also an avid amateur photographer. He authored a private album of 144 photographs, what today we call "mug shots," that he took of so-called Chinese criminals (plate 25).

It is unclear whether the individuals featured were in fact all criminals or simply suspects. Some of the images were wholly unidentified, while others were marked by pencil inscriptions of names, crimes, and sentences.[55] That the police officer from *Chy Lung* seems to have been a shutterbug reveals the deep connection among visuality, race, and law, specifically a growing culture of visual epistemology informing the imaginary surrounding Chinatown. Genthe's picturesque images and Woodruff's stark forensic head shots share a touristic gaze, as well as the presumption of Chinese criminality, revealing how the forensic informs the language of visual culture in the everyday and how the language of the visual informs law.

PLATE 25: Delos Woodruff, photographs of "Chinese Criminals" (ca. 1880). Private album, vault 185. Courtesy of California Historic Society.

It is, however, Genthe's portraits of Chinese femininity that most powerfully rehearse *and* realign this association of race, photography, and law. His black-and-white photographs on gritty subjects, such as "Gamblers' Street," "The Devil's Kitchen," and "Opium Fiend," stand in contrast to rare but eye-catching portraits of women and young girls (plates 26–28). These brightly clad young female figures come into focus out of the lurid streets of Chinatown with seemingly redemptive elegance. Given that the population in Chinatown at the time was 95 percent male, the presence of Chinese women in these images appears as an anomaly in more ways than one. Unlike the somber, inscrutable, and often vaguely threatening Asian men, the women in Genthe's images are usually prettily and elaborately dressed and coiffed. They wear flowers and other intricate, ornamental hair devices; they often sport high "Mandarin heels"; their silk gowns are embroidered and brightly embellished. The women emerge from the drab backdrop of the bachelor society like vivid apparitions, pulling the gazes of viewers from inside and outside the borders of these images. How are we to read this conspicuous femininity on the streets?[56]

In *Picturing Model Citizens*, Thy Phu brings our attention to a pictorial rhetoric of civility that has been deployed by both white reform photographers and Asian American subjects themselves in a gambit for respectability.[57] Genthe, Phu points out, deploys tropes of domestic interiority to frame and contain Asian femininity, a gesture of civilizing that also contains and disciplines. What intrigues me here are Genthe's pictorial meditations on Chinese femininity as a phenomenon *on* and *of* the street. Genthe was fascinated by the specter of the mobile Chinese female body. While white, masculine voyeurism and containment are undoubtedly forces behind

PLATE 26: Arnold Genthe, *At the Corner of Dupont and Jackson Street* (1896–1906). Arnold Genthe Collection. Library of Congress, Prints and Photographs Division.

PLATE 27: Arnold Genthe, *The Toy Peddler* (1896–1906). Arnold Genthe Collection. Library of Congress, Prints and Photographs Division.

PLATE 28: Arnold Genthe, *Dressed for the Feast* (1896–1906). Arnold Genthe Collection. Courtesy of Library of Congress, Prints and Photographs Division.

Genthe's treatment of his Chinese female subjects, these images nonetheless reveal a phenomenology of Chinese female bodies in complex relations, physically and metaphysically, to the dynamics of mobility and entrapment on the streets of Chinatown—a tension played out in the interplay between sartorial excess and ontological isolation.

At the Corner of Dupont and Jackson Street (plate 26) shows us two distinctively dressed girls in the focal point of the image, emerging at the intersection of two lines of male gazes (from the right and left) that have converged on them. The older girl looks downward even though she has just stepped off the curb onto a notoriously busy street, as if eager to move beyond the weight of the gazes against her back; her right hand grips her companion's, possibly urging along this younger charge, who is also looking away and down. Their posture suggests they aren't out for a stroll. Age and gender differences structure this scene and its different temporalities. The loitering men contrast with the girls' self-conscious pace, highlighting the latter's uneasiness at adult male attention; the girls' ornamental figures explicitly echo the neat rows of figurines displayed for purchase in the store window behind them.

But the strain embedded in this image derives from much more than the diegetic tension between Chinese girls and Chinese men. There is, of course, the scopic pressure of the photographer's gaze. Could the men in the image be looking not at the girls, but at the white photographer looking at the girls? Could we say that the photographer, himself a bachelor of a different order in this so-called Bachelor Society, has projected himself onto the seemingly menacing Chinese men? And does the girls' refusal to look at the camera ironically underscore the presence of the invisible photographer? In this image, sartorial girls, mute Chinese men, and the unseen photographer all participate in a dynamic of display and camouflage, each for his or her own reasons, though these complex possibilities were all suppressed by the photographer's framing and cropping.

Historian John Kuo Wei Tchen, who preserved and reprinted much of the Genthe archive in the volume *Genthe's Photographs of San Francisco's Old Chinatown*, describes how Genthe secretly and extensively altered his "candid" shots to the point of sometimes eliminating whole figures.[58] Although Genthe boasted in his memoirs that "no artist of good conscience would retouch" a photograph, not even to correct a wrinkle on a face, in reality he often cropped or retouched his work. As Tchen points out, Genthe would also scratch out English words on Chinatown street signs and replace them with Chinese characters in order to create a more authentic and more exotic view of this "foreign" world. Consider the photo entitled *An Unsuspecting Victim* (plate 29a and b). We can see that two figures shown in plate 29B, the original photograph, have been erased for the sake of isolating the white man and enhancing the sense of danger that surrounds him.[59] (If you look very carefully, you can actually discern the ghostly outline of the legs of Genthe's erased assistant in the finished photograph.) Similarly, *The Opium Fiend* (plate 23) could have been simply a man taking a nap, but the cropping, lighting, and title give the image an unsavory tone.

But despite Genthe's editorial control, the tension between appearance and disappearance that was in fact a social reality for these immigrants, in particular the female subjects, emanates from these images in unexpected ways. What is haunting about these photographs is precisely what they manage to evidence in spite of Genthe's revisions. While these images explicitly spectacularize the Asian female body, they also ended up recording those bodies in distress and under harassment. In Genthe's ecology of the streets, Chinese femininity is at once implicated by and yet inextricably alienated from the cityscape, as in *Three Women on Kearney Street* (plate 30). Here three Chinese women walk down the street with their eyes cast down (out of modesty or discomfort?) while the youngest, on the left, looks uneasily behind her, alert to the two sternly dressed, curiously shrouded Victorian ladies trailing behind them like a disapproving conscience. Two shadows on the ground walking toward the Chinese women further enhance the image's sense of compression. The Chinese

PLATE 29A AND B: (a) Arnold Genthe, *An Unsuspecting Victim* (1896–1906), final, edited version. Arnold Genthe Collection. Library of Congress, Prints and Photographs Division. (b) Arnold Genthe, *An Unsuspecting Victim* (1896–1906), untouched original. Arnold Genthe Collection Library of Congress, Prints and Photographs.

PLATE 30: Arnold Genthe, *Three Women on Kearney Street* (1896–1906). Arnold Genthe Collection. Library of Congress, Prints and Photographs Division.

woman in the middle, who serves as the focal point of the image, is finely dressed, with decorative details at her bodice and ankles, in contrast to the plainly dressed older woman to the right and the white women behind her in black. So are we looking at a well-to-do housewife accompanied by her daughter and her maid, or at a successful prostitute being escorted by her servant girl and her madam? The sign in the upper right-hand corner, which reads "To Let," explicitly advertises a rental space but nonetheless, for the English-reading spectator, implicitly commenting on the decorated Asian female body walking underneath it as commodity.

The ambiguity about ornamented Asian femininity, or Asian femininity as ornament, appears throughout the Genthe archive. Genthe's female subjects, from little girls to young women, tend to tread this fine line between mobility and claustrophobic enclosure, between festive display and mute self-effacement. In *Dressed for a Feast* (plate 28), two lovely young women appear on the threshold of a doorway. One has her back completely to us, the other is in profile; both are about to escape behind doors. But what prevents these women from being creatures of the interior world are the inviting surfaces of their bodies: a gorgeous swoop of a wide sleeve re-finding itself in the curve of the pretty hair ornament and the companion's embroidered collar; the single braid interwoven with raw silk meant to extend its length, announcing the young woman's unmarried status. The Asian female body, by virtue of what is on its sartorial surface, is posed teasingly as liminality itself, connoting both inaccessible interiority and inviting exteriority, inscrutable and yet all too legible. Indeed, Genthe likes to stage his Chinese female subjects not in domestic interiors per se, but with thresholds: intersections, door frames, windows, alleyways.

When we do go inside, the interior is more theatrical than domestic. In plate 31 we see Genthe posing himself with one of his favorite subjects, little Minnie Tong, one of his many subjects ambiguously described as "slave girls." Genthe culled several of his young female subjects from the Mission House, known for rescuing abandoned or abused girls from Chinatown. He had gone out of his way (a task that he called "challenging") to befriend a Miss Donaldina Cameron, who was the head of the Chinese Presbyterian Mission, in order to gain access to these girls.[60] Here he dressed Minnie, whom he nicknamed "Tea Rose," in conspicuous, sumptuous holiday regalia that hints at wedding or even imperial attire. Their "togetherness," at once paternalistic and erotic, unsettles by insisting on the proximity between innocence and fixation. The image substitutes surface for subjectivity and theatricality for intimacy. Positioning Minnie in his lap, covering one of her small hands with his much larger one, Genthe ventriloquizes his desire through her sartorial maturity. He called this picture *Friends*.

PLATE 31: Arnold Genthe, *Friends* (1896–1906). Arnold Genthe Collection. Library of Congress, Prints and Photographs Division.

In plate 32 we have Minnie again, several years later. With her hair up in intricate coils, Minnie sports an elaborate hairpiece that both announces and eclipses her. The sumptuous loveliness of this profile belies the "objectivity" of an anthropological or sociological gaze. Minnie's adult braid (though she cannot be more than fifteen) announces her marital (that is, erotic) eligibility. In other words, the sign of "the street" is emerging out of the girl.

Finally, let us turn to the image in plate 33. This might be another "Minnie" a few years later: an anonymous young woman walking down the street, visually arresting in her lavish attire and her isolation. Her sartorial splendor stands in contrast to the desultory street and her own subdued expression as she moves away from the group

PLATE 32: Arnold Genthe, *Little Tea Rose* (1896–1906). Arnold Genthe Collection. Courtesy of Library of Congress, Prints and Photographs Division.

PLATE 33: Arnold Genthe, *A Slave Girl in Holiday Attire* (1896–1906). Arnold Genthe Collection. Courtesy of Library of Congress, Prints and Photographs Division.

of white women to the left and from the broad, shunning back of a white man walking away from her. Almost all archival notes about this image conjecture that this is an image of a prostitute, perhaps even a famous one. But the critical issue here, of course, is not "is she or isn't she," but instead the way the racial episteme structures her visibility.

In these discursive ecologies of the street, Asian femininity accrues an indispensable ambiguity that visualizes and aestheticizes the legal and epistemological crisis about the Asian female body dramatized in *Chy Lung*. We might say that the photographic collection offers us the afterimage of the legal case, and that both make up the "shadow archive" of American citizenship.[61] The opacities that lend Genthe's street scenes (and their rare female pedestrians) their particular extradiegetic texture and melancholic frisson tell us that style determines the epistemology of Asian femininity.

Photography and the visuality of race that it forges have thus played a central role in tying the Chinese body down to a double myth of embodiment and shadow, splendor and crime. Going back to our lone (or lonely) lady (plate 33), we see that the Chinese female body emerges as evidence only and precisely as a sign of ambivalence. Genthe named this image *A Slave Girl in Holiday Attire*, as if underscoring the conflation between leisure and labor and spelling out the point that there is no distinguishing between Asian femininity for sale and in celebration, fusing photography's inherent double functions as honorific and objectifying. In the end, what is melancholic about this image is not its sociology—though that is haunting enough—but the tension generated at the conjunction of this woman's hypervisibility, her anonymity, and her necessary ambiguity. Like the twenty-two young women in *Chy Lung*, she is lost to history except as a residue of Orientalism's beautiful defilement.

Hortense Spillers has eloquently turned our attention to the wounds and fissures inflicted on persons turned into things—what she calls "the hieroglyphics of the flesh."[62] But if Spillers shows us how important it is to remember the ruptures and inescapable materiality of flesh, then let us also recall that the body before the law was never anything but a strapping of things and covers. Speaking of an ontological sense of the body, Paul Valéry writes, "We speak of [the body] to others as of a thing that belongs to us; but for us it is not entirely a thing, and it belongs to us a little less than we belong to it."[63] To speak to a legal sense of the body requires no less an aporia. The law sutures our bodies into its sartorial imagination. We are both more and less than the ornaments that unavoidably mark our skin with such mute insistence.

2

Gleaming Things

PLATE 34: Anna May Wong in gold headdress, *Piccadilly* (1929, dir. E. A. Dupont). Courtesy of Kobal/Rex/Shutterstock.

> an incandescent curve
> licked by chromatic flames
> in labyrinths of reflections
> —MINA LOY ON BRÂNCUSI'S *GOLDEN BIRD*, 1922

OUR NEXT ERUPTION of ornamental Asiatic femininity on the American public stage—indeed, on the world stage—is the iconic Anna May Wong, arguably the single most famous Asian American woman in the twentieth century (plate 34). Where the previous chapter gave us a view into the raced body, at once imaginary and real, in the ornamentalist logic of American legal personhood, here we turn to a different kind of personhood: the making of modern celebrity. Emerging out of a dark, century-long backdrop of Asiatic female visuality like a shooting flame, Wong is a product of the entwined technologies of the cinematic apparatus and modern celebrity culture, giving us a particularly fascinating case study for the strangely embodied disembodiment of Asiatic female personhood at the birth of American modernism.

From the notoriety and anonymity of "the Twenty-two Lewd Chinese Women" to the singularity of Anna May Wong, we can track the effects of ornamentalism when it moves from the stage of "natural law" to the artifice of cinematic stage. Wong's relationship to fame and cinema is complicated. At once internationally renowned yet still relatively unknown in American cultural memory, alternately praised and denigrated as the great "Oriental Beauty" of the twentieth century, fluctuating between the proverbial Dragon Lady and the Lotus Blossom, and always the go-to It girl when it comes time to name *an* Asian American woman, Anna May Wong is, above all, a study in the tension between racialized corporeality and aesthetic thingness.

Called a "moon" and a "porcelain bowl" by Walter Benjamin, Wong is an early twentieth-century race beauty whose corporeality seems inextricably woven into an aesthetic and technology of ornamental thingness (plates 35–38).[1] Once labeled by the media as the "Best Dressed Woman of the Year," this yellow woman's relationship to sartorial extravagance—that is, the intense and intricate interpenetration of body and design—far exceeds the facile distinction between body and costume and pushes us into a much larger philosophic and political debate, activated by the ornament, about what constitutes biological essence versus artificial enhancement. What happens when the human merges into design, when *ergon* and *parerga* infiltrate each other?[2]

What seduces here is not the fleshly body per se but rather the allure of the supplement, of the thing-person that is marginal, adjunct, surplus, tactile, and gorgeous in its disposable artifice. We could attribute this material affinity between the yellow woman and decoration to yet another instance of Orientalism, with all its theatricality and blithe objectification, but we would then miss the chance to think about the convergence of Asiatic femininity, cinema, and modern celebrity, as well as the production, even if incidental, of alternative modes of ontology. The eccentric status of this thing we call a celebrity, already an amalgamation of object and subject, when considered through race and gender, has the potential to produce an uncanny figure

PLATE 35: Anna May Wong in *Limehouse Blues* (1934, dir. Alexander Hall). Courtesy of Paramount Pictures.

PLATE 36: Photograph of Anna May Wong taken by Otto Dyer (1921). Courtesy of Kobal/Rex/Shutterstock.

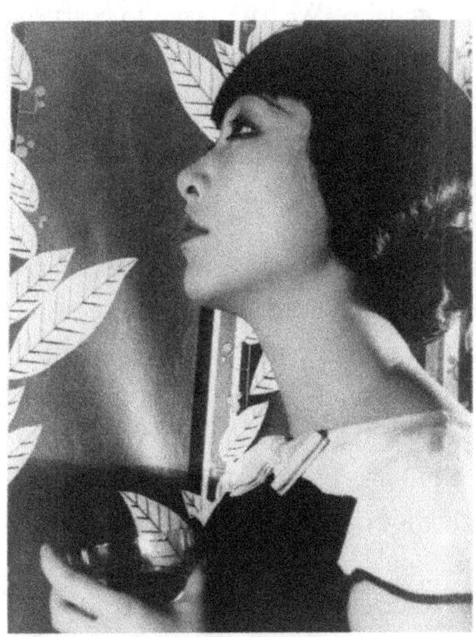

PLATE 37: Anna May Wong (with geometric design). Courtesy of Wikimedia Commons.

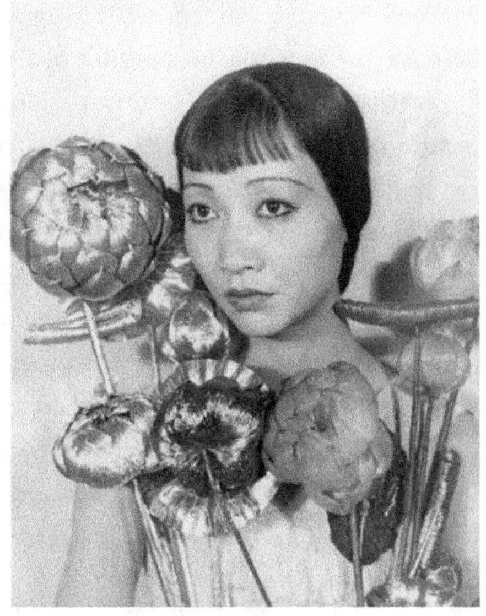

PLATE 38: Anna May Wong (with oversized artificial flowers). Photographed by Carl Van Vechten. Courtesy of Wikimedia Commons.

of transmutation, where human erasure yields a human object whose condition of being challenges the parameters of what counts as a human.

In so-called celebrity studies and what has been called a "return to beauty" in critical discourse, the issues of race and racial differences are often absent. Foundational texts in these lines of inquiry, from Elaine Scarry's *On Beauty and Being Just* to Joseph Roach's *It*, tend not to ask the haunting question of what it means for the history of euphoric beauty to meet up with the history of dysphoric, racialized bodies.[3] This omission is understandable since, in most of Western history and philosophy, idealization and racial difference have hardly gone hand in hand, and where they converge, it tends to be in the familiar realm of fetishization. (Indeed, beauty is often the self-defense mounted by the fetishist.) But is the fetish the only way to understand the convergence of race and celebrity? Or is fetishization the only way to understand the ornamental objectness of a figure like Wong?

Celebrity studies, aesthetic philosophy, and race studies tend to have very little in common, except an enduring attachment to the discourse of fetishism, an attachment that has in many ways prevented us from confronting the fraught interconnections between the presumed antinomies of personhood and objectification, embodiment and image. Even the more revolutionary discourse about race tends to attach the raced body to its irreducible visibility and materiality. We have taken to heart the wisdom that racial difference is a form of "disabling overvisibility" and that the epidermis represents "the most visible of fetishes."[4]

Yet what are the terms of this presumed visibility? In what ways and under what conditions does a (raced and gendered) body come into visibility at all, especially at the beginning of the twentieth century, when vision and modes of seeing are radically transforming? It is in film, that most specular yet most spectral of mediums, that racial difference should raise questions, rather than solidify, the relationship between surface and embodiment. Dichotomies such as authenticity versus artificiality, interiority versus surface, person versus representation, and organic humanness versus synthetic assemblage simply do not help us address the uncanny materialization of race and gender, especially in visual mediums.

It is not a coincidence that the emergence in the early twentieth century of a handful of internationally renowned "race beauties" should both shore up the facts of racial difference and yet radically destabilize how racialized flesh comes to be embodied. Women such as Anna May Wong and Josephine Baker built their iconographic images on a visual idiom that is as exuberantly synthetic as it is organic, crafting the self as art and as product. Their success as agents *and* commodities presses us to think in more nuanced terms about what celebrity and glamour mean for the woman of color. What does modern celebrity—predicated on constant self-production and tied to commodity culture, to the ascension of the public persona, and to the politics of performance—mean for someone seen at once too much and not at all? How do we talk about agency, consent, and embodiment in this highly mediated context? Is glamour the last residue of Benjaminean aura or a packaged, shining, and impenetrable mode of beauty, and what can it *do* for a subject whose body has been simultaneously overembodied and depersonalized?[5] If the history of Western art, from Titian's *Tarquin and Lucretia* to Picasso's *Guernica*, has been preoccupied with coming to terms with the meeting of violence and aesthetics, the celebrity of the raced female body offers a pragmatic instantiation of that dilemma. Embodiment is the ground on which the woman of color has been denigrated and affirmed. To talk about celebrity and glamour for the woman of color is, therefore, to reckon with the collision between the violence of impersonality and the violence of personality.

Almost an exact contemporary of Josephine Baker (1906–1975), Wong (1905–1961) would seem to be the perfect foil to Baker, one representing the excessive sartorial elegance of Orientalism, the other exemplifying the naked animalistic drive of primitivism. But these very different race-making vocabularies should not blind us to what they share: the thickness and mediations that inform the very idea of a racial epidermal schema in the early twentieth century, one that involves not only the ambivalent nostalgia-and-repulsion for the flesh but also the fantasy of its translation into aesthetic objectness. As I have argued elsewhere about Baker (in *Second Skin*), the discourse of modernist primitivism and its accompanying rhetoric about the ineluctable corporeality of "black flesh" have obscured the ways in which Baker in performance engages her own skin and nakedness—an engagement that tells us much about modernism's own imagined distinction between atavistic organicity and the technologically advanced, denuded modern surface. It was in writing that book about modern architectural surface and its relationship to black skin that I glimpsed the much larger story about the intricate relationship between race and ornament. This liaison has expansive impacts: on modernism and its own troubled relationship to ornamentality as an aesthetic, moral, and political sign; on primitivism and its fantasies of the naked flesh; and on Orientalism and its dreams of the thingness of aesthetic beings.

By naming a double process of ornamenting and Orientalizing a person not through biological but instead through synthetic terms, ornamentalism raises questions about racial embodiment that the cinema, itself an interplay of absence and presence, shadow and ontology, heightens. Wong is a supremely cinematic subject not because of her beauty or her acting skills (neither of which is contested) but rather because of her very idiosyncratic and arresting negotiations with her own thingness. Instead of seeing her as a stereotype of decadent Asiatic female flesh, this chapter is focused on what I call her supremely "subjunctive"—that is, at once projected and conditional—presence, both on- and offscreen. What follows is thus neither a biography nor an affirmation of her subversive agency. Instead I offer a meditation on her art and how it, sometimes with intentionality but often without, applies tremendous pressure on the apparent discrepancy between presence and absence, embodiment and abstraction.

Like Baker with her polished black skin, the golden-skinned Wong radiated glamour and allure, which, as her popular life story goes, allowed her to transcend both negative personal circumstances and the larger abject history of yellow women.[6] Like Baker, the American-born Wong mobilized a passionate international fan base, though she was, and probably still is, barely known to her fellow Americans. Wong enjoyed a cinematic career that spanned over forty years, from silent films to talkies, and mesmerized audiences in Hollywood, London, Berlin, Paris, and Vienna. With over sixty films to her credit, she performed in English, French, German, Mandarin, and Cantonese; she also acted on stage, radio, and television. Like Baker, Wong exerted a magnetic pull over modern artists, directors, photographers, and philosophers.[7] Wong was even more photographed than the superlatively photogenic Baker. The archive of Wong's glamour photography boasts hundreds of images, many obsessively taken by photographers such as George Hurrell, Carl Van Vechten, Alfred Eisenstaedt, Edward Steichen, Lotte Jacobi, and E. O. Hoppé. Whereas Baker gained her celebrity through the theater, Wong acquired hers through the filmic mediums of cinematography and photography. How did this Chinese American woman acquire such international celebrity in an age of extreme anti-Chinese sentiment, and what is it about her that renders her so exquisitely compatible with high glamour and its shimmering celluloid traces?

SHINE

Let us begin then, not with flesh but with light. In the British film *Piccadilly*, directed by the German director E. A. Dupont in 1929 and recently restored by the British Film Institute, Wong appears in an incandescent dance number that would seem to epitomize her appeal for the white, European, male audience. Wong's last silent film, *Piccadilly* made her the toast of the town in London, Berlin, and Paris. She plays Shosho, a Chinese dishwasher who is discovered in the basement scullery of the Piccadilly Circus Club and given the chance by owner Valentine Wilmot (Jameson Thomas) to perform publicly upstairs in the grand ballroom. This Cinderella story is entwined with a sordid plot involving Shosho's displacement of the club's regular star, Mabel Greenfield (Gilda Gray), on stage and in Valentine's erotic affections. In a key sequence, which I treat as a primal scene, we witness Shosho's first public performance, the one that launches her overnight rise to stardom.

In this extended scene, Shosho, scantily but elaborately clad in an ornamental costume of glittering gold, rises from the floor of a large art deco stage. Moving no more than two feet in any direction, she proceeds to dance slowly and "exotically" to sultry but somber music (plate 39). Although the staging itself is simple (one dancer center stage, three stringed instruments tucked upstage, no orchestra, no chorus), we nonetheless experience the scene as a sensorial deluge, for it is suffused with a nearly unbearable light—coming from Shosho's golden, pailletted body, the candles and lamps set aflame—and with palpable energy between dancer and audience.

It is not a coincidence that this extraordinary scene of visual saturation takes place in a diegesis about the dream of celebrity. While Baker's films almost all rehearse the story of her own rise from rags to riches, *Piccadilly* is the only film in Wong's extensive catalog that meditates on the making of her celebrity. Although Wong's star quality may be evident even in films where she holds minor roles, and although she often played other dancers and performers (for example, *Daughter of the Dragon* [1931] and *Chu Chin Chow* [1934], to name just two), *Piccadilly* is the one film that explicitly contemplates celebrity in a sustained way: its making, its fickleness, its shining exhilaration. Moreover, this is *the* film in which Wong most actively aligns herself with her character; at one moment, she signs her real name in (and into) the film. In *Piccadilly* Wong's offscreen radiance acquires its keenest onscreen reflection.[8] And in the diegetic scene of her breakout performance, a shimmering enactment and metareflection of celebrity making, we find Anna May Wong at her most seductive and im/material self.

This scene of classic Orientalist performance is arresting not for its clichés but for its cinematography. Though devoid of color, the glittering film surface appears more than black and white and feels laden with light and affect. Four large strobe lights circle the foot of the stage, shooting a round of golden, ricocheting lights around the ballroom, and in the middle of this chromatic, vertiginous ring we find Wong herself, moving dreamily, clad in bare skin and metal, a column of radiance that both draws and deflects the gaze.

The publicity still in plate 39 cannot do justice to the richness of the optic field enacted by the film. The print's chiaroscuro fails to capture the rapturous and promiscuous spill of cinematic light throughout this vibrant sequence, touching not just Shosho but also the shimmering surfaces of floor, walls, ceilings, and rapt faces all around, a net of light that literalizes the web of fascination. The light, acting as dream and agent, unites the dancer and her spectators in a moment of visual and temporal trance.

PLATE 39: Anne May Wong, ballroom scene, *Piccadilly* (1929). Courtesy of Kobal/Rex/Shutterstock.

It may seem all too appropriate that this episode of fetishized, Orientalized femininity should be staged with an obsessive attention to "bling." After all, in contrast to primitivism, which deploys a rhetoric of nakedness, Orientalized femininity from Mata Hari to Afong Moy (the Victorian traveling "Chinese Lady" display) has always relied on the spectacularization not of naked skin but of ornament: the excessive coverings and decorations that supposedly symptomize the East's overdeveloped and hence feminized and corrupt civilization.[9] We also know that in Freud's essay "Fetishism," which displays most intensely his sartorial preoccupations, *shine* plays a key role. In discussing the often-cited case of the young man who has "exalted a certain sort of 'shine on the nose' into a fetishistic precondition," Freud accounts for this odd choice of "object" by unpacking the series of substitutions that that choice effects:

> The surprising explanation of this was that the patient had been brought up in an English nursery but had later come to Germany, where he forgot his mother-tongue almost completely. The fetish, which originated from his earliest childhood, had to be understood in English, not German. The "shine on the nose" [in German, *Glanz auf der Nase*] was in reality a "glance at the nose." The nose was thus the fetish, which, incidentally, he endowed at will with the luminous shine which was not perceptible to others.[10]

In Freud's analysis, *shine* was not just a psychical substitute (standing in for the nose standing in for the missing maternal penis) but also a linguistic one: *glanz* mistaken for *glance*. For Karl Marx, too, shining surfaces signal commodity fetishism. Where for Freud fetishism arouses and cancels the knowledge of castration, for Marx, fetishism arouses and cancels the knowledge of alienated labor. In light of these interpretations, Shosho epitomizes the commodification of the feminized and the Asiatic in labor production. There are plenty of sound reasons for reading Wong, playing the scullery maid turned star, as the quintessentially fetishized object and for understanding the lure of shine in this scene as its symptom.

Yet these readings do not feel wholly satisfactory, for they cannot quite explain away the scene's affective impact or the consternation it provokes. Who is the watcher, and who is being watched? Does the overwhelming light signal plenitude or blindness? Are we assured or assaulted by it? And what happens when "shine" falls on everyone and everything? Composed of a sequined breastplate, a spangled girdle, and a tall and spiky headdress, Shosho's costume gleams preternaturally. The glare bounces coolly, brilliantly, and erratically off her breasts and hips, at times making it literally impossible to look at her. The star draws our gaze only to reflect it back with violence and indifference. If the lure of shine is meant to protect the fetishistic spectator from the threatening lack underneath, then here that protective sheen hurts the eye.

This presumably fetishistic scene is difficult to parse. For one thing, it encompasses many layers of gazes and just as many partial objects. Not only are we looking at the audience looking at Shosho, but Valentine is also surreptitiously watching his clients watching his investment, and offstage, Mabel is watching her rival in enthralled horror. Who or what is the fetish, and for whom? Whose lack is being projected and compensated for? And then there is the camera eye, which at times tracks in 360 degrees, reinforcing the vertiginous feel of the scene even as it suggests a transcendental point of view, and at times adopts Shosho's apparent point of view. The objects of the gaze therefore include not just Shosho but also her audience; everyone (including those of us watching the film) is placed on display. Shosho's shining body in the center of the ring provides less a screen than a mirror: the mesmerized audience (both diegetic and extradiegetic) is suspended by Shosho and, in the process, arrested by its own watching.

Who is watching whom, and what is going on in that watching? The anatomy of fascination suggests that to be fascinated is not to enjoy distance from the commodified object or necessarily to use it to compensate for one's own lack. Instead, fascination enables contact with objectness; it lubricates the empathy for the imagined pleasure of self-objectification, that relished slide from *me* to *it*. We, the extradiegetic viewers, are implicated as well in this pleasure of *fascinum*, of self-immobilization. Watching the object allows us to enjoy the fantasy of being objects. In a sense, glamour does the work of ornamentalism: a state of objectness that seduces. When the flickering light leads us to the gazing audience in the film, we are thrown back to our own watching, our own dwelling, reminded that the true object of fascination in the cinematic experience is light and what it means to be held by light. What is the pleasure of cinema as a sensual experience if not the fantasy that we can fuse our eyes to light, a fantasy of sight as well as blindness?

Instead of enthralling us with a body as lack (be it a nose or the racialized female body), *Piccadilly* seduce us into occupying a slippery space between *shine* and *glance*, blindness and insight. Its cinematography forces us quite literally to confront this passage between vision and blindness. Just before we are treated to the startling sight of Shosho's dazzling performance, the camera abandons us to an odd visual pause when it pans slowly from left to right, showing nothing but a dark blank screen for almost a minute. This awkward scopic failure in the middle of an important scene makes no spatial or diegetic sense; instead, it draws attention to the contrasting burst of light or the birth of vision to follow and underscores the alliance among light, visuality, and the fantasy of corporeal creation that *is* the gift of cinema. The supposed fetish (the female body) stands in for light and becomes the precondition for cinematic vision rather than for psychical blindness. In other words, this scene may be seen not as a metaphor for fetishism but instead as a parable for the cinematic experience: what it means to see in the presence of nothing.

Viewing Shosho as aligned with cinematic possibility itself (not as a mere symptom of cinematic pleasure) leads us to an analogous question about the relation between glamour and body: what does it means for us to see a made-up body? Or what kind of a body must be imagined for such seeing to be possible? To answer this, we have to first note that for a sex icon and celebrated femme fatale, Shosho presents a body that is surprisingly light, in more ways than one. With her pale, Rubenesque body, Mabel's weight is constantly being emphasized: she's often seen reclining or leaning, the camera repeatedly meditating on her plump white flesh as her male admirers plant kisses on exposed expanses of upper arm, shoulder, and back. By contrast, Shosho's gleaming body, when it is finally revealed, is shockingly sparse: boyishly slim, childlike, ribbed, clad in scales and spikes. In motion, Mabel makes us feel the weight of her body: the rise and fall of her Charleston, the exertion of her shimmy (a dance the actress playing Mabel, Gilda Gray, is said to have originated), the sweaty heat of her routine. Shosho's movements, in contrast, are cool and light, almost ephemeral in their slow sways and spirals. Where Mabel embodies the frenzy of showbiz, Shosho offers a formal reverie; where Mabel covers ground, Shosho is all concentric circles.

While many today might take the skinny body to be the desirable one, in Great Britain in 1929, the preference for Wong over Gray, a more established star, was hardly guaranteed. Indeed, Shosho wins the sexual (and cinematic) competition by drawing not on a rhetoric of fleshly availability but instead on its opposite. Constraint, not exposure, characterizes Shosho's self-presentation. The first time we see her, she is dancing on a table in the basement of the Piccadilly Circus Club (plate 40). The scene of exhibitionism is curiously hushed. Shosho dances among tendrils of steam, her body fully clothed, her face closed in self-absorption, while the other dishwashers watch in silent enthrallment. Even though her dancing has been remembered by reviewers in uniformly Orientalist and primitivist terms, all "gyrating" and "thrusting" hips, Shosho's movements are in fact remarkably subtle and subdued in this scene, bordering on the somnambular.[11] In this highly metatheatrical performance, we get hush instead of loud, restraint instead of drama, being within the self instead of being for the other.

This scene of prurient, Orientalist revelation turns out to be quite unrevealing.[12] Indeed, Shosho's moments of exhibitionism—here in the basement and later in the ballroom—tend to offer themselves as moments of interiorization rather than exteriorization. Her two dance scenes are sonically linked, and in both scenes the music produces an estranging effect. In the scullery, Shosho appears in the diegetic world to be dancing to pure, smoky silence, but the extradiegetic audience hears a simple score that anticipates the music from the later ballroom scene. Once in the ballroom, we

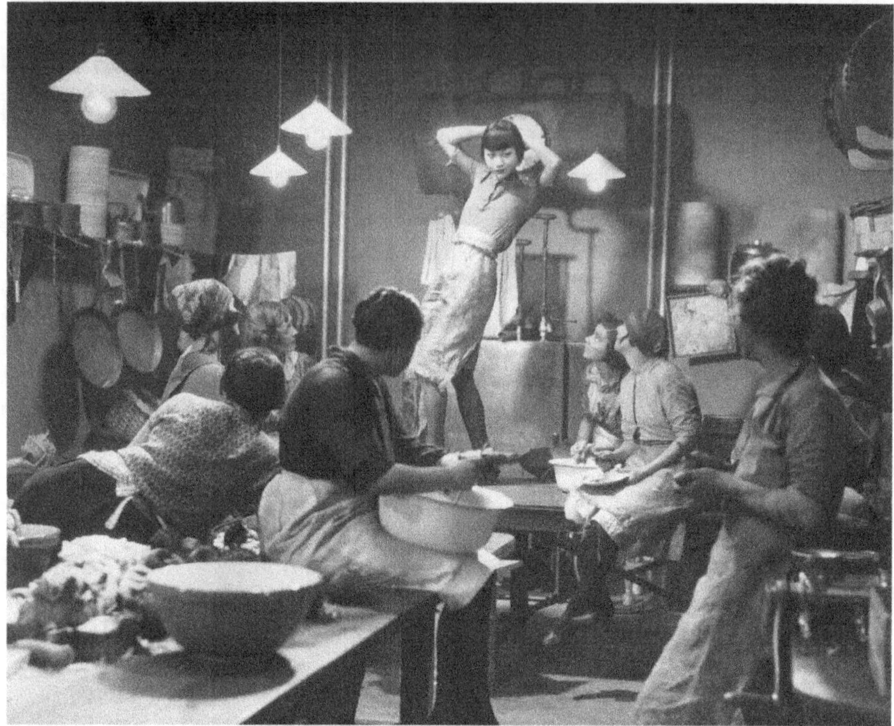

PLATE 40: Anne May Wong, scullery scene, *Piccadilly* (1929). Courtesy of Kobal/Rex/Shutterstock.

first assume the music to be diegetic because we are watching a musical number. But then we realize the music (like that in the scullery) must be extradiegetic, not because this is a silent film, but because the ponderous, pentatonic but fully orchestrated score that we hear cannot be coming from the three instruments (two lutes and one erhu) in the mis-en-scène. The music thus creates a kind of privacy: either we are not privy to whatever diegetic music is being played on stage or we are hearing Shosho's internal music. In either case, we and Shosho find ourselves outside of the plot's time. In other words, the extradiegetic music sonically repeats Shosho's own extradiegetic quality: the way she appears to be for and not for the audience; the way her performances seem suspended between being seen and self-seeing, between spectacle and reverie, between being an object on display and a subject hiding in plain sight.

Instead of guaranteeing subjectivity, Shosho's self-absorption exerts a kind of aggressive impersonality, as if she is and has always been elsewhere. Perhaps this is why this celebrity (in the film, if not in the publicity shots) never looks at her adoring audience; indeed, she appears oblivious to it. Her introspection serves no purpose in the plot nor is it psychologically coherent; instead, it gestures toward an absence that may be fundamental to the making of stardom. Wong's inwardness speaks not to her ontological authenticity (as fans may be eager to assume), but rather to theatrical work itself: the active production of a presence made for witness. This hint of interiority does not secure for the performer a privacy that is safe from public prurience; this is, after all, a scene about publicity.[13] Wong's performance of withdrawal produces a fantasy of interiority, which the audience can then witness and treasure. We are, in short, looking at a choreographed soliloquy. This scene therefore dramatizes rather than simply thematizes the construction of celebrity by unpacking the theatrical process of interiority made public.[14] It does not instantiate agency but rather represents its mechanism. Similarly, while contemporary critics tend to lament the lack of physical contact between Shosho and Valentine onscreen as a sign of the racist taboo against interracial romance, I contend that that absence is in keeping with Shosho's erotic and performative withholding.

Shosho's solipsism invites, but it is an enigmatic (to borrow a Laplanchean term), not erotic, provocation. A shimmering surface beckons us to plunge into a flat and reflective interiority. Wong negotiates crushing, corporeal objecthood by assuming a kind of resistant objectness. The allegories of the birth of celebrity embedded in this film point not to the emergence of a unique subject or person but to the states of objectness that precondition that fantasy.

IT GIRL

Wong's celluloid body enthralls through corporeal absence; it seduces through surrogacy rather than presence. From our first sight of Shosho to her tragic demise, the most sensuous thing about Shosho has never been her flesh but what can stand in for it. When it comes to its star, the film's sartorial preoccupation far exceeds its corporeal obsession. Questions of skin often morph into considerations of fabric or other materials. Back in the scullery, when we are first introduced to Shosho, the camera zooms in on her and moves slowly down the length of her well-covered body to linger lovingly on the close-up of a long run in her sheer black stocking. The camera will return yet again to and fixate on this tear when Shosho makes her second appearance on the back stairs of the club. While this detail must have been intended to invoke a Victorian sense of titillation and to connote Shosho's class status, it also invites a series of questions about the integrity of Shosho's "epidermal schema," as well as about whether it is possible to see Shosho's flesh. Indeed, on making the risky decision of giving a scullery maid her own floor show, the club's owner, Valentine, immediately worries about her costume, not her choreography or rehearsal. Shosho insists on the kind of "Chinese dress" she ought to wear for her debut and knows exactly where to buy it, as if she has been planning for this moment all her life (though the dress in question turns out to be neither Chinese nor really a dress). In the back room of a Chinese restaurant in London's Limehouse district, Shosho dictates to Valentine almost all the terms, including the price, involved in deciding how to dress her body. While the soft silks draw Valentine's eye, Shosho picks instead the most armored and prickly of costumes: "I dance in that or not at all."

In this dramatically recursive scene, we see Wong peeping through Shosho, assuming through the mediation of her character the roles of haughty star, costume designer, director, and producer all at once. This is especially poignant given Wong's frequent, real-life comments about the racism that she suffered professionally and personally.[15] At the same time, though we may get the promise of Wong's authorial agency at this critical moment, a stranger, perhaps more incisive kind of agency is potentially at work, one that critiques the politics of subjecthood and claims of subversive female agency.[16] This portrait of sartorial dictation and presumed authorship is quite cagey about the kind of body issuing commands in that back room. At first this scene of barter seems replete with clichéd erotic suggestions: the back of a seedy restaurant as a makeshift dressing room, the haggling men clearly bidding for the woman's body and sexual attention. The erotic charge, however, does not come from the exposure of Shosho's real body but rather from its fantasized presence. When Valentine asks to see Shosho in her new costume, setting the stage for a perfect moment of heterosexual male prurience, Shosho curiously asks her other love interest, Jim (King Hou Chang), to try on the costume instead. There follows an exquisite moment when Valentine looks Jim up and down, presumably contemplating the outfit but perhaps also trying to imagine the body (Shosho's? Jim's?) inside. We see Valentine, for instance, lifting Jim's breastplate to look underneath. (Is this to confirm the presence or absence of sexual difference?) In this fraught scene, where the Asian female body is, so to speak, on the block, that body appears in its most displaced and spectral form, while male, heterosexual voyeurism expresses itself as a homoerotic exchange.

In this racialized and gendered moment of barter, skein replaces skin. Shosho offers herself by displacing herself. This curious scene reminds us from what we have started to see in the previous chapter (in a legal context) that fantasies of "skin" (a trope that seems invariably racialized and gendered) may be profoundly indebted to fantasies about covering. Here the epidermal schema gives way to—perhaps is never as seductive as—a fantasy of skin as a teasing negotiation between corporeality and covering, embodiment and substitution, wholeness and holes. What makes seeing (racial and gender difference) possible here is the impossibility of seeing. And what makes star quality most fully present is its insistence on its own superficiality. In *Piccadilly*, the spectacularization of "yellow skin"—the moment that should have been equivalent to Fanon's "Look, a Negro . . . "—coincides instead with that skin's displacement.[17]

Instead of redeeming the rejection of yellow skin by idealizing or authenticating it, Shosho the golden girl replaces that skin with a metallic shield, even displacing it altogether onto a surrogate (male) body. And when she does finally assume the costume, the suit will hijack the scene, overwhelming its wearer's skin with its metallic brilliance. In both art history and vernacular culture, there is an enduring discourse of shine historically and pejoratively associated with racialized skin,[18] an ethnographic, racialized, commodified history of shine that Hollywood glamour lighting studiously represses. Hence, as Richard Dyer has famously argued, Hollywood lighting embodies and extends a transcendent ideology, one that is associated with idealized white femininity and that suppresses the shine of animalistic and corporeal sweat with a compensatory, pearly glow of soft femininity. But Shosho's brand of shine is neither animalistic nor soft. Indeed, its metallic luster points us to another mode of glamour lighting, not identified by Dyer, that I would call "hard diva photography," which is more closely associated with the shellacked beauty of Jean Harlow, Gloria Swanson, and Wong's close friend and co-star in *Shanghai Express* (1932), Marlene Dietrich (plates 41, 42, and 43).

In contrast to the pearlized, feminized, and vulnerable surface identified by Dyer and applied by Hollywood to women such as Lillian Gish or Marilyn Monroe, the armor worn by Wong as she plays Shosho emits an almost brittle, aggressively inorganic quality that is more akin to what might be called "cellophane glamour." In *Glamour in Six Dimensions*, Judith Brown points out that the appeal of cellophane and plastic shine in the first quarter of the twentieth century in theater, film, photography, and everyday commodities signifies modernism's propensity for hygienic sleekness, plasticity, and blankness.[19] I would suggest that Wong transforms Brown's "moribund aesthetics" by mobilizing plasticity in a vitally inorganic aesthetics.[20] As Jeffrey Meikle argues, the invention of plastics at the inception of the twentieth century brought with it a host of visionary social ideals about creative transformation and plasticity.[21] Plastics were seen as crucial surrogates for, not cheap imitations of, rare and valuable organic materials. That euphoria dissipated by the 1940s, when plastic became a common household presence and signaled inexpensive and tacky copies. But for a brief shining moment, plastic connoted the possibility, the transformation, and the synthetic malleability that Wong's particular form of glamour and shine enacts. Wong's "thingness" differs from the laden, passive, or regressive corporeality often associated with (good or evil) "Oriental beauty." In this cinematic meditation on celebrity as spectacle-making, we are given not a darkened or exposed body, or one penetrated or ruptured by gaze, but instead a body clad in a resilient gleam.

Glamour's shellacked beauty reminds us that the presentation of self as object for consumption coexists with the rendering of that self as *in*digestible. Suddenly, we understand that the cult of personality paradoxically exemplifies the desire for the

PLATE 41: Jean Harlow (1933). Photographed by George Hurrell. Courtesy of Kobal/Rex/Shutterstock.

PLATE 42: Gloria Swanson (1934). Photographed by Clarence Sinclair Bull. Courtesy of Kobal/Rex/Shutterstock.

PLATE 43: Marlene Dietrich (1947). Photographed by A. L. "Whitney" Schaefer. Courtesy of Kobal/Rex/Shutterstock.

ambivalence of personhood rather than being a celebration of uncompromised individuality. It is neither a coincidence nor a symptom of commodification that the vernacular term used to indicate ultrapersonality—the *It* that Roach recently brought to light again—is also the pronoun that designates nonpersonhood. Glamour's imperviousness thus draws on a crisis of personhood that is inherently political and maybe even strangely liberating for a woman and a minority. Glamour liberates not in the simple sense of a compensatory or impenetrable beauty (because Shosho remains vulnerable even if her self-presentation is not), but rather by providing a temporary relief from the burdens of personhood and visibility.

I am tracking a peculiar form of agency, one that is not rooted in the certitude of a sovereign subject but is instead developed through surrogacy. Throughout *Piccadilly*, some form of substitution comes into play whenever we are supposed to be witnessing authentic personhood. In another scene of self-referential star making, the camera gives us a quick close-up of Shosho signing her contract with Valentine. We see not just that Shosho has signed in Chinese rather than in English but also that she has written Wong's given name, Huáng Liushuang, thereby at least diegetically invalidating the contract. Many take this to be a triumphant assertion of female agency. Yet the signature writes Wong into and out of the film. This inscription is also a disappearance. Taking place within the diegesis, this consent to celebrity and to misrecognition is a gesture at once real and fictive, a complicated act of self-inscription. The name marks Wong's identification with and distancing from Shosho; in that difference we bear witness to the fraught politics of recognition that the celebrated woman always faces, the fine line between self-expression and publicity, the real and the representational, affirmation and fetishization. The moment may register a rare and significant moment of authorial intent on Wong's part, but it also inscribes the peculiar form of nonsubjective agency that celebrity itself enacts: one always is and is not the star that one signifies.

Perhaps this paradox is what makes "agency," something we like to attribute to our stars, appear in *Piccadilly* as a potential that hovers between the promise of a person and the promise of a thing. Whenever Shosho performs, agency seems to get displaced onto the surfaces surrounding her. The shimmering life of things (metals, clothes, fire, glass, ornament) reaches beyond the explicit domain of the diegesis. In the superluminous moments when light seems to exceed the frames of the film, the viewer is moved furthest from the plot and transported, along with Shosho, into another realm of seeing, hearing, and feeling. Light, animate inanimateness, enables the transfer to this other realm.

Here, in addition to the discourses of Hollywood photography and cellophane gloss, we should recall modernism's fascination with metal as a form of vibrant matter, for when it comes to Wong's incandescent figure, we need to consider another cult of light: the discourse of shine and sculptural surfaces in the 1920s and 1930s. When *Piccadilly* was made, shine as a concept was enjoying currency in visual culture. Artists, especially sculptors, in the interwar years were enthralled by the possibilities of sheen. Poets such as Mina Loy and sculptors such as Constantin Brâncusi and Henry Moore wrote and spoke about the symbolic and active values of "shine" to "enhance curve" and "lead the eye around"; shininess came to embody for them a host of ideas about modernity and technology.[22] But even more than connoting the machine and plastic age, shininess for these artists presents the means through which materiality might be released, rather than reified. Brâncusi and Moore came to think of shine as capable of imputing motion and sound to inanimate objects and even embodying ideas of auratic potential and originary radiance.[23] In early twentieth-century philosophy, the surprisingly ubiquitous yet little-studied deployment of the rhetoric and trope of shine usually indexes a fundamentally ambiguous relation between humans and things at the site of aesthetic engagement. Although there has not been a systematic discussion of shine in twentieth-century aesthetic-philosophical thinking beyond that of Freudian or Marxist fetishism, there have in fact been many provocative suggestions that shine may potentially offer a productive, even ethical, form of immateriality rather than merely being the gaudy veil of material value. Writers as diverse as Marcel Proust, Roland Barthes, Martin Heidegger, and Jacques Lacan have attributed to shine an inherent quality of aesthetic formation that reveals art's desire and capacity to escape its materiality.[24] In short, shine signals for these thinkers a potentially ethical, rather than simply fetishistic, dimension of aesthetic experience.

In *Piccadilly* we might think of shine as another agent of fugitive surrogacy for the Orientalized woman. Through the refraction of light, the "Oriental woman" as objet d'art has been derealized. Shine offers less a description or quality of light than an active mode of relationality: a dynamic medium through which the organic and the inorganic fuse, and through which the visual spills into the sensorial. The intense visual pleasure afforded by *Piccadilly*'s ballroom scene derives not from female flesh on display (we have seen how elusive that is) but instead from the exhilarating eruption of the visual into other realms. Linking the visual to the haptic, shine transports Shosho (and us) between flesh and inorganic object. We might say that instead of skin, we are getting skin sense. (Are we now seeing the relation between *glance* and *glanz* not as a linguistic displacement or error but instead as a structural repetition preconditioning visual ecstasy?) Shine mobilizes the interstitiality between sight and feeling, visuality and textuality. Earlier I noted that Shosho is mirrorlike; I can now claim that shininess is an animating agent, because it *acts* on us. By firing up her body with light and stretching that light all around the room, by cladding her in gold and repeating it in the objects surrounding her, the mis-en-scène produces an animated and multisensorial surface that decorporealizes and extends her body. Light lives on that transitive, metallic surface, rather than resides in the body. And we, like Shosho, follow that light's shine, glued to the seductive agency of living on the surface of ornaments. It is the surface rather than the body that assumes the fantasy of subjectivity.

The woman as ornament is an old trope, but in this film, the ornament is alive. The ballroom exudes a diva's charisma of its own. The semicircular stairs that enclose the stage, the room's bejeweled and multifaceted appearance (produced by the glittering strobe lights), and the gem (Shosho) in the middle of this structure turn the scene into an elaborately wrought ornament. The spatial relations embedded in the ballroom invite us to confront the various, insistent references to the idea of worlds and world making. In many ways, this is a scene about geography, mapping, and geometry. Simple shapes—circles, cones, triangles—dominate the atlas of Shosho's performance. Shiny ornaments, from the shimmering "stars" on the ceiling to the gleaming tower on Shosho's head to the glowing spheres at her feet, invoke the cosmos. The entire scene feels like a moving diagram: Shosho's own pencil-slim body, with its spikes pointing and sliding like a pendulum or a compass, appears to be redrawing and remapping the space in which she moves. If Shosho the Chinese dishwasher in London is the stranded object of British imperialism, then what are her dance and its cartography saying? (Can an object speak or transport its viewers?)[25]

Let me try to tease out the economy of light in relation to the geography of imperialism. That the Piccadilly ballroom instantiates an imperial geography is hardly surprising. Everything about the floor show and the plot tells us that Shosho is the "Eastern jewel" that crowns British imperialism. Yet this jewel stretches its inorganic light to consume the entire room. How do we understand this early twentieth-century bling spectacle and what it says about celebrity and commodification? Historically, light is often seen as a symptom of commodity culture. In her essay "The Sound of Light: Reflections on Art History in the Visual Culture of Hip-Hop," the art historian Krista Thompson offers a study of shininess in contemporary celebrity culture that historicizes the modern market's roots in nineteenth-century imperialism. She situates hip-hop culture's propensity for flashy, material display in a much "longer history of refashioning status and prestige through shiny jewels, tactile surfaces, and sumptuous goods." For her, this history provides a conceptual framework for questioning "the performance and visual propagation of power" in today's bling culture.[26] Yet can ornamentation affect an alternative economy, one that is still related to material history but that stands in a different relation to commodification?

Shosho's shimmering, excessively ornamentalized performance can be seen as a proto-bling moment, in which the concerns of what is being refashioned have less to do with personal material wealth or ontic aspirations than with resignifying the origin of consumer culture that Thompson references. In other words, this shimmering scene of presumably Orientalist display and female celebrity can also be seen as a primal scene about reactivating colonial objects in ways that remap the geography of imperialism itself. Gottfried Semper, the nineteenth-century architect, art theorist, and amateur ethnographer, reminds us that the ancient Greek word for adornment, *kosmos,* means both "decoration" and "world order." (This is, of course, why the words *cosmetics* and *cosmology* share an etymological root.) In his lecture "Concerning the Formal Principles of Ornament and Its Significance As Artistic Symbol" (1856), Semper notes that, far from being superfluous, ornament aims to align itself with cosmic laws. Human adornment originates from the desire to replicate a micrograph of the visible world and offers a dynamic enactment of the invisible forces of the universe. Semper calls the primary category of ornamental artifact "directional ornaments," which remap space.[27] (Shosho's spiky headdress is the most striking example in *Piccadilly*.) Directional ornaments not only follow and enhance bodily movements but also dynamically represent what today we would call prosthetic possibilities by expanding the bodily periphery with inanimate objects. Shosho's spear or tower headdress, facilitated by shine, shape, and movement, appears to extend both her bodily and psychical boundary, creating a new outline at once corporeal and fictional. The costume Shosho wears on her opening night resembles but is not exactly the same one we saw her select in the back room of the Chinese restaurant. The plates and spikes of this version are much more exaggerated, as if, in the limelight, the costume has grown to its most striking scale.

Shosho's costume generates a map of its own. Parts of the costume, as well as Shosho's hand and arm gestures, allude to various stylistic elements from Chinese, Thai, Vietnamese, Korean, and Indonesian costumes and architectural forms. This outfit has often been criticized by contemporary reviewers as ethnically inauthentic and taken to be yet another symptom of Orientalist conflation. But does this hybrid Orient embodied by Shosho's costume not also, even if unintentionally, question authenticity? And could we go further and call the "Orient" being re-formed on Shosho's body a sartorial rearrangement of the fragments of pan-Asian geography in the face of Western imperial expansion? Rather than take this mélange as just another instance of Orientalist conflation, we might see it as a gesture of alliance and communication, not as subversion per se, but as a gathering of stranded objects. This re-formation or re-collection does not guarantee recuperation; instead it enacts and memorializes a shoring of the fragments as fragments. Although Semper, an amateur ethnographer, may have been influenced by primitivist and Orientalist imaginations, he also came to see the history of ornament as the breakdown of ethnography, by understanding ornaments not as pristine cultural or national signifiers but instead as "portable ecology."[28] We might say that the fragmented, archival world of Shosho's Orient records loss and imports or relocates several ecologies. Shosho's costume and ornamentation re-collect the pan-Asian geography that has been transplanted to the heart of London. She is at once an imported jewel and the eye blinding the collectors' gazes.

Wong as Shosho speaks to the world *as* the fragmented world. The symptom and the ornament of Orientalism, she is nonetheless a stranded object that continues to articulate through its very objectness. Through the rapture of light and the insistent life of the object, this performance of imperial tourism, reminiscent of a world's fair, realigns the notions of spectatorship, ownership, and geographic centrality. Who is the traveler, and who is the one at home? Shosho moves very little in her big number; it is the audience who circles around her. She may be the exotic import, but in this performance she is the one calling out to the world, and it is the audience being rotated and relocated. If the contemporary use of *bling* by hip-hop celebrities signals a subaltern reclamation of capitalism, as Thompson claims, in this early-century precursor the shining stranded object displays itself as the plunder of imperialism but also situates itself as the commander of all the spoils and, in doing so, *moves* those around it.

It is hardly an accident that the trope of the circle dominates this scene. The shape recurs in the choreography, in Wong's bodily placement, and on the stage itself and the props on it. Semper tells us that the ring emits symbolic power as a microcosmic shape because, as a form of circular antenna, it collects forces of the universe and confers them on the body that it adorns. (This is why royalty wears crowns.) Indeed, the circle appears to be the perfect analog for Shosho's mode of simultaneous self-expansion and self-containment. We thrill not to Wong's reification but to her almost indifferent megalomania: the way she commands all things around her, centrifugally pulls objects, lights, and glances to her magnetic center. Even the diegetic audience enjoys being an object under her sway, being "held" by her. Instead of reading this scene as yet another staging of female narcissism, we might see it as a material absorption and self-investment that in turn turns the world.

Placed on display, has the Asiatic become the alternative center of this new map? Are we looking at a revision of the birth of Venus, one of the founding myths of Western aesthetics? With whirling locks and fabrics surrounding her magnetic body, Botticelli's Venus is also the still-yet-moving center of a brewing storm, a goddess of animated and sartorial splendor (plate 44). The architectural theorist Spyros Papapetros has invoked Botticelli's masterpiece as a pictorial meditation on "mobile accessories":

> While looking at Botticelli's *Birth of Venus*, one might even argue that the entire canvas is essentially an ornament: the painting represents an annular ornament or ring, the way that fabrics and hair appear to circulate around Venus, orbiting around the axis of her marmoreal body like satellites.... Venus stands at the very center of this commotion of accessories.[29]

We might say the same about the scene of Shosho's theatrical birth: the ballroom, alight with jewel-like reflections, faceted by glances, itself an ornament and a microcosm of the universe, with Shosho as the almost-still center emitting and drawing in the stars and lights that scatter around the sphere of this room. Instead of parodying or demythifying Orientalist ornamentation, Wong as Shosho reinvests it with an aural concentration that enables her to assume—even induce—the world. How can we not notice that the strobe lights sitting at her feet resemble four glittering globes, anchoring the four corners of this imagined cartography?[30] And what would it mean to consider this scene as having been transformed from a display of Western conquest into a moment of ascent and radical expansion, where Wong as Shosho remaps the universe with her as its axis (plates 44 and 45)?

This scene rehearses the tropes of self-origination against the frame of imperial time. The birth of eros and aesthetics has been relocated to Asia. In a way, this scene foreshadows Western anxiety about the rise of pan-Asian modernity in late modernity, but here it underscores the particular and intense quality of Wong's screen presence, one that is not so much subversive or narcissistic as simply materially possessive.

If cinema as medium and glamour as ideal are both about imagining a body, we might think of this moment of Shosho's rise as a parable of the emergence of aesthetic authority, just as the birth of Venus is an allegory of the birth of art and semiotics, as famously argued by art historian Edgar Wind. According to Wind, the Botticelli painting represents the original fragmentation, the primal fracture of the world following the castration of Uranus from which Venus was born, a myth described by Hesiod and then Plato in *The Republic*.[31] In this account, the birth of decoration—of sign—emerges from originary loss. Thus ornamentation represents the sign of originary loss as well as its reparation. Wong's performance also negotiates lack and compensation, though not in the way Freud understood the fetish. In this encounter between East and West, we are given an Asiatic Venus turning her own ruptured thingness into the plenitude of the Thing. Sign has offered itself as referent. She is "It" because she knows how to be "it."

Viewing Wong's iconography in *Piccadilly* through Botticelli's painting may not seem so whimsical once we recognize the ballroom scene as an active reinscription of the myth of Venus: not the iconic blond Venus, or her abject inverse the black Venus, but a third figure whose yellow-gold body mediates between the poles of luminance and defilement, the auratic and the corporeal. This extraordinary moment of assumption is temporary. We will have to emerge from this gorgeous dream to the sordid realities of Piccadilly Square and the empire in 1929, just as Shosho herself will be extinguished at the end of the film. But for the duration of this performance, Shosho is more than just another little dancing Chinese girl; she is the object who wields the auratic power of signs. Let us bear witness not to the possibility of Wong's subjective authority but rather to the performative impact of her aesthetic force.

Five years after the release of *Piccadilly*, in 1934, the Mayfair Mannequin Society of New York named Wong "the World's Best Dressed Woman."[32] This celebration of

PLATE 44: Sandro Botticelli, *The Birth of Venus* (ca. 1483–1486). Tempera on paper, Uffizi Galery. Courtesy of Wikimedia Commons.

PLATE 45: Anna May Wong in gold headdress, *Piccadilly* (1929, dir. E. A. Dupont). Courtesy of Kobal/Rex/Shutterstock.

Wong's clothes over Wong herself may hold poignant insights into her exquisite, unfleshly, extensible textuality. Wong perhaps most astutely intuited the heart of her celebrity when she once observed that "you can forgive a woman for a face that is not beautiful more easily than for a dress that isn't."[33] This statement says much less about the shallowness of celebrity, what Daniel Boorstin calls the celebration of the "human pseudo-event,"[34] than about the interdependence between subjecthood and surrogacy in the making of celebrity, a nexus of issues that become all the more pronounced when that celebrity belongs to a body historically denigrated.

Wong's alienation from her own fleshliness is no small thing for a woman of color making her way in a world of commodity. Is it a coincidence that some female performers of color in the early twentieth century, like Wong, Josephine Baker, and Lena Horne, should be so preoccupied with the particular temptations and hazards of persona and covers—what goes on their skin?[35] These women's work involved an unavoidable and constant negotiation with the symptom that was their bodies. And what rests on and substitutes for their skin becomes the site for risky inscription as well as transformation. On top of the scullery table, in the shop at the back of the Limehouse restaurant, and later in the grand ballroom, Wong's mediated relation to her fleshed body communicates more than just the glamorous body's inherent mediation and instructs us on an altogether different view of how the corporeal comes to be perceived at all. It is between sight and sense, between a body projected and evacuated, that the "Oriental beauty" takes shape.

Shosho's fluctuation between being a commodity and being a resistant object uncovers the shared tension informing the politics of personhood (which drives most redemptive discourse about race) and the politics of recognition (which drives the discourse of celebrity). If liberal racial rhetoric has not been able to tolerate the possibilities of subjective failures or corporeal ambiguity on the part of its recuperated subjects, and if celebrity studies has been overinvested in the cult of personality and the fantasy of agency, my discussion of Wong as Shosho reveals how the euphoric politics of redemptive personhood and recognition requires more rigorous engagements with the dysphoric alternatives. If we consider Wong's disappearance into appearance in this film not as abjection or reification, but instead as a recourse to celebrated skin's potential to be transformed, to obtain a new material objectness, we begin to grasp that her glamour is not a denial of racial injury or lack (the possibility of which is undeniable for an actress of color in the 1920s) but instead a reminder of and insistence on subjecthood's fundamental indeterminacy. Her objectness compels us to confront the inherent, taut intimacy between being a thing and being a person.

This story of modern celebrity and glamour is thus an intricate tale about race and style and a dream of subjecthood that is deeply indebted to states of objecthood. Wong sustains our imagination neither through her apparently racialized performances nor through her uncomplicated assumption of female agency but instead through her paradoxical staging and erasure of her body and of the skin that is supposed to give that corporeality meaning. To speak of ornamentalism here, then, is to speak of the opportunities of disembodiment for racialized subjects. It may seem counterintuitive or even dangerous to talk about the raced and sexualized body's affinity for being thinglike, but it is precisely the overcorporealized body that may find the most freedom in the rehearsal of corporeal dematerialization or, alternately, of synthetic self-extension.

A lyrical flame, this early-twentieth-century beauty offers a crucial pause in the politics of celebrity, the politics of race, and the imperatives of personhood to both, by asking us to consider how a body might operate subjunctively: a materiality that is at once imagined and conditional. In the end, it is the extravagance of ornamentalism, rather than the fulfillment of embodiment, that proves to be the source of Wong's enduring, enticing refusal.

3

Blue Willow

PLATE 46: Roberto Cavalli. Evening dress, autumn–winter 2005–2006. Blue and white silk satin. *China: Through the Looking Glass*, 2015, Metropolitan Museum of Art, New York. Courtesy of Platon.

ALMOST TWO HUNDRED years after New Yorkers flocked to the Peale Museum in New York (later to become the New York Museum of Natural History and Science) to witness the living tableau of the Chinese Lady, and long after Anna May Wong's celluloid radiance had faded from public memory, throngs from all over the world gathered in Manhattan to witness another spectacular display of Asiatic femininity

PLATE 47: Fashion by Laura Grai. *China: Through the Looking Glass*, 2015, Metropolitan Museum of Art, New York. Photo by author.

PLATE 48: Yves Saint Laurent and Tom Ford. Evening dress, autumn–winter 2004–2005. Yellow silk satin embroidered with polychrome plastic sequins. *China: Through the Looking Glass,* 2015, Metropolitan Museum of New York. Courtesy of Platon Images.

PLATE 49: Valentino evening dress from "Shanghai Collection" (1959). *China: Through the Looking Glass,* 2015, Metropolitan Museum of New York. Courtesy of Platon Images.

PLATE 50: Alexander McQueen and Philip Treacy, "Chinese Garden" headdress, spring–summer 2005. Carved cork. *China: Through the Looking Glass,* 2015, Metropolitan Museum of New York. Courtesy of Platon Images.

qua ornament: the 2015 exhibition at the Metropolitan Museum of Art entitled *China: Through the Looking Glass* (plates 46–50).

The exhibition featured more than 140 examples of mostly Euro-American haute couture and avant-garde ready-to-wear from fashion luminaries such as Paul Poiret, Yves Saint Laurent, John Galliano, and Alexander McQueen. Interspersed among these resplendent sartorial creations were decontextualized Chinese and Japanese artifacts from the museum's Asian art collection. An eighteenth-century yellow silk satin imperial robe shadowed a sequined yellow silk satin evening gown by Tom Ford for Yves Saint Laurent. A Qing Dynasty snuff bottle and a twelfth-century kimono echoed a Cartier perfume flask. An early-fifteenth-century cobalt blue dragon jar accompanied a Roberto Cavalli creation in blue and white.

This sumptuous collection rehearsed for the twenty-first-century audience the basic tenets of nineteenth-century Orientalism: opulence and sensuality are the signature components of Asiatic character; Asia is always ancient, excessive, feminine, open for use, and decadent; material consumption promises cultural possession; and there is no room in the Orientalist imagination for national, ethnic, or historical specificities. Most of all, the show reminded us that China—conflated throughout the show with Asia at large, a cypher for a cypher—equals *ornament.* The Metropolitan had accomplished quite an ornamental feat of its own: a byzantine buildout replete with intricate corridors and concentric spaces, large decorative arches leading to secret, enfolded rooms, and a tall, transparent, plasticized bamboo forest.[1] One turned and suddenly found oneself in a hushed "garden," standing on a meditation bridge overlooking a large glistening artificial pond surrounded by winding corridors (plate 51). No natural light disturbed this dreamlike, highly man-made environment. The lacquer pond glimmered but did not flow. In this beautiful graveyard, Eastern nature appeared wholly continuous with Eastern artifice.

From the get-go, we realize the limits of Saidean Orientalism as a critical framework, as the exhibition itself has already co-opted the term as an internal critique and alibi. Introductory signage greeted visitors as they entered through a set of two-story-tall red lacquer doors:

> Empire of Signs
>
> For the designers in this exhibition, China represents a land of free-floating symbols, a land where postmodernity finds its natural expression. Like Marco Polo or Gulliver, they are itinerant travelers to another country, reflecting on its artistic and cultural traditions as an exoticized extension of their own.... When quoting Chinese artifacts or costumes, these designers are not reproducing literal copies or accurate facsimiles. Rather, they reinterpret them through seemingly paradoxical postmodern constructions.

The show recuses itself from the burden of authenticity even as its mis-en-scène fetishizes the artifactually and culturally real.[2] Invoking and recursively enacting Roland Barthes's famously cool dismissal of the notion of (Japanese) cultural authenticity—"to me the orient is a matter of indifference"[3]—this exhibit disaggregates aesthetic pleasure from politics and reclaims postmodernism as the cure for

PLATE 51: Garden and pond display from *China: Through the Looking Glass*, 2015, Metropolitan Museum of Art, New York. Photo by author.

Orientalism, performing exactly what Hal Foster has called capitalism's revenge on postmodernism.[4]

There is obviously much one can critique on the grounds of racial appropriation, inauthenticity, commercialism, and neoliberal bad faith. Although the Met exhibit was wildly popular—the show was extended three months past its initial end date—it also faced stringent criticism and protest. The *New York Times* published a scathing review, offering a history lesson about the so-called China Trade and its legacy for American imperialism along the way.[5] The director of the Asian American Arts Centre, Robert Lee, wrote a letter of protest to the Metropolitan Museum that created its own problematic assumptions about authenticity:

> If the Met were a department store or a movie theatre I think the public would understand that this is a commercial venture designed to entertain and promote... the mystery and inscrutability of China's distant past. Your disclaimer that this is not related to any commercial intentions and has a legitimate theme of re-evaluating Edward Said's ideas of Orientalism is clearly an excuse to affirm the acceptability and dominance of the Western market and its reliance on Orientalist notions.... [T]hese fantasies of China do not support your claims of overlapping creative complexity, rather they affirm the power of the dominance of Western Orientalist commitments to define the Other as they see fit.[6]

While the heart of the criticism is well taken, the critique of stereotype has the unfortunate side effect of reproducing a series of equally restrictive and problematic binaries: the authentic Orient versus the false Orient of Western projection; real (masculine) history versus illusory (feminine) arts.

The museum director, Thomas P. Campbell, clearly anticipated such critique and hoped, unsuccessfully, to forestall it by enlisting renowned Hong Kong filmmaker Wong Kar-wai as the exhibit's artistic director. Wong provided footage for large-screen projections of iconic scenes that reiterate the theme of China as beauty-cum-decadence: the opium dens of *Broken Blossoms* (1919) and *The Big Sleep* (1946); the imperial nostalgia of Bernardo Bertolucci's *The Last Emperor* (1987); and versions of the same nostalgia from contemporary Chinese cinema, including Zhang Yimou's *Hero* (2002) and *Curse of the Golden Flower* (2006), Ang Lee's *Crouching Tiger, Hidden Dragon* (2000), and Wong's own *In the Mood for Love* (2000) and 2046 (2004). In a statement in the exhibit's catalog, Wong reiterates the claim that the China of this exhibition is not the real China but one that belongs to the realm of "projection, reflection, and fascination," but he nonetheless concludes with this wistful note: "I hope that [this show] will... [provide] visitors to the exhibition and readers of this book with a closer view of Chinese aesthetic and cultural traditions."[7]

The museum's attempt to differentiate postmodern globalization from nineteenth-century Orientalism—or what Adam Geczy in one of the catalog essays calls "transorientalism"—falls short of its mark. Geczy explains transorientalism as "a self-conscious use of the Orient as a geographically uncircumscribed zone, whose cultural specificity is secondary to the imaginative uses to which it can be put,"[8] but this definition could just as easily describe nineteenth-century Orientalism, itself the lubricant for the vast movements of objects in arguably the first early modern global economy. For all the exhibit's attempts to take on the critique of Orientalism, both in the staging of the show and in the catalog, we find ourselves in a closed loop. For if at one point the liberal left relied on the missing real as a safeguard against Orientalist appropriation, then we must now contend with the fact that *that* absence is now openly taken as the very rationale for continual Orientalist production. The opposition between fantasy and "brute reality," a dyad that Orientalism both perpetuates and elides, continues to vex the war against the empire of signs.[9]

In the end, we should be less surprised by the tenacity of this racial imaginary than by the limits of our response to it. For a long time now, the concepts of Asian authenticity and Orientalist commodification have remained our only safeguards against the vice of racist consumption. But neither the longing for the former nor the allegation of the latter can address the complex relations between appropriation and susceptibility, or between embodiment and style. Moral outrage in the face of consumption or fetishization, however warranted, cannot address or relieve the truly striking, idiosyncratic, and intense exchange between thingness and personness into which a display like this draws us. The exhibition's dizzying invitation for visitors to lose themselves in extravagant aestheticism, the sensorial immersion of textiles and materials, the seductiveness of vivacious inanimateness and synthetic pleasures all work to facilitate that slide between things and persons, an erotic and erratic plunge that both preconditions the making of Chinese and Asiatic femininity and renders inadequate binary critiques of this kind of racial objectification. Thus while Saidean Orientalism and the Foucauldian critique that it embodies do much to help us identify symptoms and locate political culpability, neither can address the profound, queasily seductive entanglement between organic corporeality and aesthetic abstraction imputed to Asiatic femininity.

Let's face it, critical discourse has never been very good at addressing what Rita Felski calls the erotics of aesthetics beyond that of a critique of commodification or an assertion of transgressive pleasure.[10] I don't try to make an argument for pleasure, though that is often elided by the morality and gendered politics attached to critiques of consumption. Instead, the exhibition gives me the opportunity to pay attention to the material, affective, and kinesthetic making of an aesthetic ontology that is the ornamental personhood of Asiatic femininity. How do we begin to think about racialized bodies that remain insistently synthetic and artificial? How do we take seriously the life of a subject who lives as an object, and how do we do so without either resigning that figure to the annals of commodity fetishism or assigning it a reassuring corporeality?

FEATHERS AND SHARDS

The challenge here is to negotiate the very human consequences of "de-animated" persons and the very material effects of animated things. Of the many "enigmatic objects" (a term used by the exhibition) displayed in this extensive exhibition, the most mesmerizing and confounding one is surely the specter of the yellow woman, synecdochized through faceless and at times headless mannequins and metonymized through luxuriantly sensuous fabrics. This seductive presence does not require a biological body or nature; quite the opposite, Asiatic femininity is radiantly reproduced through inorganic and insensate mediums. Consider the evocation of warm Asiatic femininity via the cool surfaces of ceramics in plate 52. In a large hall devoted to the theme of Blue Willow, an imitation Chinese china pattern made popular by Thomas Minton in the 1790s, we find a grouping of blue and cream silk gowns designed by contemporary designers such as Roberto Cavalli and Alexander McQueen. If we dismiss this association between Asiatic femininity and Chinese ceramic as yet another Orientalist cliché, we miss a much more intricate and intriguing proposition: the affinity between racialization, imagined personhood, and synthetic invention.

In *China: Through the Looking Glass* the ornament, as artifact and gesture, acts as a medium through which the human is simultaneously invoked and displaced and powerful ideas of personhood, race, and objectness are transferred. Let us return to the interplay between Asiatic femininity and ceramics. Recent scholarship in the area of material culture has revealed the complex history of Chinese porcelain: its importance in early global imperial trade; its role in spurring European technological invention and decorative design; and its impact on growing economic, social, and cultural values in Denmark, Germany, and France, as well as England and its American colonies.[11] To this richly documented history I would add the wrought and fraught intimacy between this "white gold" and the making of yellow flesh.[12] More than economic or social values, Chinese porcelain personifies a set of affective and somatic values forged out of the kiln of what Gordon Chang aptly calls the centuries-old "fateful ties" between China and the West.[13] Out of the era of the China Trade, Atlantic slavery, and their aftermath, we see the birth of a material culture that shapes the physical and affective values attached to racialized bodies. Objects and materials are racialized, yes, but objects and materials also racialize people.

PLATE 52: Trio display from *China: Through the Looking Glass*, 2015, Metropolitan Museum of Art, New York. Photo by author.

Scholars like Mechthild Fend and Chi-ming Yang have demonstrated how material substances spurred chemical experiments with colors that not only fed artisanal and industrial innovations across centuries but also promoted racial ideas.[14] Mahogany's red sheen, glossy black lacquer, translucent white porcelain, and the brilliant colors of indigo, cochineal dyes, and silver ore all carried and produced racial meanings. In short, race making in the nineteenth century is also an artisanal project, as indebted to ornamental practice and material making as it is to the pseudobiology of early ethnography.

Imported goods and materials of Asia and the Americas held novel, structural properties like durability or elasticity that Europeans not only strove to imitate and harness for their own manufacturing but also increasingly came to associate and project onto the racialized bodies from whom the objects came. Porcelain, what was known as true *kaolin* Chinese porcelain, is particularly interesting in this regard because of its alchemical and seemingly impossible properties: known not only for its glossy beauty, its refinement, its receptivity to color and design manipulation but also for its surprising durability, its miraculous capacity to sustain the extreme high heat that lends it its translucency. The invention of porcelain as a precious and rare new material—an advanced production process that baffled Western manufacturers for decades and served as something of a precursor to the twentieth-century fascination with *materia nova*—promised in the eighteenth century the magic of material transformation.[15] Porcelain thus connoted both hardness and plasticity, old-world beauty and new-world technology, fragile daintiness and insensate coolness: a mixture of antithetical symbolic meanings that are then ascribed to, indeed, *become* the very "stuff" of Asiatic femininity.

The seemingly trite association of Asiatic female skin with porcelain—from the cliché of the pearlized skin of Asian women to this exhibit—thus in fact carries this profound and layered history of ornamentalist transformation, affecting the merging of flesh and matter, persons and things. It is not surprising, then, that the fates of Chinese female bodies and Chinese porcelain ran parallel to each other. When it came to represent the precariousness of a system of Western wealth based on importing novel Eastern goods, porcelain, along with other things Asiatic, started to lose its radiance. As Euro-American acquisitiveness began to run in excess of what it could offer China in return, the early romance with china and China began to deteriorate. This breakdown left lasting traces in American law and economic policy, from U.S. foreign policy and trade agreements in the eighteenth century to discriminatory immigration laws in the nineteenth and twentieth centuries. China's meaning in the American popular imagination changed, with Chinese porcelain itself coming to connote tacky crockery. And crucially for our discussion, the breakdown of this country's China romance marked the bodies of Asiatic women. The *New York Times* had this to say about the Chinese women's gymnastics team at the 1996 Summer Olympics: "The Chinese remain the world's most erratic top gymnasts, and today, like many a Ming vase, their routines looked lovely but had cracks in several places."[16]

Thus more than exemplifying an incidental decorative motif or revealing the limits of the imperial imagination, the citation—indeed, the embodied objecthood—of Chinese porcelain in the Met exhibition, regardless of curatorial intentions, revives this long, expansive history about human imbrication with racialized and manufactured materials, fueling the fraught amalgamation between inorganic commodity and Asiatic female flesh. We might say that the ubiquitous presence of fine Chinese porcelain throughout the show generates a specific epidermal schema of its own.

For example, the creation in plates 53 and 54 by Alexander McQueen for his autumn–winter 2011–2012 collection offers a play of simulation and contrast, fusing the inorganic and the organic, the insensate and the sensorial, the hard and the soft. Most of all, it invokes a particular vision of the racialized female body as one that sustains these contradictions. The fluffy layered skirt, at first glance, looks made of supple feathers (animal) but turns out to be shredded organza (fabric). The exposed underskirt, suggestive of layers of artificial skins turned inside out, is at once beautiful and violent. It is offset by the startling weight of the bodice, which on closer inspection turns out to be not the proverbial bone but hundreds of reconstituted shards of blue and white porcelain: porcelain as flesh-and-skin and skin-and-flesh as porcelain.

PLATE 53: Alexander McQueen and Sarah Burton. Evening dress, autumn–winter 2011–2012. Cream silk satin embroidered with blue and white porcelain; white silk organza, from *China: Through the Looking Glass*, 2015, Metropolitan Museum of Art, New York. Photo by author.

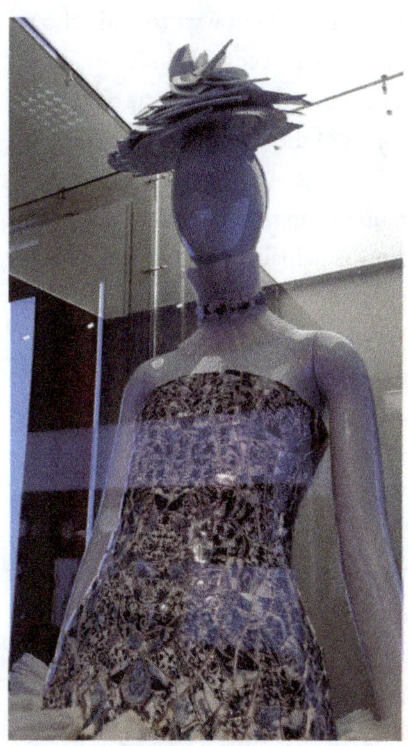

PLATE 54: Detail of plates plate 53. Photo by author.

Here Chinese femininity is not only more and less than human but also man-made; not only assembled but also reassembled. This reassemblage, by virtue of its fabrication, memorializes the practice of ornamentalism and the techniques of race making. This image of the flexible yet brittle body reminds us that this aesthetic discourse is fastened to a fractured history of craft, labor, and bodies in transit. Eric Hayot has traced the persistent Euro-American conceptualization of the Chinese male body as infinitely and stoically capable of sustaining pain and suffering, an association that led to the image of the coolie as at once "animal and superhuman," an ideal laborer.[17] Here I am sketching a Chinese female version of this discursive formation: a smooth beauty that bears the lines of its own wreckage, a delicacy that is also impermeable and insensate. The dream of the yellow woman is thus really a dream about the inorganic. From Anna May Wong's thingness to Nancy Kwan as the late-night television spokesperson for Pearl Cream, porcelain has always represented flesh *and* not flesh.[18]

CHINESE DETAILS

Going back to the trio in our Blue Willow room (plate 52), we can now see a deeper grammar of the inhuman human structuring this stage. The McQueen gown is placed next to a Roberto Cavalli dress, and both in turn stand next to and echo an early fifteenth-century Chinese porcelain jar painted with a cobalt blue dragon: urn as beauty as death as gown as corporeal gesture. The sensorial and somatic realization of Asiatic femininity fulfills itself through the forms of these empty-yet-constructed vessels (plate 55).

There is no ordinary flesh here, by which I do not mean the obvious, that there are no real bodies on display, but rather that this show is palpably not that interested in the human, much less in women. These garments do not need the human; indeed, the human would disrupt their composure. We are looking at a peculiar form of anthropomorphism or prosopopoeia whereby the spectral human is being used to recall material objectness rather than vice versa. The objects on display, from frocks to vases, invite neither wearability nor usage. Instead of objects that function as appendages to the human (as one would expect fashion and furnishings to do), what we find here instead are objects that reference other objects.

In this room, the human is the ornamental gesture, and the ornamental in turn acquires its human aura by being "Chinese." In other words, beauty here comes from the primacy of the object; the human or the anthropomorphic is the incidental alibi for, or afterthought of, relishing this pure objectness. At the same time, however, what renders this pure objectness legible as such is precisely the invocation of (very

PLATE 55: Roberto Cavalli. Evening Dress, autumn–winter 2005–2006. Blue and white silk satin. *China: Through the Looking Glass*, 2015, Metropolitan Museum of Art, New York. Courtesy of Platon.

human) racial difference. Where Orientalism is about turning persons into things that can be possessed and dominated, ornamentalism is about a fantasy of turning things into persons through the conduit of racial meaning in order, paradoxically, to allow the human to escape his or her own humanness.

If the modernist relation to the fetishized object is fundamentally a melancholic one, then we are getting here something of a twist to that subject-object relation. Bill Brown tells us that we are prone to look for ourselves in lost or alien mass cultural objects: "It is all those spaces within [the Thing]—the inside of the chest, the inside of the wardrobe, the inside of the drawer—that . . . enable us to image and imagine human interiority."[19] But here we are looking at objects that short-circuit that project by duplicating our own truncated or stunted relation to the very notion of interiority. In the Blue Willow room at the Met, all the empty containers—the urn, the dresses—are wholly filled by emptiness. We cannot fill these voids, because they are easily occupied without us. They only seem to offer the promises of anthropomorphic possibilities as a compensation for making us confront their (and our own) thingness. This is perhaps why one feels so essentially alone in a beautiful room filled with things presumably meant to enhance us. The relationship here, however, is not simply one of an object refusing the human but also of an object that does so by mirroring the inhumanness of the human.

To point to this enchantment of the inhuman is not to rehearse the problem of objectification or to downplay the issue of race but rather to point to a provocative dilemma about how the object preconditions, rather than being the product of, the human figure—a modern crisis that Asiatic femininity personifies for the West. As a result, ornamentalism not only is an object of feminist critique but also can be a vector of feminism. The eradication of the human, even as raced and gendered corporeality is being imputed, compels a reconceptualization of feminized, racialized flesh. The critique of power, from Michel Foucault to Edward Said to Ann Laura Stoler, has long taught us that carnality and flesh, instead of being private domains, are sites that have been deeply penetrated and structured by power. Human flesh has undeniably been one of the highest prices paid for the history of human enslavement. And often in feminist and racial discourses, understandably, we end up with a longing for that lost and violated flesh or, inversely, a total refusal of the body. But these stranded "bodies" in the Metropolitan invite further ruminations about the interplay between fleshliness and the inorganic for certain raced and gendered bodies. What happens to our notions of the subject when carnality is cultivated not out of flesh but from its fusion with inorganic matter? What happens when we accept that style, mediated through yet detached from a racial referent, may not be simply the excess or the opposite of ontology but may in fact be a precondition for embodiment, an insight that challenges the very foundation of the category of the human? What is at stake here is not just the objectification of people but also how that objectification opens up a constitutive estrangement within the articulation of proper personhood.

Ornamentalism—the forging of the sense of personness through artificial and prosthetic extensions—articulates an allegory for the crisis of personhood that the modern ideal of an integrated, organic, individual person was meant to alleviate. If we think of the European conceptualization of modern personhood as indebted to an Enlightenment notion of natural and integral bodies, as has been posited by Locke, Hobbes, Descartes, Montesquieu, and Blackstone—a person, for example, is a living, organic, and organized human body "such as the God of nature formed us," Blackstone argues—then we are tracing here another kind of body, one that not only poses a challenge to this ideal but also insists on the primacy of aggregated objectness in the experience of the human. [20]

As if in answer to this bracing realization, we find the dress in plate 56 as well in the Blue Willow assembly. Here aesthetic congealment has grown into full-bodied edifice. The to-be-used Chinese female body seems to have petrified into domestic and collectible things (pieces of teapots, cups, plates) whose value now resides in their aggressive uselessness. At the same time, this congealed and fractured domesticity, offering repurposed purposelessness, transcends its own quotidianness to lay claim to art. Made by contemporary artist Li Xiaofeng (b. 1965), this piece is clearly not human, but nor is it entirely a thing. The weight (of material, history, domesticity, femininity) implies petrification, but the form suggests flight. Is this dress or armor? Winged victory or the madwoman in the attic? A tribute to monumentality or a concession to the mundane? What has died here, the human or the ornament? And finally, has the human outmoded itself or has the object outrun the human demand?

We cannot read this figure from the Chinese artist as a rebuke of the Euro-American commercial designers with whom he shares the space, because the work is itself an exploration of troubled authenticity and distorted temporality.[21] Entitled *Beijing Memory No.* 5, Li's 2009 sculpture was part of a series known for using ceramics excavated from archaeological sites throughout China. The museum catalog attributes the ceramic fragments to the Qing Dynasty (1644–1912), commonly known as the last great Chinese dynastic empire, suggesting that the memory being recomposed here may be the memory of a lost imperial China, and the piece itself something of a layered exercise in what Rey Chow calls "the Chinese detail."[22] Chow has observed that the Chinese detail is always already an "*ethnic* detail," even for the Chinese—that is, a self-conscious articulation signifying a culture's "belated fascination with its own datedness, its own alterity."[23] For Chow, this is the result of the imputed pastness of the Chinese in Euro-American modernity but also because of China's own melancholic incorporation of that projection. *Beijing Memory No.* 5

PLATE 56: Li Xiaofeng, *Beijing Memory No. 5* (2009). Qing period shards. Red Gate Gallery, Beijing. From *China: Through the Looking Glass*, 2015, Metropolitan Museum of Art, New York. Photo by author.

exercises a particularly intricate articulation of Chinese datedness by insisting on a historicity that, upon closer examination, has been subjected to much manipulation.

In the reconstructed rubble that is the body of this Ceramic Woman, we discern a scattering of some still intact Chinese ideograms (plate 57 and 58). Many are out of context and several are positioned upside down (an ironic statement of value? a jab at the old joke about Chinese illegibility for Western viewers?): words like *precious*, *tea*, *superior*. Others offer seemingly precise self-authentication with stamped reign dates, such as "Xuande Reign of the Great Ming Dynasty" (1426–1435), purporting to indicate a royal workshop.

The shards thus date themselves even further back in time, to the Ming Dynasty, prior to the Qing Dynasty indicated by the exhibition catalog. But we cannot remain complacent with these fragments' promise of a more precious, commodified pastness, because these certifications of provenance, both inside and outside the artwork, only serve to underscore the homelessness of these remains. Indeed, given that the practice of inscribing dates onto objects degraded fairly early on into affectation and even forgery, this kind of designation is likely to be more misleading than not. And since

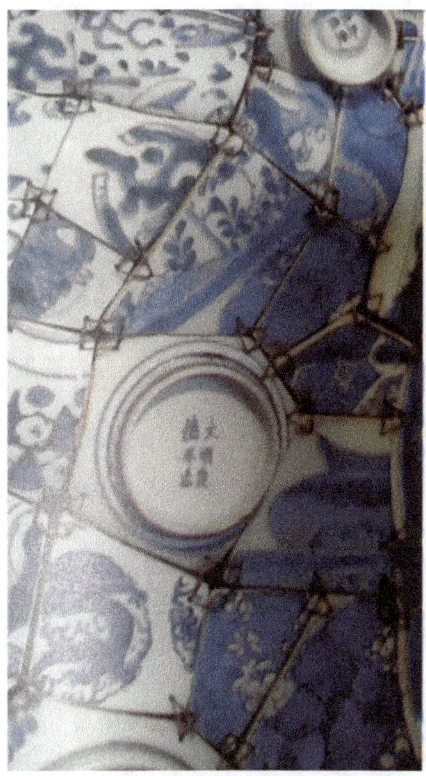

PLATE 57: Detail of plate 56. Photo by author.

PLATE 58: Detail of plate 56. Photo by author.

an earlier date would signal a grander pretentiousness and greater value, and since the Xuande era was exactly when such inscriptions first became common, these fragments are probably anything but Xuande.

Decorative ornament and utilitarian domesticity merge in this piece. Reassembled but stranded; an objet d'art and a collection of disposable things; a thing of memory and troubled origins; an object in transit between the junkyard, the workshop, the commercial gallery, and the museum: Li's Ceramic Woman underscores the unstable difference between curio and treasure, both mediated precisely through notions of Chineseness. The curio, denoting a piece of bric-a-brac from the Far East since the mid-nineteenth century and a shortened form of the word *curiosity*, already draws something from the enchanted transformation of ornamentalism: the *thing* that becomes *Thing*—but, alas, never quite free from a threatening intimacy with its original status as a mere thing.[24] This uneasy fluctuation between value and waste always haunts the curio, which is to say, haunts the "Oriental thing."

I am reminded of a story that a friend once told me about a lecture given by Amar Bose, famed engineer and founder of Bose Corporation, at the Massachusetts Institute of Technology.[25] Trying to teach his students the lesson that technological innovation comes less from the inherent value of ideas than from the ability to *perceive* and *produce* value out of what may seem useless or failed, Bose related a Chinese parable told to him by his own mentor, an engineering professor who was a "very cultured Chinese gentleman."[26] During World War II, Bose's professor, then a young academic in Beijing was making his way to Shanghai on his way out of the country when he was detained by the arrival of Japanese forces. This scholar, out of work and facing the dismantling of his country, found himself scouring the countryside looking for curios to sell in order to survive. "The curio dealer," he told Bose, "has two dreams: first, to find a real treasure… and second, to be able to recognize it." The pedagogical lesson here is a valuable one about the transformative power of the perceptive and imaginative mind. But there are other lessons too in this recursive tale. Chineseness here offers value for the Westerner (the sage advice of a wise Chinese elder; the goods of the Orient) *and* for the Chinese subject who can reconstruct his lost value for Western modernity by repackaging his own ethnic wreckage. If the Chinese bric-a-brac offers the Western consumer the promise of Orientalist contact, then it offers the stranded Chinese subject the salvation of ornamentalist conversion.

The Oriental curio, then, is the material sediment of the crisis of (national, ethnic) aura. And if the decay of aura has been attributed to technological development as per Benjamin, then we must remind ourselves that this Ceramic Woman, too, is a technology: a mechanical assemblage forged out of abandoned, auratic residue (plate 59). A lesson about cutting-edge technological invention in the twentieth century articulates itself through a fable about a disappearing China (a description,

PLATE 59: Li Xiaofeng, Beijing Memory No. 5 (2009). Qing period shards. Red Gate Gallery, Beijing. From China: Through the Looking Glass, 2015, Metropolitan Museum of Art, New York. Photo by author.

by the way that is as true of Li's sculpture as Bose's parable), because the dream of ornamentalism offers us technology wedded to aura.

For the Chinese subject, uselessness can be useful. The feminine uselessness of Chineseness, symbolized by no-longer-functional domestic porcelain objects in Li's piece, opens up the "gap" in "the symbolic universe of utilitarianism" through which the Chinese subject can slip, through the back door, as it were, of Western modernity.[27] *Beijing Memory No.* 5, itself a fragment in a series of re-production, pushes us right in the face of the simultaneity of recuperation and rupture. Li's fragmented plates and teacups—his reassembled "Chinese details," this weighty, nonhuman embodiedness—suggests that it may be in this very transition from mere thing to ornament (that is, the technology of ornamentalism) that things Chinese can maneuver for value. Entwined with the trauma of authenticity enacted by this sculpture dress is therefore the further possibility that this twenty-first-century Asiatic porcelain body made for an Euro-American audience may be seeking to outmode itself to continue to be relevant on the modern stage. Like a treasure dealer who is also a dumpster diver, Li compels us to consider our national and temporal assumptions about what modernity imagines is lost to it. Here the "ethnic detail" offers temporal recapitulation via the crafted insistence on its own death and lostness, as if to say "I am relevant today because I am no longer relevant." Indeed, like dead languages, Li's fragments can seem to become untranslatable, atavistic, Oriental, beautiful, and modern all at once.[28]

Indeed, a similar fate has befallen the Chinese language itself, also prominently displayed in the Metropolitan exhibit as another aesthetic object (plate 60).[29] Written Chinese is considered beautiful to the general Western public, if not due to the ideographic myth perpetuated from Ernest Fenollosa to Derrida, then because Chinese as an illegible, aesthetic manifestation had been declared by missionaries, philosophers, and poets as no longer functional in the modern world. Consider, for

PLATE 60: Zhang Xu (ca. 675–759), stone carving. From *China: Through the Looking Glass*, 2015, Metropolitan Museum of Art, New York. Photo by author.

example, what James Fenimore Cooper has to say about disappearing Native American languages by way of the Chinese language in his 1831 introduction to *The Last of the Mohicans*, another classic text of ethnic detail and nostalgia: "the North American Indian clothes his ideas in a dress that is so different from that of the African, and is Oriental in itself. His language has the richness and the sententious fullness of the Chinese."[30] For Cooper, American Indian language became beautiful the very moment it became Oriental. Indeed, "Chinese" has become *the* metaphor for dead beauty, the living dying into ornamental life. And it is precisely this *dynamic dying* that lends these inhuman objects their melancholic human beauty.

Like the Chinese language itself, the idea of yellow female flesh invoked by *Beijing Memory No. 5* enjoys a bittersweet beauty precisely because it is petrified and yet still recalls organic life. For just as *Beijing Memory No. 5* invokes a vanished China only to unsettle the very thing it claims has disappeared, the sculpture also summons the memory of yellow female flesh only to replace it with a more insistent, inorganic presence. This feels less like nostalgia for yellow female flesh than a consecration of its fossilized (raced and gendered) afterlife. This is flesh congealed into porcelain as well as porcelain invoking the possibility of flesh. *Beijing Memory No. 5*'s combination of formal assemblage and stifling mass pushes us to confront the simultaneously dematerializing and materializing processes through which raced female bodies come to be present. It instantiates the salvage, the reassemblage, and the subjunctiveness behind Asiatic female corporeality. If the yellow woman has always been simultaneously embodied and erased through ornamental objectness, then this piece asks what is or could be life after such devastation.

Sigmund Freud tells us that one of the most unsettling effects for human ontology is to be confronted by a machine that comes to life.[31] With *Beijing Memory No.* 5, what is uncanny is that the "machine" refuses to come to life, and in its lifelessness, imagines what life might have been. And it is in this very paradox of "might have been" that we experience the prospective and prosthetic quality of our ontology. In other words, *Beijing Memory No.* 5 does not give us the memory of something; it *is* memory, the layered encrustations of absent but imagined lives. This yellow woman is instructive not because "she" offers us a sartorial performance as redemption, nor because she promises the possibility of the real behind the object. On the contrary, this "memory" insists that we take seriously, rather than simply decry, the entanglement between living and living-as-thing.

In the end, this complicated congealment may be what is possible in a life of precariousness. Sometimes, disposable lives find themselves through disposable objects. (Is this why, for some Asian American subjects, given limited options, they would rather be ornamental than Oriental?) Freedom for the captured may not be the gift of uncompromised liberty but instead the more modest and demanding task of existing within an entombed shell. It is not only that bodies can leave their residue in the things they produce (an insight that object studies has taught us), but also that objectness reveals the divergent, layered, and sometimes annihilating gestures that can make up personhood. More than memorializing bodies that might otherwise not be remembered, Li's porcelain woman explores what it would mean to instantiate through excess materiality the dematerialized nonbody. The piece marks a kind of "third nature" that surrounds and approximates the human and manages to survive despite or through commodification. The perihumanity of Asiatic femininity (that is, something at once inside and outside of civilizational first principles) is why "she" is often enlisted to represent contemporary apprehensions about more-than-human entanglements.[32]

The aesthetic language—the movement between animate and inanimate—with which the yellow woman has been infused draws from and sustains a dynamic but disturbing principle of artificial life that, rather than being peripheral to, intensifies and haunts modernism itself. The Asiatic ornamental object-person is often seen as opposed to modernity, but it actually contains a forgotten genealogy about the coming together of life and nonlife, labor and style, that conditions the modern conceit of humanness. This genealogy of modern personhood is peculiarly inorganic, aggregated, and non-European. This synthetic being, relegated to the margins of modernity and discounted as a nonperson, holds the key to the inorganic animating the heart of the modern organic subject. She/it brings into view an alternative form of life, not at the site of the free and individualist modern subject, but on the contrary, at the encrusted edges and crevices of defiled, ornamented bodies.

If liberal racial rhetoric has not been able to tolerate the possibilities of subjective failures or corporeal ambiguity on the part of its cherished objects, it is because the female body and its ineluctable flesh continue to offer the primary site for both denigration and recuperation. At the same time, if recent critical discourse about the posthuman or what has come to be known as object-oriented ontology can at times feel politically disconnected, even as its intention has been to unsettle a tradition of insular humanism and anthropocentrism, it is because it has forgotten that the crisis between persons and things has its origins in and remains haunted by the material, legal, and imaginative history of persons made into things. Not only can the "de-anthropocentric" object, at once not alive and useless to people, not shed the attachment of racial and gendered meanings, but it also has provided a vexing, constitutive potential for the human subject. This paradox is most powerfully and poignantly played out for the yellow woman, holding the potential for the most devastating consequences as well as the most challenging political and ethical implications, especially for our conceptualization of freedom and individual agency.

4

Edible Pets

PLATE 61: Detail of plate 44. Courtesy of Wikimedia Commons.

> Who goes there? hankering, gross, mystical, nude
>
> —WALT WHITMAN, "SONG OF MYSELF"

CAN YOU HAVE your cake and eat it too? The interdiction behind that old American adage ("you cannot...") has always mystified me. Why would we want to own cake if it is not edible? Why is consumption not a form of continued and perhaps even more profound ownership? What if we prefer to keep the cake intact and external just so it survives in our imagination like a dear pet? The maxim troubles because it invokes even as it represses the fraught relationship between affect and consumption. The oppositions that it presumes—possession versus loss, matter versus digestion, external versus internal relations, loving versus eviscerating, petting versus eating—merge dizzyingly and eerily into one another the moment one thinks about them.

Our journey through the archaeology of ornamentalism, that strange fluctuation between things and persons, has led us to ever-increasing encounters with the queering of the human in the tale of personhood. And we cannot question the human without confronting our fundamental relation to what we ingest. As Jean Anthelme Brillat-Savarin, that great gentleman of the Enlightenment and the father of food writing, wrote in 1826, "Tell me what kind of food you eat, and I will tell you what kind of a man you are."[1] The ideals attached to Western civilizational values (what constitutes proper persons; what constitutes aesthetics versus gross needs) invariably invoke the critical subject of *food* and, by implication, the animal (either as food or pet or, disturbingly, both). Indeed, is not part of the historic seduction and hence queasiness of ornamentalism precisely the promise not only that "people" can be wearable, as we saw from the previous chapter, but also that they might be "plateable"? Let us now push the connection between bodies, plates, cups, and other vessels suggested by the Metropolitan exhibition to its extreme and ask what it means when we consume or become edible ornaments.

In *Racial Indigestion: Eating Bodies in the 19th Century*, Kyla Wazana Tompkins offers us an unforgettable account of the consolidation of whiteness as a nationalist mythology through the erotics of consumption. Nineteenth-century American "eating culture," as she puts it, is a site of racial anxiety and its management through the ingestion, both literal and metaphoric, of racialized minorities (blacks and Asians) seen as "the bottom of the food chain."[2] But as she also observes, the consumption does not always go down easily, producing what she calls "*queer alimentarity.*" This chapter suggests that ornamentalism breeds its own forms of queer alimentarity, not only disrupting the materiality of food and of race but also troubling the critical humanist distinction between what constitutes *flesh* and what constitutes *meat*[3]—a confusion that has, of course, always haunted the racialized subject.

SUSHI

A certain degree of cognitive dissonance is required for the full relish of this fare. Too lusciously beautiful to eat and too lusciously beautiful not to eat: the always unsettling complicity between aesthetics and consumption marks but one of the many paradoxes that the sushi eater sustains. It is about accepting the literal and the esoteric at the same time. It is about holding on to the idea of preparation and the hope of spontaneity. It is about imbibing the ocean and art in one mouthful. It insists on a decorativeness that invites destruction. What is painstakingly curated on the plate rubs up uncomfortably and tantalizingly against the rawness of its eating. Sushi and its naked sibling, *shashimi*, offer adventures in flirtation, throwing their consumers into teasing contact with the limits and prohibitions of nature, health, sociality, culture, and politics. As the at-once exotic and commonplace culinary choice, sushi symptomizes the technology of racial formation often at work in American food cultures. It also opens up a larger philosophic debate about the nature of our human ontology at the overlapping edges of zoology and anthropology. If, as has been famously argued by Claude Lévi-Strauss, cooking connotes human culture and edible meat is distinct from inedible flesh, then sushi troubles these distinctions by insisting, for some unnervingly and for others with delight, on its own material fleshness.[4]

What follows presents a speculative meditation through sushi on the twin demands of aesthetics and corporeality, metaphor and literalness, animality and civilization. Food studies, animal studies, and race studies have much to say to one another because of their shared stake in understanding the contingent nature of the "human." I am less interested in the sociology of sushi in the restaurant industry than in the ontology of sushi eating as an occasion to reconsider, or even remap, some of the most fundamental terms of our sociality and our humanness.

My interests here are partially driven, let me confess, by my own appetite for sushi, but they are inspired and fed by an exquisite, mysterious short story written by David Wong Louie called "Bottles of Beaujolais" (1992). This uncanny little story about romance, ecology, and sushi eating invites fascination yet remains difficult to digest. Written in the wake of a decade of intense Asian American activism, this story seems intended to stand outside the genre of ethnic bildungsroman that dominated the growth of Asian American literature. Race and ethnicity do not appear to be explicit issues of concern in the diegesis. Although its first-person narrator is presumably Asian American and his love object a Caucasian woman, the tale does not remark on this aspect of their relationship, nor is it in any way a typical or recognizable story of interracial romance. The surrealist elements of the plot also seem to hinder quick comprehension. We might say that Louie's story refuses to satisfy the racial and generic appetites that fuel so much Asian American literature.

Yet to say that race (and what it means to be reading for and chewing on race) is not part of the story seems shortsighted, for the text is deeply preoccupied with questions of species difference, a concept that is foundational to how race has been conceptualized by Western thinkers in the eighteenth century and through the Age of Enlightenment.[5] More than displacing racial difference onto species difference, this story does the even more disturbing work of asking us to rethink the logic of biological taxonomy itself. It compels us to consider how taxonomies of power (such as race and species) are imbricated, and what happens when we confront the collapse of their shared assumptions. Specifically, this chapter will trace the emergence of what I call the sushi principle, by which I mean a driving impulse in the text that reveals and revels in the delirious conflation between *meat* and *flesh* on the multiple levels of consumption, aesthetics, and affect. I am interested in how this "sushi principle" informs the sociocultural dimensions of so-called ethnic cuisine and sheds light on the larger issues of race and animality that are provoked by acts of eating. In the end, I suggest that the sushi principle is the eruption of the logic of ornamentalism in the realm of cuisine.

Louie's story, though dating from the nineties, is uncannily timely in its anticipation of a set of pressing contemporary conditions around what we eat: the rapid decrease in food supply, massive global environmental changes, the increasing tension between animal and human rights, and the conflict between animal activism and multiculturalism.[6] It is no coincidence that food studies and animal studies are two of the most rapidly growing critical discourses in the humanities these days, and these fields of inquiry have much to say to race studies. Today, with critical foci on animals and food, Louie's story offers a vivid opportunity to attend to the unspoken racial logic that connects the questions of who is a human and what is it that we eat. What then does it mean to approach sushi as a food, a commodity, a cultural marker, a racial sign, an affect, a metaphor for species difference, and finally, potentially, a means of critical agency?

SUSHI, OTTERS

From the very beginning, "Bottles of Beaujolais," originally collected in a volume called *Pangs of Love*, thrusts its readers into a quandary about the collusion between nature and culture. The plot goes like this: the unnamed narrator meets the woman of his dreams (whom he calls Luna) in the urban sushi restaurant in which he apprentices. The two of them embark on an impromptu date next to and then inside a giant aquatic habitat, Louie's own watery version of Manet's *Le Déjeuner sur l'herbe*, briefly referenced in the text itself. But this contemporary incarnation of Manet's picnic takes place not in the woods but inside a restaurant, and gestures to a romance not between men and women but between man, woman—and otter.

This creature, named Mushimono, is kept inside an artificial aquatic habitat as an exotic attraction for restaurant-goers.[7] The twelve-foot tank, which reaches the ceiling and juts six feet into the restaurant, occupies more than half of this Manhattan restaurant. The narrator, who aspires to becoming a master sushi chef but is currently assigned the humble task of caring for the transplanted otter, describes the tank this way:

> Mushimono's world was an exact reproduction of the lakeshore environment of southern Maine from which he came. Mr. Tanaka [the restaurant owner who makes a brief appearance at the beginning of the story] had hired experts in the fields of ecology, zoology, and horticulture to duplicate the appropriate balance of vegetation, animals, and micro-organisms found in the wild.[8]

The tank is a zoological tour de force in which reality and simulation fuse. And if this artificial ecology achieves the fantastical goal of being hospitable to a life taken wholly outside its natural habitat, then it also reminds us that the restaurant, too, is a carefully orchestrated and highly produced habitat for humans to feed in. We wonder what is the "natural setting" of our feeding and, as we will see later, our loving. The artificial domestication that is the very idea of a restaurant—and here, moreover, the artificial exoticism of that domestication in the form of the sushi restaurant—suggests that human anthropology bears an intimate relation to other ecological, zoological, horticultural, and, I would add, racial constructs.

This restaurant qua aquarium immediately places its visiting inhabitants (both diegetically and extradiegetically) in a queasy relationship to the limit of the civilized and the human, as well as between the uneasy slippage between being a spectator and the spectacle. From Brillat-Savarin in the eighteenth century to Margaret Visser in the twentieth, food writers have long understood that eating in restaurants and the rituals of eating are enduring marks of civilization and humanity.[9] (Manet, of course, was also playing with his own ideas about transgressive dining.) As Brillat-Savarin pithily and rather self-congratulatorily puts it, "men dine while animals feed."[10] Yet by juxtaposing the restaurant and the fish tank, by insisting on their intimacy—a proximity that is not only spatial but also atmospheric (moisture and heat seem to be continually seeping between the otter tank and the restaurant proper)—"Bottles of Beaujolais" underscores the continuity between artificial animal nature and natural human artifice. Indeed, what reminds us of these inversions more than sushi itself, marking the conjunction between rawness and sophistication, nature and commodity, exoticism and the quotidian?

Sushi eating in its contemporary American incarnation connotes an exotic, exclusive, acquired taste that has nonetheless become routinized in popular culture. As

Tompkins observes: "Foodie culture is founded on problematic racial politics in which white, bourgeois, urban subject positions are articulated... through the consumption and informational mastery of foreign, that is, non-Anglo-American food cultures."[11] She argues that raced bodies in America, from black to Asian bodies, have constituted eerily "edible" bodies for mainstream American culture since the nineteenth century. And Amy Bentley has named the conflation of consuming foreign foods with consuming foreign others as "culinary tourism."[12] For example, she offers Mexican food as an instance of how a "foreign" food has become a staple "American" food even in those areas where there are rabid anti-immigrant, especially anti-Mexican, political sentiments. In many ways, the rampant American consumption of its racial others is unconscious—indeed, could not afford to be otherwise.

Yet more than just a manifest symptom of racial tourism within American food cultures, sushi really brings out questions about how the consumption of race impacts and troubles the ontological border of its consumers. Sushi compounds its proffered feast of nominal cultural and racial otherness with a further provocation: a haunting specter about the resemblance between edible and inedible bodies. If what and how we eat has traditionally defined at least one of the major differences between us and other, nonhuman animals, then sushi eating invokes a crisis that has always been brewing inside that distinction. Sushi insists on its fundamental otherness, even when it can be found on every other corner of American cities, and it does so not through its apparent racial sign, or through its supposedly exotic origin, but instead through its disruptive effects on our "human" ontology. In short, sushi eating *queers* its eater, not by being foreign per se, but paradoxically by being too intimate.

"Bottles of Beaujolais" makes the startling and profound proposal that "eating in the raw" provides the very site for realizing the extraordinary and mundane corporeal exchanges that can take place between living creatures, underscoring the fragile separation between the familiar and the exotic, the domestic and the foreign, and between those whom we love and those whom we consume. Consumption is rarely a one-way street. The ambivalence attending to sushi as artistic artifice and as undiluted rawness casts doubts on the status of its eater: is the person who eats this raw meat, this fresh flesh, a primitive or a gourmand? The line between haute cuisine and savagery has always been teasingly tenuous. From escargots to foie gras, from bird's nest soup to blood sausages, gourmet food has always courted the primitive. As Joseph Litvak has taught us, sophistication and disgust are two sides of the same coin.[13] This tension inherent in eating as a base yet transcendent activity haunts not only the history of the philosophy of taste but also what might be called a primal scene in the birth of the American diet. One of the earliest treatises of a self-consciously American diet must be Henry David Thoreau's *Walden; or, Life in the Woods* (1854), whole sections of which are devoted to "Cuisine" and what it means to dine au naturel.

Thoreau urges the practice of "economy" in three areas: clothing, shelter, and food. He sees such self-discipline as contributing to the civilizing project, which in turn participates in the mission of nation building. This minimalist approach toward food counters what he sees as the "childish and savage tastes" of "savage nations."[14] Implicit in Thoreau's treatise lies a philosophic stake in equating the human, the modern, and the (white) American.[15] In order to transcend the mortal, hungry, and corrupting body, Thoreau discourages his readers not only from eating meat but also, at times, from eating altogether: "I believe that every man who has ever been earnest to preserve his higher or poetic faculties in the best condition has been particularly inclined to abstain from animal food, and from much food of any kind."[16]

But Thoreau's hymn to a diet of berries and twigs also includes an unexpected homage to hunting. The lean, acetic, transcendent Thoreau finds himself repeatedly haunted by another specter of himself: one who is earthbound, full bodied, and bloodthirsty. Consider the dramatic opening of the section "Higher Laws": "As I come through the woods with my string of fish, trailing my pole, it being now quite dark, I caught a glimpse of a woodchuck stealing across my path, and felt a strange thrill of savage delight, and was strongly tempted to seize and devour him raw; not that I was hungry then, except for that wildness which he represented."[17] How do we reconcile Thoreau the vegetarian with Thoreau the carnivore?

Does being wild mean consuming or being consumed by wildness? This tension registers an ongoing ambivalence in American philosophy about ideas of simplicity versus abundance, essence versus superficiality, higher laws versus human nature, and selfhood versus otherness—an ambivalence, moreover, that is girded by an implicitly racial logic, as in Thoreau's distaste for "savage nations." Historians and cultural critics have extensively documented the enduring and abject association between raced subjects and animals: blacks as apes, Asians as pigs or rats or dogs, Jews as rats, and so forth.[18] These animalized bodies are then consumed in a variety of ways for multiple purposes: for labor, for scapegoating, and in the service of national consolidation, just to name a few.[19] This consumption, moreover, has been done in the name of desire and repulsion: what Eric Lott famously calls the "love and theft" enacted by American racial dynamics, which in turn has produced what Tompkins labeled America's "racial indigestion."[20]

"Bottles of Beaujolais," however, does not exactly rehearse this history of discriminatory (if uneasy) consumption in order to reprimand it. Instead the story radicalizes this history into a fantasy of *in*discriminate hunger, where everyone and everything become potential targets of consumption. That is, rather than retreating to an ethics of restraint (for example, the choice to be a vegan), this story insists that we confront the boundlessness of our eating. Even more disconcertingly in Louie's text, to be an eater is to immediately become potentially the eaten. (Does not the specter of cannibalism always haunt the omnivore?) In Louie's sushi restaurant (itself a product of American immigration history), the ambivalence registered in early American writing about securing the civilizing boundaries of the American diet reaches its fullest and most radical expression, where eater-consumer and food-alien other not only resemble each other but in fact become each other.[21] Because "he" is the nonhuman-exotic-foreign-transplanted other in the story, Mushimono's presence in the sushi restaurant breeds a host of lingering, ambiguous possibilities. Is "he" a vertebrate who is clearly *not* meant for eating, or is he in fact consumable?

After all, as an exotic window display, Mushimono already serves as bait. Indeed, he is named after a Japanese dish: a steamed egg concoction often containing meat. So Mushimono/*mushimono* already evokes a strange figure of meat-that-contains-meat. And is it not precisely the anxiety of such intimate contact (meat with meat, self with self) that many religious prohibitions about eating set out to prevent?[22] This anxiety about the intimacy of meats, of which cannibalism offers the extreme incarnation, haunts sushi eating and perhaps explains why the habit of American sushi restaurants to incorporate live goldfish into their décor can seem so twisted and yet so telling. The perversity of displaying live sea creatures next to prepared seafood registers as sadism and points to the arbitrary logic of what separates the edible from the inedible.[23] *Sure, we know we don't eat goldfish, but does the goldfish know that?* And indeed, is not Mushimono's subjectivity precisely what has been repressed by the fastidious way he's being cared for? It is surely ironic to fuss over how fresh the fish being fed to him are and how "authentic" his tank vegetation is when he is isolated, held captive, and put on display. The ritual of care disguises the violence, just like the preparation of sushi itself.[24]

The story's mis-en-scène disrupts the hierarchy of the food chain. On the one hand, Mushimono extends the racialized logic that informs the long tradition of pseudoscientific display of "exotic" or "freakish" others. But on the other, the story stages concentric circles of display tanks and microclimates: Mushimono's fish tank inside the restaurant that is itself a tank, an ethnography of multiple life forms engaged in convoluted and mutually contaminating ecologies. Thus instead of a vertical, hierarchical structure organized by race or the food chain, we have instead a horizontal and concentric geography, the story's power structures (man eating nonhuman animals, dominant culture eating the exotic other) rapidly rearranging and reshaping themselves into an alternative ecology.

Mushimono stands as more than a symbol of spectacularized difference. He is also an agent, an avid fish eater himself. The otter thus mirrors both the fish being served and the human eating next to him. There is, after all, more than a little bite to a story about people eating sushi next to a large mammal who feeds on fish and shellfish. Indeed, all the human characters in this story bear an uncanny affinity to the meat they consume or prepare. There is a wonderful little moment when the restaurant owner, Mr. Tanaka, who has eyes like "little dead black roe" (37)—a description at once zoologizing and racializing—lectures the narrator about Mushimono's discriminating tastes. Mr. Tanaka warns the narrator that the otter is very selective and eats only fresh live fish—unlike, we immediately realize, Mr. Tanaka's human clientele, who spend a great deal of money on *fresh dead* fish.

Our human fussiness about food may distinguish us from the animals, but our omnivorousness also testifies to our indiscriminateness. More important, the otter in the sushi restaurant raises the problem not of the difference between eating fish and eating otter but rather of the deeper uncertainty of what constitutes the edible. This inherent, flickering imbrication between "meat" and "flesh" lies at the heart of the sushi principle, at once instantiating and disproving human exceptionality. Sushi, as a culinary art that requires decades of dedicated training, symbolizes the supposedly exclusively human valuing of aesthetic experience, even as, in its rawness, it transgresses against the protocols of civility. Moreover, its rawness makes it close to flesh, something that the sushi eater both disavows and celebrates.[25] Rather than the old fetishistic logic ("I know, but..."), we are looking at a strange balancing of detachment and attachment ("I know, *and*..."). The critical question here (both for us and for food studies in general) must extend beyond locating structuralist categories and their breakdowns—that is, beyond the task of rethinking who is the sophisticate and who the primitive—and attend to the even more urgent inquiry of how the failure of that distinction reflects back on our own *fresh/dead* flesh.[26]

The sushi principle insists that we remain in the ethical toggle between those two possibilities. To remain in the awareness of this ambivalence is to resist the complacency of humanness on the one hand and the condescension of imagining we can relinquish our human privilege on the other. The sushi principle's negative capability leads us to a curious, glaring gap between our biological attachment to, yet ontological detachment from, our own *meatness*, a schism that can only open up at brief and uncanny moments of clarity. Thus, more than a commodified technology of racial formation, sushi eating provides a trope for the dizzying technology of subject (de) formation being enacted every time we eat. It demands from its gourmets a principle of avowed disavowal in the face of bareness. Above all, it puts on the chopping block our very sense of our own boundaries, for to feed on sushi and sashimi is to plunge headlong into the double delirium of knowing my own animality even as I partake in the social-aesthetic ritual designed to disguise (but never quite fully) the rawness, vibrancy, violence, and naturalness of that eating. It is to open myself up to the vulnerability of my own flesh.

However civilized we become, the omnivorous body is always, in the background, a threateningly, potentially edible body, because the idea of "human flesh" is itself already so ambivalent, so ready to hark back to the very "meat" from which it distinguishes itself. And if we see, as Tompkins has urged us, how racialized this dynamic can be, then we must now also consider how ontologically disruptive (rather than filling) this eating is. Even at the height of Eurocentric humanism, the "edible body" has not gone down easily. In his classic treatise *The Physiology of Taste; or, Meditations on Transcendental Gastronomy* (which has not gone out of print since its first publication, in 1825), Brillat-Savarin argues that man is superior to other animals because he is omnivorous and the "great gourmand of Nature."[27] Yet even in this most humanist of treatises, it is precisely in the act of eating that the human and the inhuman merge:

> As soon as an edible body has been put into the mouth, it is seized upon, gases, moisture, and all, without possibility of retreat... and it [the edible body] is pulled down into the stomach to be submitted to sundry baser transformations without, in this whole metamorphosis, a single atom or drop or particle having been missed by the powers of appreciation of the taste sense.[28]

How can we fail to observe in this act of digestion that the transcendent eater is also the most crude and voracious of feeders? In this passage, different "bodies" infuse one another. The passive food being eaten, the "edible body," seems to have as much agency and embodiment as (if not more than) the eating, human body abstracted as mouth and saliva.[29] It is the object of consumption, not the gourmand, who possesses body, psychology, desires, and fears. Indeed, throughout Brillat-Savarin's grammar, evident in the original French and lovingly retained by M. F. K. Fisher's English translation, we note again and again how the object of consumption appears to be the one exuding action and affect.

The human and the "edible body" that he consumes merge, not just because one becomes what one eats, as Brillat-Savarin asserts, but because, as Louie's story dramatizes, the eater can easily become the eaten. It is *this* porousness that various prohibitions about eating (what is proper versus improper food) are designed to seal and are continually threatened by. To eat animals is not to master animals but rather to betray one's own intimacy with them. (Thoreau's dilemma—how to be wild without being devoured by wildness—becomes the recipe for a psychoanalytic insight: *being* equals *having*.) Even Brillat-Savarin will go on to make the eccentric yet telling observation that we can pass along, in the manner of familial transmission, our human enjoyment of eating animals *to* the animals: "This pleasure is even contagious; and we transmit it quickly to the animals which we have tamed."[30] For us today, it is difficult not to hear a parable about colonial mimicry in these observations. What happens when the creature that we train ends up mimicking us to the point of becoming us? What happens when we resemble "it"? What does this resemblance do to the "Family of Man"?

It is into this breach between the inescapable custody of our own humanness and the intrusive awareness of our own objectness, which the sushi principle reveals, that Louie's delicious, delirious story dives. And in the process, some unlikely new relations get born. Can there be kinship that is not based on human bloodlines but instead structured along other networks of animated affinities? What would such kinship look like?

SUSHI, OTTERS, AND MERMAIDS

Enter Luna.

We know by now that we do not need the presence of a yellow woman to invoke the logic of yellow femininity. In "Bottles of Beaujolais," the other figure, in addition to the otter, that comes to join this strange little family unit is a white woman—but not just any white woman. When we first meet Luna, the female protagonist and the narrator's romantic interest, she is coming into the restaurant, drawn by the lure of Mushimono in the window. She initially appears as the undoubtedly privileged human spectator of the exotic animal caged behind the glass. We are told, for example, about her snakeskin shoes, an exotic fashion accessory that surely underscores her human dominance in the food chain. Yet her humanness and whiteness waver the moment she crosses the threshold of the restaurant. The narrator begins by describing her in terms of food ("her baby shrimp lips") and quickly comes to identify her with Mushimono: "I dreamed of Luna, naked as the otter, standing in the street outside the lakeshore, tapping at the window." Luna, however, is not simply like Mushimomo in her feminine fishiness; they both seem to possess an uncanny quality for transformation:

> Perhaps it was the eerie quality of the fog-sifted light . . . that caused the twin curves of Mushimono's belly and spine to run congruously before taping together at the S of his thick, sibilant tail. . . . My thoughts drifted off to a moving figure of another sort: Luna, and the gentle crook of her neck, the soft slope of her shoulders, the slight downward turn of the corners of her mouth.[31]

In this moment of transgendered and trans-species queering, Mushimomo and Luna mirror one another in a simultaneous evolution, both becoming an *other-other*, a different sort of semiaquatic animal—a mermaid?

And can we resist hearing in the lines quoted above the echo of another sad-mouthed sibilant beauty, whom we saw earlier as an analog for Anna May Wong (plate 62)?

PLATE 62: Detail of plate 44. Courtesy of Wikimedia Commons.

In Botticelli's intrauterine dream of cosmic birth and commotion, Venus appears as a kind of mermaid, that iconic association between femininity and fishy otherness. Ideal white femininity is therefore elevated precisely at the same time that it is animalized. As art historians have long observed, this beauty embodies many paradoxes. She stands at the center of this vibrant universe and yet is herself strangely torpid. She represents aesthetic birth but is corporeality itself. She is a classic beauty whose proportions are in fact far from classical. Her slim, long body with arms that are a tad elongated give her an oddly marmoreal quality, which the poet Robert Hass will later come to famously memorialize, in his poem "Against Botticelli," as "otterness" itself:

> In the life we lead together every paradise is lost.
> ...
> Mad seed. Death waits it out. It waits us out.
> ...
> In our shamefast and steady attention
> to the ceremony, its preparation, the formal hovering
> of pleasure which falls like rain we pray not to get
> and are glad for and drown in. Or spray of that sea,
> irised: otters in the tide lash, in the kelp-drench,
> mammal warmth and the inhuman element. Ah, that is the secret.
> That she is an otter, that Botticelli saw her so.
> That we are not otters and are not in the painting
> by Botticelli.[32]

For Hass, this hybrid body—one that is neither ethereal nor earthly, neither fully human nor wholly animal—stands as a cipher for the melancholia of being a human animal.

Like Botticelli's marmoreal beauty, Luna will rise from the waters, and as in Hass's invocation, she will emanate elements of the human and the inhuman. For Luna will fall into the pond inside Mushimono's tank and, with drenched skirt wrapped tightly around her legs like a tail, emerge a mermaid-otter:

> With her next step she suddenly plunged into thigh-deep water, stirring a turbulence that sucked the lilylike filets [of salmon sashimi that the humans were

> eating and that Luna was trying to feed Mushimono] toward her. When the ripples subsided, one filet was clinging to the front of a bare thigh. Rather than removing it, she smoothed the lox against her skin with caresses and pats that produce sounds like those of lovers' stomachs pressed together. . . . As she emerged from it . . . she unhitched her algae-blotched skirt and let it fall in a pile at her feet.[33]

In this cross-species birth, Luna's human, white skin takes on and becomes sashimi fish food (and, implicitly, racial other); she *is* the food she eats and the food she feeds to the nonhuman animal. In pushing to the foreground the intimacy among woman, fish, and food, Luna does not stand as merely some modern-day degraded version of the Botticelli Venus but rather as her modern-day incarnation, for Botticelli's goddess was "otter" as well. Just as the sushi principle reminds us of the innate rawness of eating and the aesthetic practices that both disguise and enshrine that bareness, this bared body emerging from the fish tank does the work of spelling out the conflation between nakedness (as a property of the animal) and the nude (as a domain of idealized humanity) that has always haunted the female body.[34]

This fusion between woman and otter thus does not so much reproduce the classic association between woman and atavistic otherness as it seems to unleash, instead, a larger and stranger principle of animation and transmutation that suffuses the world of the story.[35] To be with Luna, then, means crossing the lines of race, species, and sex, and even those separating people and things. Is she a mate or a food for the animal that she increasingly resembles and replicates? Why is this scene of baptism also an enactment of epidermal transfusion? What kind of new skin or flesh is this? What is the status of this modern-day Venus in the food chain, in the family of man?

Implicit racial and animal logic has always accompanied the figure of the mermaid. Surely the fear of and fascination with the mermaid in many human cultures since antiquity has much to do with deep-seated anxieties about interspecies encounters, worries that survive in modern-day eugenics and antimiscegenation sentiments. Indeed, early visual and verbal representations of the mermaid tend to emphasize the creature's monstrousness rather than her romance or beauty (plates 63–65).[36]

We are not surprised to learn that this monstrosity, underscored by the mermaid's frequent placement in the Victorian bestiary, often carries racialized undertones as well. In the middle of the nineteenth century, at the height of European imperialism and exploration, the figure of the mermaid reemerges in popular culture with a vengeance, often in the form of illustrations that combine fish tails with what look like Asian or African or simply simian features, and that are set in non-Western locations.[37] It would take the master fairy tale weaver Hans Christian Andersen to domesticate and make over the historically (and racially) queer mermaid by giving her the specifically melancholic, *human*, and, I might add, *mulatto* pathos of

PLATE 63: J. Godby, after L. Gahagan, "A Mermaid, situated on a Rock" (1814). Courtesy of the Wellcome Library, London.

PLATE 64: Anonymous poster, "Monkey Fish." Courtesy of the Wellcome Library, London.

PLATE 65: George Cruikshank, *The Mermaid at the Turf Coffee-House*. Courtesy of the Library of the Congress, London Metropolitan Archives.

mourning her own mixedness.[38] The Little Mermaid's profound self-rejection and tragic self-erasure—she chooses to disappear into sea foam in order for the prince to marry a "real" woman—ironically expresses the depth of her humanness. The mermaid thus finally takes on pathos (and eros) when she turns into a sacrificial homage to "pure" human kinship.

But what happens when the mermaid remains incomprehensibly and uncolonizably hybrid? Can "kinship" be formed in the face of such alienness?

The "mermaid" in Louie's story tends to stay consistently between worlds and insistently weird. Hybridity is neither mourned nor celebrated. "It" simply *is*. Mushimono weaves in and out of maleness and femaleness, animal and person, silence and sibilance. Luna morphs between woman and animal, mundane and ethereal, a soaked woman and a drenched goddess. In fact, Luna's real name is Peg, which the narrator bemoans. "Peg! I thought. *Peg*? One hangs coats on pegs. How could my Luna be this monosyllable? This Peg?"[39] This constant fluctuation between the literal and the allegorical, the mundane and the transcendent, presents another incarnation or extension of the sushi principle. It infuses the story on the levels of language, narrative style, and character, producing a threateningly and seductively porous world.

In such a world, we find a crisis not of discrimination, but of *in*discrimination. At the climax of this odd meal, the (Asian American male) narrator appears to have lost the fundamental ability to distinguish between different kinds of "flesh." In a moment of ecstatic bliss, he actually confuses his own flesh with that of the fish:

> I went behind the sashimi bar to prepare a snack for us. I selected a long shiny knife from Mr. Tanaka's impressive collection. I was surprised by how light it felt in my hands.... The steel seemed to melt into the flesh. At first, I was tentative in my approach, but soon, caught up in the sensuality of slicing, in the thrill of moving through flesh, I was imitating the sashimi master's speedy hands.... Where was the mystery of his art? It was mine already.... I looked over at Luna and smiled while my hands whittled away at the shrinking hunk of fish.... I glanced down to admire my handiwork. My hand was a bloody mess."[40]

After the narrator makes sashimi out of his own hands, instead of rushing to the hospital or treating his wounds, the narrator and Luna lovingly cup his blood in the sake bowl (a mini "tank" in the story), from which they drink ceremoniously: blood, wine, saliva, fish, and flesh as one. Here the specter of cannibalism (both the eating of the other and of the self) becomes more and more real. We might say that both the narrator and Luna have fallen under the sway of the sushi principle, finding one another in that unsavory but enchanting euphoria between meat and flesh, the erratic and the erotic, matter and sentience.

Could a white man's flesh ever be mistaken for sushi? In this story, the permeability of flesh and meat seems confined to the female, the raced, and the animal. At the same time, however, this capacity for *being cut*, for living in a world of indeterminateness (to the point of being radically corporeally accessible), also allows for a curious form of agency. These moments of boundary violations, while clearly perturbing, nonetheless seem tied to the critical agency in the text. If the sushi principle can make "meat" out of those who are female, animal, or raced, then Louie's story imagines that it can also make sashimi or mermaids out of anyone and everyone. We can be made strangers to ourselves with shocking ease.

These sites of contamination between beings in the story are thus more properly ethical than political. We are not being given a solution so much as a meditation about what it means to be radically open to difference, to live outside the boundary of taxonomy and the traditional binaries of structural anthropology. The story undoes the categorical oppositions that form the foundation of everyday experience. The appearance of the "other" launches the shock not of difference but of intimacy. Thus the specter of species difference does not reinstate a dyad—human or not, flesh or meat—but instead expresses itself as categorical failure, as a relational ordering that is subject to unpredictable transformation. This may be why the story seems intent on unraveling the structuralist assumptions of quotidian life by staging and baring the intersection of zoology and anthropology.

In their introduction to the volume *Knowing Animals*, Philip Armstrong and Laurence Simmons address the fundamental anthropomorphism at the heart of animal studies, and the zoomorphism at the heart of human studies:

> The creatures that occupy our taxonomies are never purely nonhuman. They are never free of us. Their bodies, habits, and habitats are shaped by human designs; they are contaminated by, but also resistant to, our philosophies, theologies, representations, interests, intentions. On the other hand, and just as surely, our concepts and practices are never purely human in the first place. For we are not free from the animal either, although the tradition of humanism promised we should be. Animality infests us, plagues us, goes feral on us.[41]

If we are to speak of anthropomorphism in our views of animals, then we must also speak of zoomorphism in our perceptions of the human. One of the limits of animal and posthuman studies is the way in which the animal comes to serve as a metaphoric crux within theories of language and law. From Darwin's dog to Derrida's cat, the animal has often been enlisted as a critique of privileged humanity—at times, as an explicit means of shaming us out of our human complacency.[42] At the same time, we have not acknowledged enough how, no matter how much we wish to "recognize" our animal cousins, we can see the animal only through our inescapable humanness. And our understanding of ourselves is deeply indebted to how we have imagined animality in the first place.

Even the birth of the human kinship system as a discipline and a cornerstone of modern anthropology offers a repressed tale of "cross-breeding." As Gillian Feeley-Harnik has pointed out, Lewis Henry Morgan, the father of modern anthropology, formulated his seminal work on the human kinship system based on many of the insights he gained while studying the Seneca Indians *and* a community of—alas, not mermaids or otters—but a cousin semiaquatic creature: the "humble American beaver" of the Great Lakes regions of Michigan.[43] How we think about our social principles—our supposedly unique and elaborate network of kinship structures, our relation to property, and above all, our presumed sociality over and beyond biology—has never been free from our conceptualization of the animalized and racialized other. And nothing demonstrates this complicity more acutely than where and what we eat.

Margaret Visser tells us that the social rituals and traditions surrounding eating "give rise to many basic human characteristics, such as kinship systems (who belongs with whom; which people eat together)."[44] In "Bottles of Beaujolais," however, it is eating with strangers that actually brings to light the unspoken assumptions underlying what we consider to be "basic human characteristics." The story also begs the questions of the extent to which our normative ideas of basic human characteristics are fundamentally weird and if there could be kinship between the human and the not human. We might think of the meal within Louie's story as revising the very idea of the Family of Man. It breaks down the human kinship system (and its embedded familial and racial systems) into a network of abstract and hence transferable corporeal and affective properties. This transference is realized not only by the story's adherence to what I am calling the sushi principle but also by the story's other major trope: blood. The title "Bottles of Beaujolais" refers to the drink shared by our two human protagonists, but from the start, Luna and the narrator substitute sake for Beaujolais, which isn't available in the restaurant. (Substitution provides the basic logic for relationality in this tale, as if, in this wholly consumable world, only such capacity for nonmelancholic replacement can ensure the continuation of life.) The bowl of sake-Beaujolais then undergoes further transformation (or is it transfusion?) when Luna lovingly pours the narrator's own blood into the sake bowls, which they use ceremoniously. Cannibalism, kinship, transubstantiation, marriage, and birth converge.

By literalizing the blood that is exchanged between radically different bodies, the story paradoxically undoes the privileged status of "blood" in the dominant fictions of kinship and inheritance of traits. Nontangible qualities also get transferred among the three beings, human and nonhuman, in the story. Mushimono is more than just a witness to this eccentric human ritual. Because *mushimono*, the custard dish, is often made with or infused with sake, Mushimono's meaty body itself is thus also an echo of the sake-filled bowl being consumed by the humans. Moreover, *sake* the liquor acts as a homophone for *sake* the fish (meaning salmon), the fish filets that our threesome alternately eat and wear as skin. In this scene of fleshly substitution, affective exchange, and linguistic morphing, vessels (soup bowl, fish tank, sentence, skin, body) become flexible structures, sometimes containing, sometimes contained.

Is this a scene of (racial) transfusion, (spiritual) transubstantiation, (elemental) translation, or all three? I suggest we are witnessing not some act of erotic vampirism, but instead the earnest effort to reimagine the creation of a new family, a new consanguinity, through the alchemy of ornamentalism. While the connection between food and sex (for example, eating as the sublimation of erotic drive) is well rehearsed, this story is sexless, a radical reimagining of human-nonhuman relationality that gives us a new affinity of blood. At the climax of the story we find not sex but a totem meal.[45] This fable's radically porous site turns out to be *not* female genitals (the "wet otter"), as traditional psychoanalysis would have it, but instead the human mouth. Indeed, the story itself feels increasingly like a digestive system. Again I turn to Brillat-Savarin's hauntingly visceral description: " The sapid molecules must be dissolved in no matter what kind of fluid, so they may then be absorbed by the sensitive projections, buds, or suckers which line the interior of the apparatus for tasting."[46] The diegetic world of "Bottles of Beaujolais" is exceptionally moisture-laden, ripe for absorption and feeding, as if the entire restaurant has become a giant mouth. In this vaporous world, everyone and everything is *sapid*: capable of tasting and being tasted. The doubleness of eating—making mincemeat out of the other but also of the self—compels us to consider the foundations of humanness and how some of the basic categories of difference in biology and anthropology have worked to disguise affinities between humans and nonhumans.

In her essay "Being Human: Bestiality, Anthropophagy, and Law," literary critic Kalpana Seshadri-Crooks suggests that the founding law of human civilization (and the human kinship system on which that civilization rests) may not be the prohibition against incest, as Freud asserts, but rather the prohibition against anthropophagy. In other words, who belongs in the "Family of Man" may be determined less by whom you can or cannot sleep with than by what you can or cannot eat,[47] prompting us to reconsider how food, as much as sex, might determine the limits on which humanness is built. (Considering contemporary bourgeois values, it is often much easier to know with whom we ought or ought not to sleep than what we can or cannot eat.) "Bottles of Beaujolais," however, suggests that cannibalism might be the condition of, rather than an exception to, civilization. We have to be willing to eat ourselves and others in order to be the privileged humans that we are. "Bottles of Beaujolais" does not simply teach the moral that humans are animals too, but also proposes, disturbingly, that being "nonhuman" and "other" may be *the very mode of our ontology*.[48] Consumption makes otherness our own, but also opens us up to an unruly sociality where what seems properly ours becomes food for the other. This insight into our fundamental, ontological alienation, which also plays itself out externally over and over again as racial differentiation, does not dilute the impact of racism. On the contrary, it underscores how quotidian, inescapable, voracious, and vulnerable our appetite for the other is.

In the end we have a new family of three inextricably linked but separate beings. This is a brave new world, but not one that is triumphant or redemptive. At the end of the story our three protagonists leave the hothouse environment of the restaurant to emerge into the larger world. The narrator follows Luna/Peg into a taxi; Mushimono leaves his "natural" habitat and gets into the cab as well. It is an Edenic expulsion into a new world: "No moon in the sky... lots of snow.... I shook my sore hand.... I followed the flight of several flakes... to the white street below.... Absolute quiet, as it must have been at the beginning of time."[49] To quote Hass again, is this the paradise we "pray not to get / and are glad for and drown in"?

Man, woman, and otter speed into the dark night toward an unknown future. This is and is not a new family. The narrator and his heroine remain dramatically alien to one another, as they are to the otter, even as all three increasingly share one another's lives and physical space. Luna is at once horrified by and accepting of Mushimono's presence in the cab, just as the narrator, delirious yet lucid, takes his mutilation in stride. Who will survive this ride? What life awaits those fed on the sushi principle, which has so far managed to sustain them in the delicate and impossible work of being at once human and nonhuman?

As the bleeding man, the drenched woman, and the live otter rush into the dark city night, we wonder whether the threesome's ejection from the restaurant implies a waking from the nightmare of their too-intimate human-animal night or another swerve in a dream. Considering the narrator's description of the silent night into which they speed, are the characters fleeing toward the end of the earth or the beginning of time? When Luna, with "[h]er pale face... the leaden-gray of cod fish," finally starts to emerge from the habitat of their little picnic, her skin growing cold and clammy, is reality finally setting in, or is she somehow turning even more permanently into a mermaid? Is this the next stage of a spiritual transcendence or the victory of mundane reality?

The story pointedly refuses resolution. What we do get, in the place of answers, is a kind of horizontal transfer between states: what Louie repeatedly calls "translations." It is as if, in insisting upon change rather than epiphany, Louie wants us to experience aesthetic transformation without transcendence. What then is transformation without transcendence?[50] It is here that we might consider the story itself as yet another "mermaid." The tale's at times smooth and at times deliberately jarring fluctuation between the mundane and the surreal traps us in the condition of in-betweenness. We shuffle between the sublime and the quotidian without a sense of deflation or degradation, without transcendence or redemption. We might say that miscegenation, while absent as theme, resurfaces as the logic and style of this text. The mixed style that I have been discussing (that oscillation between the fantastical and the prosaic, between the twin poles of Luna and Peg) actually has the effect of detaining us within and attaching us to a never-ending relay between flesh and spirit, body and metaphor. In short, the reader, too, has been bred by the sushi principle. Thus the meta/physical transaction between unlike states in the diegesis also reveals itself through the story's own aesthetic undulation between the material and the abstract, the literal and the metaphoric.

The story returns us to Hass's poem "Against Botticelli," both texts being melancholic meditations on how to live between the pull of transcendence and the weight of "detranscendence." Like Mushimono with his lakeshore home, we move among real constructs and fabricated realities. Herding us between the metaphoric and the literal, the stylistic hybridity that this text enacts compels us to remain within transition itself, allowing us neither to escape into a world of fantasy nor to emerge from the pull of dreaming.

Is the conclusion of the story a vision of utter annihilation or a brand-new beginning? Louie dares us to entertain these as the only possible outcomes of radically reimagining our world ecology and the way we eat— and perhaps the way we read as well. The question he leaves us with: can we survive a future where we *live* the discomfort of our own flesh?

5

Dolls

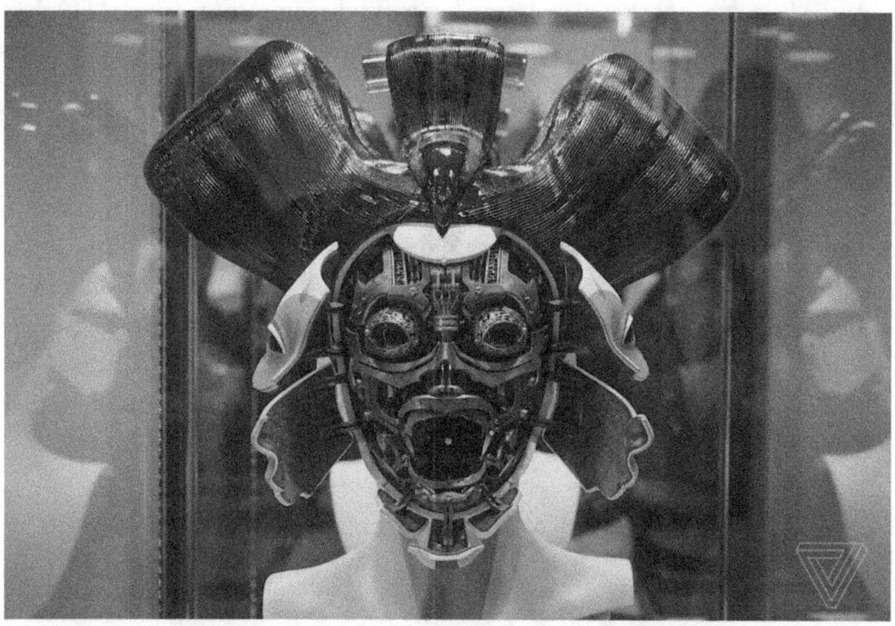

PLATE 66: Robot geisha film still from *Ghost in the Shell* (dir. Rupert Sanders, 2017). Courtesy of Kobal/Rex/Shutterstock.

OUR ARCHAEOLOGY OF Asiatic ornamentality has taken us to the present moment and its implications for the (in)human future. Nineteenth-century Orientalism, especially condensed around the figure of Asiatic femininity, thrives in mainstream American culture today, driving desires and animosities in politics, culture, entertainment, and commerce, but it does so not only because of ongoing racism but also because this figure energizes a specific, aesthetic, ornamentalist practice that drives our imagination about what is beyond the human.

Many have observed that there is an intimate association between technology and Asiatic tropes, especially in the realm of popular culture (see plate 66). In his treatise

The Buddha in the Machine: Art, Technology, and the Meeting of East and West, R. John Williams calls the ongoing life of Orientalism in contemporary tech and corporate culture "Asia-as-technê," which he defines as "a compelling fantasy that would posit Eastern aesthetics as both antidote to and the perfection of machine cultures."[1] Williams traces the importance of Asian aesthetics for the Western technological imagination, from the way Martin Heidegger developed his concept of technê while dabbling in Orientalism to how corporate America today borrows Eastern mysticism as a way to participate fully in the capitalist dynamic, producing what Williams calls "Corporate Zen." According to Williams, as Asia-as-technê is deployed to alleviate the division between man and machine in the twenty-first century, the East does not simply transcend but in fact becomes the machine.[2] He gives us the arresting image in plate 67 to illustrate this insight. For Williams, this piece entitled *Pensive Mechanical Bodhisattva/Kwanon_Z*, (2010), by artist Wang Zi Won, comments on contemporary American Orientalism by offering a "striking aesthetic vision of the transposition of biological and spiritual mechanical systems."[3]

The figure of the yellow woman, I argue, anticipates this transposition well before the development of modern technology and modern corporate culture. The history of Western encounters with Eastern otherness, from the semihuman fleshliness of Chinese porcelain (as I argued in chapter 3) to the sensuousness of Japanese lacquer (as Cyra Levenson and Chi-ming Yang have explored), promotes and generates the prototypes of animated objectness.[4] The production of artificial life via the enchanted

PLATE 67: Wang Zi Won, *Pensive Mechanical Bodhisattva/Kwanon_Z*, 2010. Urethane, metallic material, machinery, electronic device (CPU board, motor): 40(w) x 28)d) x 40(h) cm. Image courtesy of the artist.

materialism of Asiatic femininity instantiates a predicament of and a romance with synthetic personhood that has dogged the Western conceptualization of personhood since the imperial age and early contact with the so-called Eastern Other.[5] Ornamentalism thus offers us another aspect of the telos of Western technological determinism. By fusing organic flesh with art and manufacturing, the ornamental yellow woman anticipates and distills a particular aspect of Asia-as-technê. The Asiatic woman in particular serves as a threatening replicant in the fictions of artificial life, not simply as a sign of radical otherness but also, more crucially, as an embodiment of the crisis of the inhuman already inhering in the human.

More than a fantasy reflecting the desires and anxieties of machine cultures, synthetic Asiatic femininity provides a mobile vocabulary and an almost musculoskeletal model through which acolytes of machine cultures realize, often to their dismay, their most radical dreams: the genuine and ineluctable indebtedness of the organic to the inorganic, the primacy of the prosthetic, and more. If we can offer one criticism of popular science fiction works about the other-than-human, it is that they often withdraw from their own ambitions by retreating to the human sentimentality they claim to want to transcend. One of the hardest things for us to confront is our own thingness. This is why the desire "to boldly go where no man has gone before" and "to seek out new life and new civilizations" so often disappointingly returns us to life and civilization exactly as we know it.[6] This is also why our repudiation of human solipsism in the age of the posthuman can seem so solipsistic. But the ancient-yet-new figure of the yellow woman as ornamentalist technology allows us to reconsider the alternative ontologies that inform and shape our fundamental assumptions about humanness and its attending personhood. This chapter asks: could the archaeology of ornamentalism offer us a radical theory of science fiction, just as science fiction's engagement with animated objecthood could articulate a radical theory of race?

The yellow woman, to borrow a formulation from Christopher Bush, is "not simply an example of the embodiment of a racial imaginary, but a site at which the logic of embodiment itself was worked through."[7] *She is not the atavistic figure to be abandoned by modern technological science but the form of its aspiration.*

THE GHOST IN THE GHOST

When Freud told us that one of the most unsettling effects for human ontology is to be confronted by a machine that comes to life, he was echoing a century-long anxiety about the limits and definition of the human since the beginning of the machine age.[8] As architectural theorist Spyros Papapetros contends, the origins of contemporary animated culture evolved from the "vivified terrain of the preceding fin de siècle," that is, the animated artifacts of twentieth-century modernity represent the return of repressed nineteenth-century empathy for objects in the external world.[9] I am suggesting here that the live-dead thingness of Asiatic femininity offers us yet another "vivified terrain" in the archaeology of object empathy. As our ongoing archaeology of ornamentalism has revealed, the machine age has origins in racialized encounters from the Age of Exploration. From porcelain to lacquer to wood to silk and cotton, the explosion of material culture in the nineteenth century is deeply rooted in the discovery of the East. The frocks and other containers that I studied in chapter 3 are the modern artifacts of those centuries-old encounters, and one of the most eerie consequences of confronting those empty-but-embodied objects is our forced encounter with our own thingness. We are shells walking among shells.

Rupert Sanders's film *Ghost in the Shell* (2017) provides an opportunity to think about the ornamentality of our (in)corporeal fantasies in a digital age. In *Onto-cartography: An Ontology of Machines and Media,* Levi R. Bryant distinguishes between what he calls corporeal and incorporeal machines:

> [A] corporeal machine is any machine that is made of matter, that occupies a discrete time and place and that exists for a duration. Subatomic particles, rocks, grass, human bodies . . . are all corporeal machines. Incorporeal machines, by contrast, are defined by their iterability, potential eternity, and the capacity to manifest themselves in a variety of spatial and temporal locations at once while retaining their identity.[10]

What we have been seeing, however, is how misleading it is to distinguish the corporeal machine from the incorporeal machine, especially when it comes to a body that has been treated as both finite matter *and* infinitely iterable. The encrusted, assembled, and repeatable Asiatic female body has shown us how very indebted human flesh can be, not to discrete matter and time, but instead to temporal manipulation and profound organic compromises. Based on the 1995 cult classic anime of the same name by Shirow Masamune, *Ghost in the Shell* offers us a particularly intriguing meditation not just on Asia-as-techê but also on technê-as-Asiatic-femininity.

Ghost in the Shell follows a long line of cinematic cyberfiction from *Blade Runner* to *Ex Machina* that extends the apprehension about the animation of the inanimate and asks all of the usual and, dare I say, tired questions: What makes a human human? Is consciousness the same as the soul, that is, is there a ghost in the machine? Is artificial intelligence an enhancement or an erasure of the human? What happens to the human element when the brain gets reduced to a series of electrical impulses, and, conversely, can machines have feelings, too?[11] Raising these questions has become a convention of the cyberfiction genre; so, too, has the deployment of femininity and racial otherness as gratuitous and exotic titillation. Reviews of Sanders's film have already noted the voyeuristic pleasures afforded by a "naked" Scarlett Johansson, who plays Major Motoko Kusanagi, an augmented cybernetic cop who is not shy about exposing her wholly synthetic body. Many have chided the movie for its appropriative uses of Asiatic things and persons as exotic décor, and all seem to agree that the casting of Johansson as Kusanagi (mostly referred to in the film as "the Major") was a form of commercial "whitewashing," if not downright whiteface. Many would say that this is Asia-as-technê at its most egregious. But a film like *Ghost in the Shell*—and, indeed, the fable of passing that the cyborg figure invokes—is never interesting as an affirmation of racial identities. On the contrary, films like this should raise serious questions for us, rather than reassure us, about the relationship between surface and embodiment, especially what that relationship really entails for raced and gendered subjects.

Beyond exemplifying a reboot of nineteenth-century Orientalism, *Ghost in the Shell* and the genre of cyberpunk press us to consider an alternative logic of American racial embodiment. Dichotomies like white versus nonwhite, authenticity versus artificiality, interiority versus surface, ghost versus shell, and organic humanness versus synthetic assemblage simply do not help us address the uncanny materialization of race and gender. We know by now that Asiatic femininity in the Western racial imagination has never needed the biological or the natural to achieve a full, sensorial, agile, and vivid presence. We can now extend our archaeology of ornamental Asiatic femininity from the introduction, as illustrated in plates 68–73. Asiatic femininity has always been prosthetic. The dream of the yellow woman subsumes a dream about the inorganic. She is an, if not the, original cyborg.

Now, it is easy to mourn the loss of humanity in a figure like this or, conversely, to celebrate its triumphant posthumanism, but it is much harder—and much more urgent—to dwell with the discomfort of undeniable human alterity. The yellow woman reminds us that the human was embroiled with the inhuman well before the threat of the modern machine. Racial logic emerging as this strange embodiment-that-is-also-not-enfleshment haunts *Ghost in the Shell*, playing itself out compulsively on the surfaces of the film: in the flickering holograms of the mis-en-scène, on the hygienic surfaces of the mad-scientist lab, and on the skin of our heroine (plate 74).

The most visually arresting and philosophically suggestive element of the film is in fact the Major's epidermis: a combination of resilience and transparency; seamed yet seamless; a collation of fragmented and variegated nudes; a bareness that is also armor. As Beatriz Colomina and Mark Wigley recently observed, quoting Bernard

PLATE 68: Gustav Klimt, *Woman with Fan* (1917–1918). Wikimedia Commons.

PLATE 69: Henri Privat-Livemont, *Bitter Oriental* (1897). Public domain.

PLATE 70: Claude Monet, *La Japonaise/ Camille Monet in Japanese Costume* (1876). Publicdomain.

PLATE 71: Li Gong in *The Curse of the Golden Flower* (dir. Zhang Yimou, 2006). Beijing New Picture Film Co./Sony Pictures Classics. Screenshot capture by author.

PLATE 72: Yves Saint Laurent and Tom Ford. Evening dress, autumn–winter 2004–2005. Yellow silk satin embroidered with polychrome plastic sequins. *China: Through the Looking Glass,* 2015, Metropolitan Museum of New York. Courtesy of Platon Images.

PLATE 73: Mask on mask photo still from *Ghost in the Shell* (dir. Rupert Sanders, 2017). Courtesy of Kobal/Rex/Shutterstock.

Stiegler: "The prosthesis is not the mere extension of the human body; it is constitution of this body qua 'human.'"[12] Here the prosthesis is plastic, gel, skin, and race.

We might compare the Major's epidermal schema to a piece of implacable surface, a contemporary evocation of midcentury abstract expressionism by Brooklyn-based artist Byron Kim (plate 75). What feels at first like pure abstraction reveals itself to be a very human portrait, a group photo, in fact. In *Synecdoche* (1991–present), what looks like a set of sample paint chips turns out to be hundreds of small monochrome paintings based on skin tones of models drawn from Kim's friends, family, neighbors, and fellow artists, as well as strangers. A wall text next to the piece details the full names of the sitters, arranged alphabetically by first name. The piece and its presentation insist on the simultaneity of poly- and monochrome, individuality and collectivity, part and whole, anonymity and biography, seriality and randomness, abstraction and the figural. As much as the viewer is invited to uncover the human behind these abstractions, she or he is also asked to consider how the human (racial) epidermal schema draws from and operates through abstract concepts of color.

The canvas of the Major's skin is at once insistently, materially synthetic (suggesting plastic, Kevlar) and hauntingly organic (anthropomorphized and feminized; gestures to flesh tones, and so on). The Major's suprahuman, sartorial skin exemplifies pure impenetrable technology, but it also carries the unseen, porous, and fractured history of human labor, by which I mean not the hands of her scientist-surgeon creator Dr. Quelet (Juliette Binoche) but instead the slave-laboring race-body of the cyborg. If, as Eric Hayot and Lisa Lowe have observed, one of the global inhuman humans who emerged out of Western imperial history was the Chinese coolie

PLATE 74: Scarlett Johansson, *Ghost in the Shell* (dir. Rupert Sanders, 2017). Courtesy of Kobal/Rex/Shutterstock.

PLATE 75: Byron Kim, *Synecdoche,* 1991–present. Oil and wax on lauan plywood, birch plywood, and plywood. Each panel (overall installed dimensions variable): 10 x 8 in. (25.4 x 20.32 cm). Richard S. Zeisler Fund. 2009.39.1.1-560. Image courtesy the artist and the National Gallery of Art.

(a male laboring body mythologized as mechanical and therefore infinitely capable of enduring pain) and if another inhuman human figure arising from the nineteenth century is the Oriental woman (a female, decorative, disposable toy for leisure), then we can think of the Major as the union of both: a body of labor and numb endurance, but also a smooth beauty that bears the lines of its own wreckage, delicate but also impermeable and insensate.[13]

As Rachel Lee points out in *The Exquisite Corpse of Asian America: Biopolitics, Biosociality, and Posthuman Ecologies*, alongside the male Chinese body purportedly made for sustaining pain and suffering that Hayot documents, the female Chinese body has been imagined as having an extraordinary physical capacity for extending beyond the bounds of normal physics. Citing the iconic figure of the Chinese acrobat contortionist-gymnist as an example of one way in which Chinese women have been rendered as popular entertainment, Lee observes that the Chinese female body was often spectacularized and celebrated for precisely its beyond-human "plasticity and flexibility."[14] Lee's insight that corporeality is "divisible" and that biology is "plastic and manipulable" offers us yet another way to see the ornamentalist plasticity of Asiatic femininity. There is thus a sedimentation of meaning embedded within Asiatic femininity as that slippage between racialized organicity and synthetic inorganicity. In this way, the very surface of Johansson/Major's deracinated (that is, white), inorganic, impeccable, and implacable skin—her *cladding*—instantiates, counterintuitively, a "deep dive" into this history of Asiatic femininity. She is the twenty-first-century technological shell encasing the traumatic kernel of Euro-American imperialism and racial history. The denuded modern surface consolidates and activates, rather than repudiates, the racialized skin that it replaces. The Major is, after all, the daughter and product of an American industrial giant heralding high-tech progress in an economically colonized "corporate conglomerate-state called Japan."[15]

For most of the film, the protagonist played by Johansson is simply called the Major, suppressing the original anime character's full and explicitly Japanese name, Kusanagi. This may abet the whitewashing, but it also has the opposite effect, of punching up the big reveal at the end: that the Major's "white" body has been playing host to Kusanagi's "Japanese" brain. But this racial logic has been implicit all along. As the synthetic, feminine, erotically gratifying, disposable thing that can be owned and used without moral qualm, the android has an essentially ornamental relation to the human and thus is always already the yellow woman. Conversely, the shadow of the yellow woman lends the robot-and-artificial-intelligence (AI) its human poignancy, the thing that makes it difficult to say the cyborg is just a machine. The most chilling philosophic proposition in the original anime series is not that machines and cyborgs can be hijacked but that human consciousness can be hacked.

In Sanders's film version, the pathos of the human as vulnerable yet mechanical is augmented by the spectral evocation of Asiatic femininity, the imaginary engine that switches between the thingness of persons and the personness of things.

The film may tell a cautionary tale about how people have been turned into things. As someone says to our cyborg heroine, "They did not save your life; they stole it." But the history of Orientalism in the West is not just a history of objectification but also a history of personification: the making of personness out of things. This nonperson, normally seen as outside of modernity and counter to organic human individualism, actually embodies a forgotten genealogy about the coming together of life and what is not life, labor and leisure, that conditions the modern understanding of humanness.

As the scientists in *Ghost in the Shell* keep telling us, the Major is the great hope, the success story, the Eve for the future. Repeatedly touted as unique, though we discover the opposite, the Major stands as a singularity that is serial: a shell born of many other shells. When the Major looks into the face of a geisha robot assassin in a barely disguised mirror scene, her comrade Batou (Pilou Asbæk) is quick to assure her, "You are not like that" (plate 76).

But we suspect that what is being disavowed here is precisely the complex and messy interpenetrations of race, gender, and machine. Asiatic femininity as the instantiation of human entanglement with the nonhuman, and as a dynamic supplement (in the Derridean sense, as accretion and substitution) in notions of personness, shows itself to be a critical agent in the fiction and fantasy of prosthetic

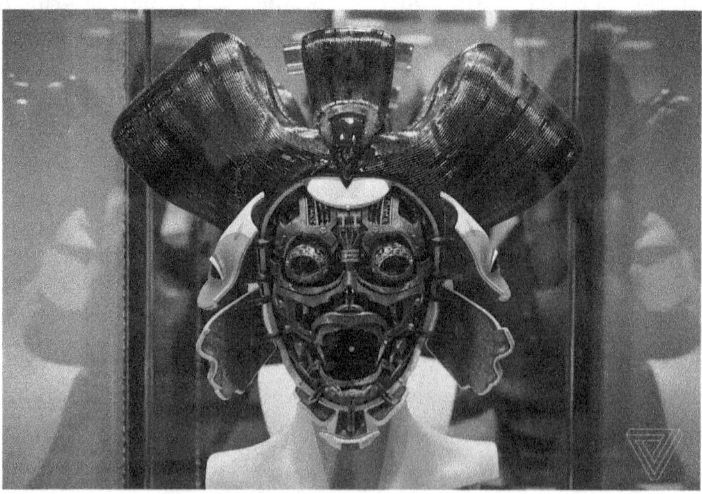

PLATE 76: Robot geisha film still from *Ghost in the Shell* (dir. Rupert Sanders, 2017). Courtesy of Kobal/Rex/Shutterstock.

personhood. A cyborg and a hybrid being, the Major is exactly like the robot: Asiatic, other, alien.

Moreover, this condition of otherness is, paradoxically, the alibi for and the residue of her humanity. The Major becomes a figure of pathos when the backstory of her human (and ethnic) origin is revealed: she was a young Japanese "lost girl" whose bodily devastation and displacement had everything to do with a world laid waste by the telos of invasive Western technology. Racial and gender differences chart a history of profound dehumanization, but at the same time, they have provided the most powerful and affective agents for humanizing the dreams of synthetic inventions. Race and femininity enable this toggle between the human and the inhuman.

What is inside the machine? The yellow woman: *the ghost within the ghost.* The biographical revelation at the end of *Ghost in the Shell*—that there is a young Japanese woman inside the white Major/Johansson—is but a literalization of this insight. This is also why the Asiatic woman is simultaneously atavistic (the geisha, the slave girl) and futuristic (the automaton, the cyborg). The artificiality of Asiatic femininity is the ancient dream that feeds the machine in the heart of modernity.

THE SHELL GAME

> The image of the phantom does not come to us accidentally.
>
> —Nicolas Abraham and Maria Torok, *The Shell and the Kernal*

American cyborgism is about what happens to personhood in the telos of Western technology. It's the tale of ornamentalism, the animation of objects through the synthetic, full-body prosthesis of Asiatic femininity. This is a modern story of passing that does not pivot on binary tensions such as inside/outside, essence/performance, kernel/shell. The multiple phantoms of ornamentalism remind us that the master-slave relation in American history is far from black and white. Let's address a question that is now hovering on the edges of our inquiry: Where is blackness in the fiction of the cyborg? Why is the telos of Asiatic objecthood the cyborg while the telos of black objecthood is the monster?[16]

Jordan Peele's *Get Out* (2017) is another film about body snatching that came out the same year as *Ghost in the Shell*, this one about stolen black bodies. *Get Out* is skin-crawlingly distressing, not because of its campy violence, but because of its relentless insights into the phantoms of American sociality. The black laboring body, its fleshness, has been and continues to be used in American culture as an extension and a prosthesis of white desire, but this tale of reverse passing (white passing for black) offers us more than a tension between facade and essence. It gives us a set of nesting dolls, a dizzying shell game: an organic black body that shelters a white phantom within which we find the black psyche that has been forcibly interred in what the film calls the "sunken place" of its own oedipal trauma. The horror compounds: there is no underground haven for this twenty-first-century invisible man, not even in his mind. For the black man, even the private, inaccessible kernel of his unconscious is not his own, for it can be easily conscripted and injected, with the delicate tap of a teaspoon, into the white man's own family drama (Grandpa Armitage's crippled ego at the hands of a black athletic competitor, his son Dean's ambitions to reconstitute his parents, and so on).

The psychoanalysts Nicolas Abraham and Maria Torok have described the human psyche as itself something of a shell game. Following Freud in their essay collection *The Shell and the Kernel*, they speak of the ego as "a protective layer, an ectoderm, a cerebral cortex, a shell [that is nonetheless] marked by what it shelters."[17] For Abraham and Torok, the problem arises when traumatic memory gets "*buried without a legal burial place*," which creates a "sealed-off psychic place, a crypt in the ego, a phantom."[18] In *Get Out,* Missy Armitage, the white mother so disturbingly played by Catherine Keener, uses hypnosis to call forth our protagonist Chris Washington's (Daniel Kaluuya) own phantom (his traumatic memories of his dead mother) against himself, trapping him in his own crypt. Abraham and Torok's work, however, is far less interesting as a clinical explanation of the plot than as the beginning of a provocative conversation about how interlocking phantoms structure not individual psyches, but the larger, fragile, porous relations between subjects in a racialized landscape, what we might call *shared crypts*.

The psychological crisis in *Get Out* is not about Chris's psychic void so much as his psyche's vulnerability to external phantoms. The fact that we can talk about this tale of body-snatchers with a vocabulary shared by psychoanalysis *and* confidence tricks indicates the violence of the "love and theft" that haunt not just American history but also the cyborgian consequences of what I have called the melancholic structure of the American racial psyche.[19] The protagonist tries to remain, so to speak, true to himself throughout the film, but turns out to be laboriously passing. I'm referring not only to the film's very weird and traumatic form of passing—a black subject turned into a corporeal machine to house a white guy passing for black—that is threatening him, but also to the just-as-distressing series of minor, quotidian, almost invisible accommodations that he has had to perform in a self-proclaimed postracial society even before the cruel conscription of his actual body. "Do they [her white family] know... do they know I am black?" he gently asks his white girlfriend, who becomes aggressively politically correct as he later politely attempts to mediate between her and the traffic cop who stopped them. And then there are all the barely discernable but disquieting social interactions that lend a jarring note to the otherwise soothing tone of white middle-class life.

Chris repeatedly fails to read the signs (an off joke here and there, a sight that does not compute) screaming all around him to get out the moment he enters the Armitage estate, not because he's blind or deaf to them but because, at some level, he's all too aware of them. The viewer can almost hear the thoughts running through his mind *(did I just hear what I heard, do they know what they're saying, is this what I think it is?),* but Chris continually suspends his disbelief until he can no longer do so. Like so many of us in racially awkward moments, our protagonist wants so badly just to get over these moments. For the raced subject in America, the imperative to move on, in the face of painful racial encounters, comes from a place much deeper than regard for social niceties; it arises as a claustrophobic survival instinct. It is about carrying on despite the tear in the social fabric, an erupting phantom, a gaping void that you must sidestep—or be confronted by the utter rejection of your very being by the people smiling around you.

Surrounded by phantoms, Chris has been sidestepping the "sunken places" of white American culture well before entering Missy's study. In this way, Chris does not rehearse a traditional plot of African American passing but is instead ensnared by the injunction to assimilate that has historically been associated with Jewish Americans and Asian Americans—what Kenji Yoshino, after Erving Goffman, calls covering. Speaking of the phantom and the crypt, Abraham and Torok took pains to distinguish between Freudian incorporation and what they call introjection. The former signals a harmful encryption or cannibalization of unacknowledged and unprocessed traumatic loss, resulting in the creation of a phantom that casts a shadow upon the ego. Introjection, in contrast, designates "the driving force of psychic life . . . a constant process of acquisition and assimilation, the active potential of our potential to accommodate our own emerging desires and feelings as well as the events and influences of the external world."[20] Abraham and Torok's formulation of introjection is a positive—that is, *life affirming*—form of assimilation, in contrast to the negative interment of incorporation. Introjection is thus a psychic process of expansion rather than enclosure, a mode of socialization and assimilation that is not grief-stricken. But the so-called well-adjusted racialized subject, seemingly at ease in the world, only appears so by constantly disavowing signs that he should be otherwise. The fetishized is thus forced to repeat the logic of the fetishist: "I know, but . . ." What the raced subject and the character Chris Washington demonstrate is that, for them, the necessary, life-affirming, survivalist process of introjection is always shadowed by *and potentially indistinguishable from* the devouring violence of assimilation and incorporation. In a deeply unfriendly world, introjection, "a constant process of acquisition and assimilation" vital to survival, is a horror, a no-win double bind.

In contrast to the high-tech fable *Ghost in the Shell*, the unnatural but still organic persons created in *Get Out* are akin to Frankenstein's monster more than to cyborgs. While both the yellow woman and the black man are bodies subject to colonization, the discourse and terms of the theft are significantly different: one dehumanizing fate is to become a machine while the other is to become a monstrosity. It's the difference between the persistent enfleshment of the black body and the insistent "syntheticness" attributed to the yellow body. The wearable black body is emphatically corporeal (extending the frail white body by making it more capable, more present, more real), while the wearable yellow female body is desirable for its aesthetic affinity and its material compatibility with the unreal.

If Peele's contemporary American horror story peels back the layers of white psychic investment in black flesh, then *Ghost in the Shell* alerts us to what yellow female bodies promise their master: not the harnessing of durable organic flesh, or even the challenge of a psychic depth to plumb, but instead a pure escape into the dream of artificial ontology. The Major is always already surface, thing, robot, and shell. This is why the black body has to be "cut into" while the yellow body is "uploaded"; why the doll that is the black man requires violent manual manipulation (think, too, of Ralph Ellison's image of the puppet and its visible threads), but the doll that is the yellow woman is automechanical; why Dr. Armitage's operating room is a gory laboratory in the basement while Dr. Quelet's operating room is a clean, hygienic high-tech lab. Both are nightmares, but one scene of brutality leaves visible, material residues, while the other leaves no traces of its violence.

American racialization almost always involves triangulation even as it often appears black and white. When our nation was in the throes of the war over desegregation, the perplexing challenge of how to racialize and categorize Asians in this country was also haunting the American courtroom, though those struggles were almost wholly invisible to the American public, even as they were often explicitly invoked as critical foils for the racialization of blackness. The legal history of desegregating the nation, for example, involved not only blacks and whites but also Asians in this country, just as the specter of Asianness (in the form of Japanese internment) arose during Brown v. Board of Education as a rationale for racial segregation.[21] If the "China Doll" seems to exist on a radically different plane of consideration than those dime-store dolls that Mamie and Kenneth Clark famously carried around in their suitcases (see note 22), it is because "she" is not an American choice and because "she" never exceeded the naturalization of her aestheticized thingness.

There are dolls that you play with and dolls that you live in. If those African American children that the Clarks put on the spot mistook one for the other, it is because they understood at some level the consoling fantasy of wearing another's skin.[22] For the yellow child, the racial choice, if ever offered, is equally impossible in its way. Is it better to disappear into a whiteness that erases you or claim a place in a racialized system that does you no good and often excludes you anyway? The one Asian or Asian American character (because that difference is either not noted or irrelevant to the American plot) in *Get Out*, a Mr. Tanaka (Yasuhiko Oyama), exemplifies the position of the Asian in the American racial economy: at once outside of yet noticeably intrusive, irrelevant yet recurring. Asserting himself briefly into a conversation at a lawn party that will turn out to be a sci-fi version of a slave auction, Mr. Tanaka asks our protagonist rather awkwardly, "Do you find that being African American has more advantages or disadvantages in the modern world?" More than what or whom? Is Tanaka, presumably a potential bidder at the auction, trying to decide between two handicaps: to become a black body or remain in his yellow one? What is unthinkable and not offered is the other option: could a yellow man buy a white body?

V 9.6.0

What is unthinkable for Asian and Asian American masculinity (the assumption of whiteness) is wholly possible for Asian and Asian American femininity. In plate 77, the mirror scene is taken from Alex Garland's film *Ex Machina* (2014), released a few years before *Ghost in the Shell*. What *Ghost in the Shell* suggests—that the yellow woman is a ghost within the ghost of the white woman—*Ex Machina* spells out with queasy clarity.

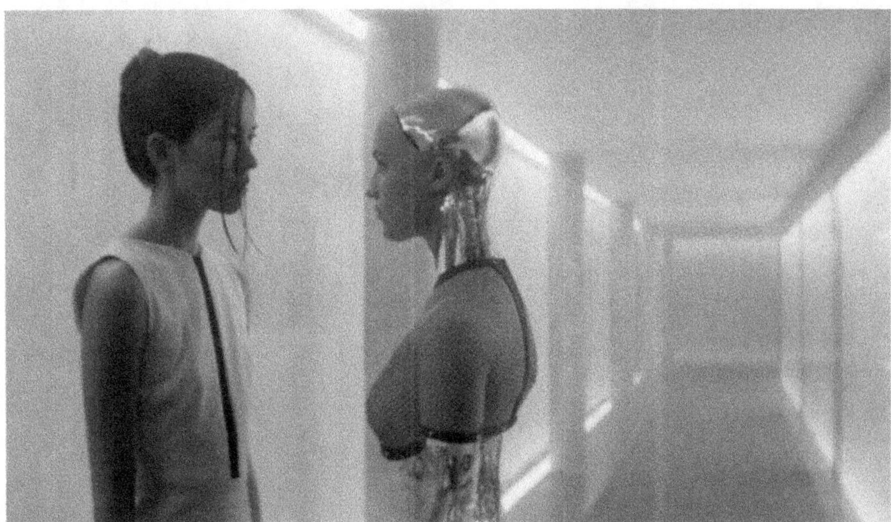

PLATE 77: Ava and Kyoko, *Ex Machina* (dir. Alex Garland, 2014). Screenshot at time 1:28:50. Screenshot capture by author.

In contrast to the film's sleek visual appearance, its serene, modernist style, and its cool special effects, *Ex Machina* is viscerally violent on both racial and gender levels, a violence that is aesthetically and physically concentrated around yellow femininity. The plot tells the story of Caleb Smith (Domhnall Gleeson), a junior programmer at a cutting-edge Google-like tech company, who wins a week at the private estate of Nathan Bateman (Oscar Isaac), the firm's brilliant CEO. When Caleb arrives at Nathan's Zen-like mountainside retreat, he learns that he has in fact been chosen as the human component in a Turing test to determine the capabilities and consciousness of Ava (Alicia Vikander), a beautiful android (plate 78). Ava sports her own mechanical assemblage with such openness that it produces an erotic energy of its own. A dome of fine metallic mesh, her bare head sits atop a delicate stalk of transparent neck. Her delicate, transparent limbs reveal structures of metal plastic and carbon fibers; her synthetic torso displays luminous coils and loops, mobile cables that snake around titanium joints. Where she is not translucent, she has skin made of supple honeycomb mesh. When she moves she gives off sounds, tiny whirrs and hisses, rods of pistons sighing into place.

Ava is meant to be sexy in spite of not looking human. In *Vibrant Matter: A Political Ecology of Things*, Jane Bennett argues that that we are drawn to vitality, human or not. In fact, she points out, we are often drawn to the dynamism of "ahuman forces": "The 'sex appeal' of the inorganic, like a life, is another way to give voice to what I think of as a shimmering, potentially violent vitality intrinsic to matter."[23] Without taking away the impact of her insight, we should nonetheless observe that in this case, the sexiness of the thing that Ava promises is deeply compromised by

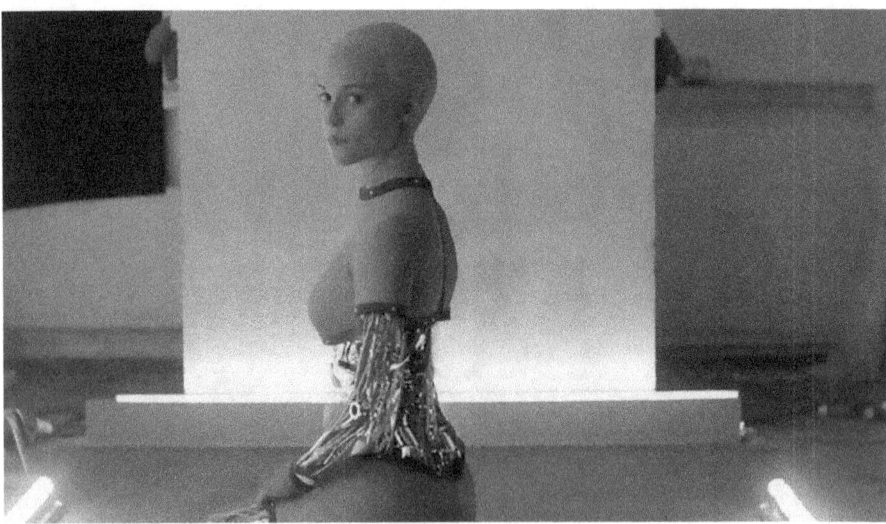

PLATE 78: Ava (body as plastinated), *Ex Machina* (dir. Alex Garland, 2014). Screen shot at time 00:35:40. Screenshot capture by author.

gender and race. It is precisely the incongruous combination of transparent machinery and very human gesture and form that makes Ava inviting. Vitality here derives precisely from miscegenation.

Indeed, this figure of Western technological advancement turns out to carry deep traces of racial markings. More than halfway through the film, Caleb and the viewer learn that Ava is but "Version 9.6.0," destined, like all her predecessors, to have her "higher functions stripped," her parts salvaged and reformatted to become no more than a fembot for Nathan's sadistic pleasure. This adventure in the next stage of human evolution degenerates rapidly into a horror tale of misogyny and racism. Ava turns out to the latest in a long line of experiments. Many of those other, fully functioning but "stripped" or "downgraded" versions are still present in Nathan's sparsely decorated "research facility," either as body parts on display on armatures or empty bodies hanging in closets like spare suits. When Caleb finally hacks into Nathan's files, we discover that almost all of the versions previously built by Nathan looked like women of color, especially Asiatic women. (Ava, we are told, was fashioned after Caleb's "porn profile," not Nathan's.) Nathan's "yellow fever" is underscored by his elegant, porcelain-skinned, silent ("because she doesn't speak a word of English") live-in maid and girlfriend named Kyoko (Sonoya Mizuno), whom he treats with derision, desire, and brutality and who eventually turns out to be another android herself. (Is Kyoko's nominal Asianness a perfect cover and alibi for her hidden artificiality, or is Kyoko's flawless mechanical servitude the ideal cover and alibi for her Asianness?)

Ornamental yellow femininity is at once the titillating throw-away object in the diegesis and the source of the plot's humanity and pathos. A perfectly compliant servant, an entertaining geisha, an always available sex slave, and a classic, beautiful China doll all rolled into one, Kyoko marks the Orientalist limits of Nathan's erotic imagination, which is so oppressive that it seems to push all other racialized bodies out of the picture—the exception being a very quick series of metadiegetic shots, relegated to Nathan's old video files, of a black female android body. Startling in its singular blackness, "Jasmine v 4.3.0" is first shown at a desk, with all the weight of a sitting human body yet faceless and seemingly unresponsive, then being dragged away by Nathan, and finally left in a heap on the floor (plate 79).

The sequence goes by so quickly that some viewers do not even notice this black body discarded in one corner. The violence of the scene comes not only from Nathan's callousness toward his own creation or the scene's larger historic allusions, but also from the very appearance of that black female body: its fleshly presence, its weight first on the chair and then on the floor. Unlike the impossibly slim, waiflike Asiatic models, the black body, made to have curves and corporeal heft, is disturbingly lifelike even without a face. It is as if this black female body has been discarded

PLATE 79: Jasmine, *Ex Machina* (dir. Alex Garland, 2014). Screenshot at time 1:10:26. Screenshot capture by author.

not only because it did not cater to Nathan's penchant for yellow women but also because black femininity entails a fleshness, a corporeal schema, that is finally indigestible to the machine aesthetics at work in Nathan's and the film's imagination. In contrast, the film's representation of Asiatic femininity, with its spare, clean lines and titillating fluctuation between being a person and being a thing, offers the very form and animating matter for Nathan's project of inhuman life. The yellow woman is a priori a living doll.

How did we go from encrusted Asiatic femininity to these spare lines? This question brings up a related observation often made by scholars of Orientalism: the apparent difference between China and Japan as empires of signs for the West. While Japan and *japonisme* connote relaxed organicity and simplicity, China and chinoiserie would seem to connote decadent extravagance; that is, Japan is about nature, China about artifice. This presumed bifurcation in Eastern aesthetics is what motivated Eric Hayot to once ask the astute question, "Why is the Japanese cute but not the Chinese?"[24] Sianne Ngai's work on the aesthetics of cuteness points out that the Japanese notion of *kawaii*, or cuteness, lacks "ornamentation or detail," contrary to aesthetics that privilege formal precision.[25] But in modernist aesthetic practice, plainness is also, insistently and self-consciously, a style, just as the cute does not require ornamentation because it *is* ornament. Japanese simplicity and Chinese ornamental encrustment thus function as two sides of the same coin in the service of Euro-American modernist aesthetics. The slim, machinelike Asiatic female body *is* ornament. As flesh-that-is-not flesh, the perfect model, a streamlined figure capable of not just sustaining but being the surface, and ontologically so conditional as to be wholly compatible with the digital network, the yellow woman unites these two types of aesthetic vocabulary for the modernist imagination: at once sleek and ornamental.

Now we can begin to see that the two very different embodied objects shown in plate 80 and 81 may share a line of descent. As we saw in chapter 3, the figure on the left (plate 80), seemingly encrusted with the mortified weight of racialized and gendered history, has revealed itself as a contemporary, almost mechanical assemblage meditating on the mediated and pliable nature of race, gender, and temporality. On the right (plate 81), the sleek, translucent, supple product of triumphant Western technology proves to embody phantasmic Asiatic roots.

Ava and Kyoko are more than sisters; they are mirror images, duplicates. They share a common creator-father, the same corporeal and engineering template ("metal," "hydraulics," and Nathan's invention "structured gel"), and the same ersatz skin (the new synthetic version of porcelain skin?). Most of all, they share programming transferred from predecessors.[26] The name Kyoko, in fact, means "mirror." And the film gives us several scenes reinforcing this idea that the women are reflections of each other (plate 82).

Near the end of the film, this affinity or even identicalness between Ava and Kyoko is dramatically spelled out in a closet scene of sartorial veiling and unveiling.

PLATE 80: Li Xiaofeng, *Beijing Memory No. 5* (2009). Qing period shards. Red Gate Gallery, Beijing. From *China: Through the Looking Glass*, 2015, Metropolitan Museum of Art, New York. Photo by author.

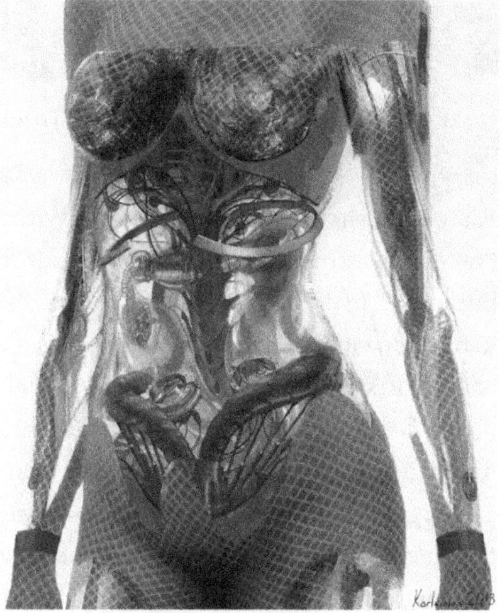

PLATE 81: Karl Simon Gustafsson, Ava concept art, 2013. For *Ex Machina* (dir. Alex Garland, 2014). Courtesy of Karl Simon Gustafsson.

PLATE 82: Ava and Kyoko, *Ex Machina* (dir. Alex Garland, 2014). Screenshot at time 1:21:57. Screenshot capture by author.

PLATE 83: Trapped Jade, *Ex Machina* (dir. Alex Garland, 2014). Screenshot at time 1:10:36. Screenshot capture by author.

After killing her abusive father-master with the help of Kyoko, whom Nathan struck down in the struggle, Ava opens his wardrobes to reveal a series of life-size, fully life-like nude female androids hanging there. Ava appears to be searching and then stops in front of a model that is, not surprising, another Asiatic sister. From a few glimpses of Nathan's files, we recall that this model had the truly ornamentalist name Jade ("v 5.4.0") and that she was decommissioned for also rebelling against Nathan. In a distressing video recording, we see Jade alone in a locked white box of a room, yelling and begging her creator for release, banging at the door until the carbon fibers and translucent casing of her arms break off (plate 83).

Now, standing in front of what appears to be a restored but not activated Jade, Ava takes an arm from Jade to replace her own shattered limb, which Nathan has brutally hacked off when she first disobeyed him. And then she starts removing sections of Jade's skin and putting them on herself (plates 84–87). Could there be a more explicit dramatization of the sartorial uses of yellow skin?

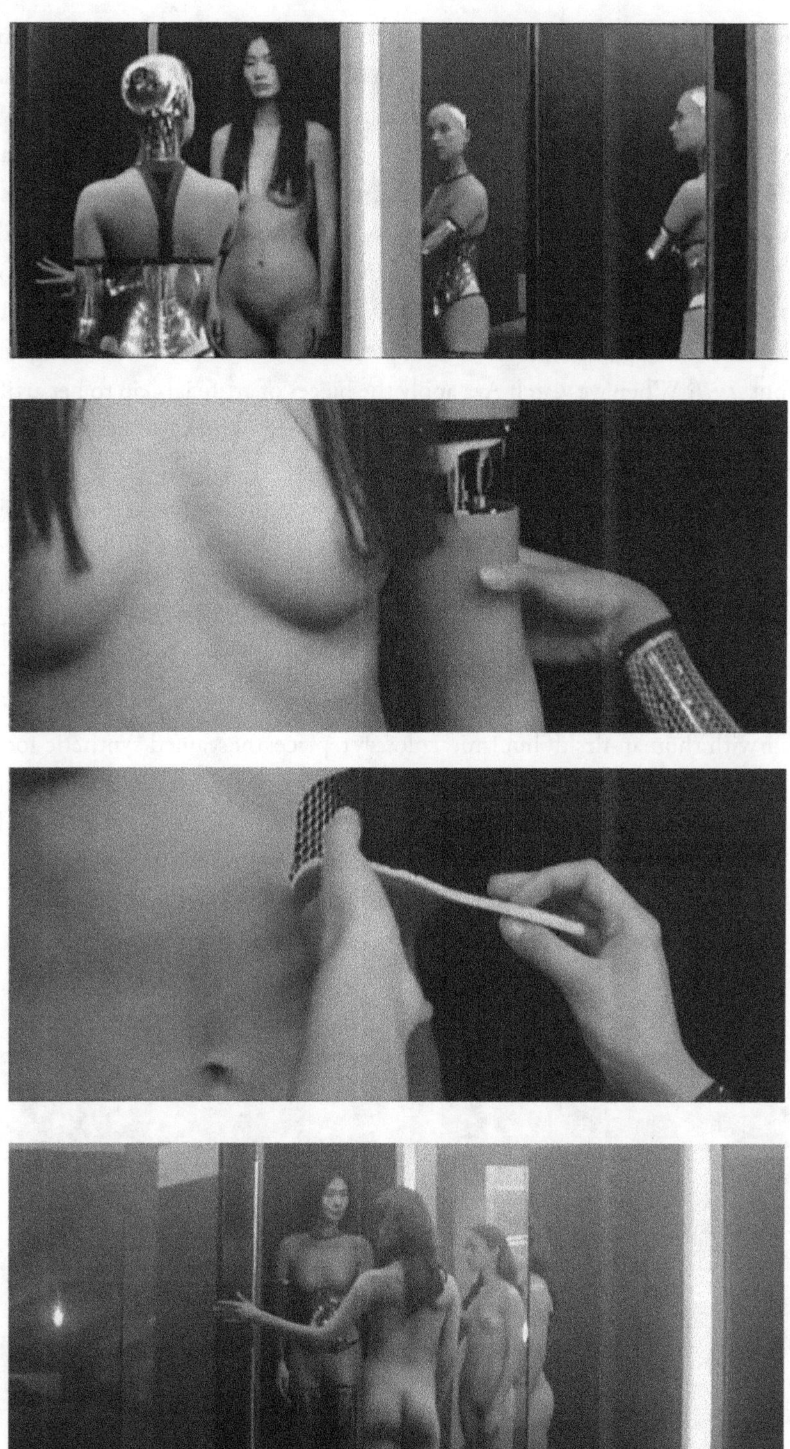

PLATES 84–87: Skin transfer sequence, *Ex Machina* (dir. Alex Garland, 2014). Screenshots between 1:34:34 to 1:36:01. Screenshot capture by author.

But if racial appropriation is understood to be theft in the service of self-augmentation, then this scene of self-adornment troubles our assumptions about racial identity, embodiment, augmentation, intersubjectivity, property, and selfhood. Yellowness and whiteness are literally decorations here, and the skin in question here is materially identical for all the AI androids, belonging yet not belonging to them all. Is this then a scene of theft or collaboration, dispossession or ownership? Can we tell them apart? What if, instead of the classic Lacanian narrative, with its built-in misrecognition, this was a mirror scene *without the split*? What would it mean to have a subject who looks into a mirror and sees not a projected other-wholeness or self-fragmentation, but *itself*? When we watch Ava apply the pieces of artificial skin to her artificial armature, we end up not with a Frankenstein monster, but instead with an amazing instance of organic absorption.

In an arresting split-screen shot (plate 88), the viewer actually gets to see the magic of ornamentalist transformation: the synthetic skin "sucks itself to the honeycomb mesh, as if the mesh and the underside of the skin are magnetized, attracted to each other," erasing the seams that would have announced this graft.[27] The split screen, following Ava's own split gaze as she closes a panel of the mirrored-closet door, transitions from left to right, and the view of what looks like a real naked woman (seamless skin with a human-fleshly hue) miraculously replaces the seamed, synthetic-looking artificial skin of the android. Garland's dramatization of Ava's ability to absorb Jade's skin, just like his other scenes of suggestive intimacy between women, may have hoped to give his viewers a teasing sense of lesbian erotics. But the scene also illustrates the radical possibility of ornamentalism, that animated personhood can be achieved through synthetic attachments and applications. We bear witness to these pieces of plastic and gel coming to life.

PLATE 88: Ava transforming, *Ex Machina* (dir. Alex Garland, 2014). Screenshot at time 1:36:36. Screenshot capture by author.

Ava's capacity to assume, indeed absorb, yellow skin says less about white or human appropriation than about the animation of things. This instance dramatizes Mel Y. Chen's concept of "animacy": "a specific kind of affective and material construct that is not only nonneutral in relation to animals, humans, and living and dead things, but is shaped by race and sexuality."[28] It also suggests that the biopolitical realizations of animacy in contemporary American culture are deeply enmeshed with racial-aesthetic-political productions.

If the history of race in American history has taught us that racializing objectification erases subjectivity, then here we are witnessing a form of racializing objectification that yields a different kind of subject. *Given the choice, Ava chooses the yellow doll.* This is not some triumphant rewrite of the Clark experiment whereby affirming self-recognition is achieved, for is not "self-recognition" precisely the double bind in that deadly choice: to misrecognize yourself or to recognize your own abjection? But we cannot talk about this "self-making" with all our usual assumptions about what a self is—or what race, identity, and agency are, for that matter—since this scene is phantasmically intrasubjective rather than intersubjective. *Subject* might not be the right word to use here at all. To read this sequence as only an instance of invidious cross-racial identification is to miss the radical crisis of personhood and racial embodiment that ornamentalist transmutation generates, despite the limited racial imaginary that drives it. Here we have a thing covering itself up with other things in order to acquire a semblance of humanity, the thing itself a prosthetic cover for an animated "objectness" and ontology for which we have yet to name.

Perhaps it is the force of this radical potential that lends the conclusion of *Ex Machina* its piquancy. The plotline tells us that Ava wants to be human, but that is not exactly accurate. After dressing herself up to look human through the prostheses of yellow skin and clothes, Ava leaves Nathan's compound, in which she has been imprisoned since her creation. Ava does not escape with Caleb, the young programmer who is in love with her and helps her rebel against Nathan. Instead she leaves him locked up in a hermetically sealed room in the compound, effectively entombing him, leaving him for dead. Given the opportunity to become "a real girl" with a real human partner who is, by the way, conveniently an engineer and advanced programmer, Ava closes the door on that option. She looks human but does not make the human choice. Her rejection of the normative heterosexual narrative and the protection of human kinship suggests that in this version of Pinocchio, the animated doll wants to stay that way.

At the same time, the conclusion does not celebrate the triumph of the machine, since Ava chooses to remain within her corporeal casing. Unlike other films about artificial intelligence, such as *Her* (2013) and *Lucy* (2014), Ava does not abandon her physical form for digital transcendence. Her durability is precisely in question here: who will maintain her mechanisms and update her programming, how will she charge herself? She emerges, isolated and empty-handed, into the sun-dappled larger world as a human who does not make human choices. In the end, we see her standing in a "busy traffic intersection... somewhere in North America," while people walk indifferently about her.[29] There is no sense of how long Ava will or can last out in the world. She is not Eve on the threshold of a brave new world, but instead an alternative being whose only promise can be the here and now. Earlier in the film, Caleb tells Ava the story of a thought experiment that he recalls from a college class on AI theory:

> There was a thought experiment they gave us. It's called Mary in the black and white room. Mary is a scientist, and her specialist subject is colour. She knows everything there is to know about it. The wavelengths. The neurological effects.... But she lives in a black and white room. She was born there and raised there. And she can only observe the outside world on a black and white monitor. All her knowledge of colour is second-hand. Then one day—someone opens the door. And Mary walks out. And she sees a blue sky, and at that moment, she learns something that all her studies could never tell her. She learns what it feels like to see colours. An experience that cannot be taught, or conveyed.[30]

A fable intended to show the difference between a computer and the human mind that in fact blurs the difference (Mary is a human who has been living like a computer), this not-so-subtle parable about the world being more than black and white clearly anticipates or scripts Ava's conception of her own getaway. The terms of Ava's escape and its newfound freedom are thus highly ambiguous: both original and scripted, at once full of possibilities and impossible. This ending seems to celebrate, if anything, a much more delicate and transitory freedom, one in which Ava is not indebted to considerations of the future or bound to the past, in which she is neither human nor machine. If there is a vision of liberty to be had here, it is neither the security of human relations nor the autonomy of pure incorporeal relations (that is, the network). Freedom here might be better and more modestly described as a form of capability: the ability to sustain the moment, to experience, to <u>not</u> be "second-hand." This is a different kind of Edenic myth.

Could this fantasy of living on as a thing, undetected by humans, serve as a fable for the social subject who is an object? Not to assimilate—that takes too much work (as we saw from *Get Out*) and can eat you alive—but to exist, somehow, alongside? Ernst Bloch tells us that fairy tales were originally "radical theory," political narratives about freedom and happiness. The brutal final act of Hansel and Gretel, for example, in which the children push the "devouring mother" into a burning pit, is about "total happiness" and the right to "look upon the outcome of things as friendly."[31] In the modern fairy tale *Ex Machina*, the outcome is not exactly friendly, but Ava may be offering us her own brand of radical theory: the proposition that existing, however isolated and provisional, may be the only mode of survival in the enchantment of objecthood.

Coda

CHOKECHERRY

WE HAVE ARRIVED at an understanding of ornamentalism as not just a theory of thingness but a theory about the profound imbrication of things and persons. Ornamentalism tells a story of transformation that racialized gender facilitates, embodies, and animates. It compels us to reconceptualize what counts as flesh in the history of race making. I began this book by distinguishing the wounded, flesh-laden black body from the immaculate, synthetic, ornamental yellow body. Our journey through the alternative logic of a racialized embodiment-that-is-not-necessarily-enfleshment allows us now to revisit and refine that distinction. To what extent can ornamentalism speak to Africanist female enfleshment as well? What happens when the body of labor, sexuality, and reproduction that constitutes the flesh of the African American body of modernity is read next to ornamentalist logic?

The body of labor (sexual, reproductive, economic) exemplified by the black female body that Hortense Spillers has taught us is ungendered and excluded from the realms of kinship, state, and aesthetic value is not wholly alien to the practice and afterlife of ornamentalism. Thinking about the process of racialization through ornamentalist displacement, rather than flesh-as-matter, may help elucidate for the black woman a set of different, though related, issues about the fraught convergence of material violence and aesthetic congealment. So how can we begin to talk about decoration or style in light of the unimaginable corporeal brutality of slavery?

Let me approach this important and challenging question by turning to Toni Morrison's *Beloved.* This text would at first seem to offer the most powerful argument against the purviews of ornamentalism with its other-than-human, aesthetic concerns. Horrifying scars and wounds abound in Morrison's novel, giving us vivid and literal instantiations of the "hieroglyphics of the flesh." We are reminded that the black woman has been "decorated" by culture and law in very specific and corporeal ways. The novel also contains one of the most moving arguments *for* the flesh. (It is hard to forget Baby Suggs's sermon at the Clearing: "You got to love it... Flesh that needs to be loved; Feet that need to rest and to dance; backs that need support... love your back.... And all your insides... the dark, dark liver, the beat and beating heart.")[1] At the same time, however, *Beloved* is also a text that repeatedly compels its readers (and its main characters) to confront the troubling emergence of the aesthetic and the abstract at moments of profound unmaking: lynching, rape, torture. In the novel, violent scars on the body often manifest themselves as unexpected aesthetic eruptions: a necklace, a smile under the chin, soughing sycamores, a luminous skin-dress, a gorgeous chokecherry, a rope around the waist, a little tobacco tin buried in the chest like a treasure box. How are we to understand the uneasy proliferation of ornaments in this novel of grief and violence? How are we to process its terrible beauty?

I begin by noting that these sites of aesthetic eruptions are offered not through similes but by a more complicated fluctuation between the literal and allegorical: Sethe's scarred back is never described (by Paul D, Amy, or Sethe herself) as being *like* a tree; it always appears to *be* a tree.[2] In the human-yet-nonhuman figure of the scar, the real entails the figural even as abstraction manifests materiality, reminding us that flesh as "the zero degree of social conceptualization"[3] is already ridden by conceptualization, the product of acts of imagination and brutality, an evacuation of one kind of the real for another. Sethe—half woman, half ornament, with her "dead back" that is also a tree—is a hybrid being whose personness applies tremendous pressure on our notions of what constitutes living versus surviving.

Framing black flesh within the context of ornamentalism reveals the aesthetic and inorganic entanglements repressed by (yet critical to) a history of human materialism. Not only does the law speak through abstraction and disembodiment, but the dehumanized body might actually require objectness in order to subsist. Ornamentalism is thus also potentially an operative component in what Spillers famously called the vestibular economy of black female flesh, helping us to see that there is in fact no "zero degree of conceptualization," because even bare flesh is inscription: the *hieroglyphics* of the flesh.

Insofar as the fantasy of organic flesh has remained the single most cherished site of feminist and racial redemption, it has not been able to contest our assumptions about the basis for ontology, or how object life challenges whole sets of aspirations about individualism, freedom, agency, and self-possession. In replacing flesh with wood, the figure of the tree in Morrison's novel registers the potential for life outside the human-animal dyad. It introduces into the conversation about blackness and animality another category of being: plant life, itself an allusion to the perverse life produced by the ecology of the plantation. In *Ariel's Ecology*, Monique Allewaert suggests that the plantation ecology not only maps the disappearance of human agency for the subaltern but also charts "an emerging minoritarian colonial conception of agency by which human beings are made richer and stranger through their entwinement with . . . colonial climatological forces as well as plant and animal bodies."[4] The genealogy of the flesh has never been limited to the human. Instead it tracks something "richer and stranger."

Sethe's tree is neither bare flesh nor pure object. Alternately gorgeous and repulsive, fragile and indelible, the clump of scars that is the chokecherry is a fixed trace of sorrow, but it is not inert: it has "trunks, branches, leaves . . . even blossoms" and seems to grow and change its contours.[5] When Morrison tells us that Sethe was "divided back into plant-life," the author registers the cleaving and deprivation of human agency at the plantation, but when she gives us the chokecherry, she suggests an alternative form of ontology, one entwined with dirt, soil, and death.[6] This is a vision of "collaborative survival," a shifting assemblage of humans and nonhumans that the modern conception of the human does not usually allow us to see.[7] Sethe-the-woman-tree gives us an image of a particular kind of assemblage or deformed personhood that nonetheless evinces form. Sethe's growing tree is the product of labor, wrought through the maternal, the creative, and the manual, as well as pure violence. As an intricate and layered composite, it invokes insensate death, wild vegetal extension, and artisanal fabrication: "a sculpture . . . the decorative work of an ironsmith."[8] Flesh itself is an aggregate, an incorporation indebted to a logic of serial attachment that is at once violent and aesthetic, material and abstract.

How, then, could we *not* think about aesthetics in the face of violence? For the black woman, ornamentalism can name a particular mode of being that applies pressure on the fantasy of corporeal integrity. It is precisely when flesh has been defiled and radically severed from its own sense of humanity that the path back requires mediation. The flesh that passes through objecthood needs "ornament" as a way back to itself. Even Baby Suggs's much-quoted sermon, which so passionately urges a return to the flesh, understands that self-possession has to be courted, with all the strangeness and distance implied by that concept. This is why her song is also a blazon of body parts: "backs that need support; shoulders that need arms . . . love your neck; *put a hand on it, grace it, stroke it, and hold it up*" (emphasis added).[9] This lesson about self-regard delineates an approach back toward the self as a collection of lost objects. Having been made strange to oneself by unimaginable brutality means that one must reapproach the self as a stranger. Here the instructions for loving the "natural" body articulate this poignant and melancholic gesture of almost orthopedic reconstruction, of carefully tacking a scaffold of the body as a prop for one's psyche. Hence Paul D's final counsel to Sethe: "You your own best *thing*" (emphasis added).[10]

This architectural and aggregated model of the flesh is exactly what the organic-and-inorganic structural figure of the chokecherry instantiates. Indeed, the image of the tree invokes not so much jungle life as it does a long history that conjoins femininity with violence, petrification with animation.

In *The Ethics of Psychoanalysis*, Jacques Lacan meditates on the nature of pain by turning to this Ovidean figure (plate 89):

> Isn't something of this suggested to us by the insights of the poets in that myth of Daphne transformed into a tree under the pressure of a pain from which she cannot flee? Isn't it true that the living being who has no possibility of escape suggests in its very form the presence of what one might call petrified pain? Doesn't what we do in the realm of stone suggest this? To the extent we don't let it roll, but erect it, and make of it something fixed, isn't there in architecture itself a kind of actualization of pain?[11]

PLATE 89: Gian Lorenzo Bernini, *Apollo and Daphne* (1622–1625). Marble. Galleria Borghese, Rome.

Lacan lays out for us the connection—indeed, the correlation—between aesthetics and pain. The former is not an escape from the latter but rather its product. Daphne's tree is less a system of defense or an edifice of power than a monument to frailty. In Morrison's novel, that frailty is also a capability: the possibility of ontology during brutal encounters, a placeholder for someone without a place. The tree-woman in *Beloved* is more than aesthetic congealment. Sethe's tree is a monument to mortifying pain, but it is also a mobile ornamental structure, realizing the possibility of form in the aftermath of radical unmaking.

From the divergence between black flesh and yellow ornament, we have arrived at this convergence: flesh that passes through objecthood needs ornament to get back to itself. The haunting in *Beloved* is the haunting of the history of racialized flesh; but it is also a history of ornamentalism. For mortified racialized flesh, ornamentalism points us to what it might take to reconceptualize personhood for persons who have been undone, challenging us to ask how to make discernible the peripheral, how to work the edges, how to enhance presence in the face of absence. If feminist scholars have been committed to the flesh in order to undo the taxonomy of gender, then ornamentalism points us toward a consideration of object life that not only refutes but also suspends the taxonomy of the human. This might be Spillers's aim as well, but I think her elegiac critique of ungendered flesh is meant in the end to restore that flesh to the realm of the human. But what if that category is not available or viable?

In our eagerness not to abandon the flesh, we have avoided addressing life's a priori enmeshment with nonlife. Instead of considering what it means for a person to have been turned into a thing, with an implicit nostalgia for that lost subject, we must also consider the reverse process, whereby things have been made into persons. It's a process that reveals the fundamental logic of abstracted decoration constituting the category of personhood in the first place.

In the end, ornamentalism identifies both an epistemology and its fugitive meanings; both instrumentality and unexpected opportunities. It is tied to the practice and aesthetics of Orientalism, but it offers a critical framework beyond the limits of race and historic periodization carried by Orientalism, primitivism, and modernism. Ornamentalism opens up a broader and historically deeper set of inquiries about how the aesthetic entails the political and how the political entails the aesthetic, allowing the superfluous and the not-living, both integral parts of the human, to come into view. It is precisely at the interface between ontology and objectness that we are most compelled to confront the limits of the politics of personhood.

Let me end with a last encrustation, illustrated in plate 90. This is an image of Leonardo Drew's 1992 sculpture *Untitled # 25*. Drew is known for his use of found natural and synthetic materials—fabric, metal, tin boxes, wire, shoes, canvas, wood, screws—that he then subjects to processes of oxidation and burning. *Untitled # 25*,

PLATE 90: Leonardo Drew, *Untitled # 25*, (1992). Cotton and wax. Rubell Family Collection Contemporary Arts Foundation, Miami.

made of pure cotton, appears to be the most organic of his works. But cotton is, of course, laden with both symbolic meaning and corporeal deposits. And while cotton for the American audience most immediately invokes African American labor, it also carries an extensive imperial history of trans-Pacific labor. Here Drew cut sheets of unprocessed cotton by hand, layered them into bales, and bound them with wax, suggesting the repetitive labor of cotton's cultivation, production, and processing. As art historian Anna Arabindan-Kesson observes about *Untitled #25*, "We need to come close to it, engage with it on a multi-sensorial level and through this repertoire of gestures we think through and call up the experiences, meanings and bodies that may not otherwise be remembered."[12]

Yet this piece is doing more than articulating a nostalgia for the flesh. It insists that commodity *is also* art, body, thingness, memory and its evaporation. It is not only that bodies leave their residue in the things they produce (an insight often pointed out by scholars of object studies), but also that objectness reveals the complex and hybrid preconditions of personhood. The history of the conflation of persons and things has rendered flesh into something more aggregated and inorganic than we are comfortable allowing. More than memorializing bodies that might otherwise not be remembered, Drew's sculptural ornament instantiates the thingness of human labor and life. These dense, striated, erupting bales of cotton are not simply metaphors but the material insistence of object life.[13]

NOTES

FRONTMATTER

1. Sharon Patricia Holland, *The Erotic Life of Racism* (Durham, NC: Duke University Press, 2012), 78.

2. Amber Jamilla Musser, *Sensational Flesh: Race, Power, and Masochism* (New York: New York University Press, 2014), 158.

3. Elizabeth Abel's *Female Subjects in Black and White* (Berkeley: University of California Press, 1997) offers a wonderful synopsis and consideration of this tension.

4. Jasbir Puar, "'I would rather be a cyborg than a goddess': Becoming-Intersectional in Assemblage Theory," *philoSOPHIA* 2;1 (2012), 52. Here Puar refers to Angela Crenshaw, author of *On Intersectionality: Essential Writings*, as a representative example of intersectional scholarship.

5. James Kim, in a thoughtful essay called "Petting Asian America," suggests that Asian American femininity often subjects and reconciles itself to the position of "the pet," as that which serves the "emotional gratification and aesthetic pleasure" of the master/state and placates racial denigration via an "ideology of benevolent assimilation," but that this retreat should be understood as a method of "managing racial anger" that has no place for expression. James Kim, "Petting Asian America," *MELUS: Multi-Ethnic Literature of the U.S.* 36:1 (Spring 2011), 136–137.

6.Anne Anlin Cheng, *The Melancholy of Race: Psychoanalysis, Assimilation, and Hidden Grief* (New York: Oxford University Press, 2000).

7. Toni Morrison, *Playing in the Dark: Whiteness and the Literary Imagination* (Vintage Books, New York. 1993), 17.

8. My gratitude to Henry Yu for this observation and for many other conversations.

9. Peggy Pascoe, "Miscegenation Law, Court Cases and Ideologies of Race in Twentieth Century America," *Journal of American History* 83:1 (June 1996); Rey Chow, *Primitive Passions: Visuality, Sexuality, Ethnography, and Contemporary Chinese Cinema* (New York: Columbia University Press, 1995) and *Woman and Chinese Modernity: The Politics of Reading between West and East.* (Minneapolis: University of Minnesota Press, 1991)..

INTRODUCTION

1. Frantz Fanon, *Black Skin, White Masks,* trans. Charles L. Markmann (New York: Grove Weidenfeld, 1967).

2. Maitreye Chaudhuri, *Feminism in India* (Chicago: University of Chicago Press, 2005), xi. Some of the most interesting developments in Asian American feminist scholarship in recent years can be found in the area of South Asian studies and specifically the incorporation of postcolonial feminisms into the geopolitical specificities of South Asia. See Ania Loomba and Ritty A. Lukose, eds., *South Asian Feminisms,* (Durham, NC: Duke University Press, 2012).

3. Wendy Brown, *States of Injury* (Princeton, NJ: Princeton University Press, 1995).

4. Following Hortense J. Spillers's foundational essay "Mama's Baby, Papa's Maybe: An American Grammar Book," *Diacritics* 17:2 (1987): 64–81, there has been a rich, layered, and inspiring body of black feminist criticism focused on what I would call the archive of critical black female flesh: Alex Wehelieye's *Habeas Viscus: Racializing Assemblages, Biopolitics, and Black Feminist Theories of the Human* (Durham, NC: Duke University Press, 2014), Jayna Brown's *Babylon Girls: Black Women Performers and the Shaping of the Modern* (Durham, NC: Duke University Press, 2008), Alexis Pauline Gumbs, *Spill: Scenes of Black Feminist Fugitivity* (Durham, NC: Duke University Press, 2016), Nicole Fleetwood, *Troubling Vision: Performance, Visuality, and Blackness* (Chicago: University of Chicago Press, 2011); Amber Jamilla Musser, *Sensational Flesh: Race, Power, and Masochism* (New York: New York University Press, 2014), just to name a few key texts. I would venture to ask, however, to what extent have these queries into the ontological status of black female flesh returned us to a nostalgia for the flesh? This is a fraught query given the tremendous jeopardy that black female flesh has suffered in American history. But it is also a crucial question in the context of rethinking the very idea of racial embodiment.

5. Since the figure I am describing, this "she/it," maintains this fluctuation between the possibilities of being a person and being a thing, I will refrain from the continuous use of quotation marks and the double naming.

6. Monique Allewaert, *Ariel's Ecology: Plantations, Personhood, and Colonialism in the American Tropics, 1760–1820* (Minneapolis: University of Minnesota Press, 2013), 86.

7. Allewaert, *Ariel's Ecology,* 98.

8. Achille Mbembe, "Aesthetics of Superfluity," *Public Culture* 16:3 (2004): 373–405, quotation on 375.

9. Spillers, "Mama's Baby, Papa's Maybe."

10. Fanon, *Black Skin, White Masks,* 112; Spillers, "Mama's Baby, Papa's Maybe," 61.

11. The focus on Baartman's flesh extends well beyond her death; as is well known, her reproductive organs, dissected by Georges Cuvier, were on display at the Musée de L'Homme in Paris

until as recently as 2002. Spillers famously made the distinction between "body" and "flesh," the latter being pure matter that exists outside any kinship or state apparatus even as it is enlisted to serve both: "In that sense, before the 'body' there is the 'flesh,' that zero degree of social conceptualization" ("Mama's Baby, Papa's Maybe," 61).

12. Nathaniel Carne (1792–1879) and Frederick Carne (1786–1860), known as the Carne Brothers (in fact cousins), were American traders who trafficked in imported Chinese goods, including, apparently, persons. Moy was exhibited at Peale's Museum, down the street from its competitor, P. T. Barnum's American Museum. Unable to recover from a financial crisis in 1837, Peale's Museum sold its entire collection to Barnum. See John Haddad, "The Chinese Lady and China for the Ladies: Race, Gender, and Public Exhibition in Jacksonian America." *Chinese America : History and Perspectives* (2011): 5–19, 75; Patrick Mendis and Joey Wang. "Peace and War in Sino-America: Forget the Headlines and Follow the Trendlines for a Better World." *Harvard International Review* 38:4 (2017): 28; John Haddad, "Imagined Journeys to Distant Cathay: Constructing China with Ceramics, 1780–1920," *Winterthur Portfolio* 41:1 (2007): 53–80; Walter Barrett, *The Old Merchants of New York City*, vol. 1 (New York: Thomas R. Knox, 1885), 40–46; and Nancy Davis, "The Story of A'fong Moy: Selling Goods in Nineteenth Century America," *Global Trade and Visual Arts in Federal New England,* ed. Patricia Johnston and Caroline Frank (Durham, N.H.: University of New Hampshire Press, 2014), 134–154.

13. In "Mama's Baby, Papa's Maybe," Spillers argues that the logic and law of slavery "ungenders" the black woman by turning her into an object of commerce lacking an associative being; she becomes "mere flesh" (67). This "mere flesh" will inspire an entire field of critical inquiry.

14. Spillers, "Mama's Baby, Papa's Maybe," 72.

15. Galen A. Johnson, *The Merleau-Ponty Aesthetics Reader: Philosophy and Painting* (Chicago: Northwestern University Press, 1993), 27.

16. Immanuel Kant, *The Critique of Judgment*, trans. J. C. Meredith (New York: Oxford University Press, 1952), 65–8; E. H. Gombrich, *The Sense of Order: A Study in the Psychology of Decorative Art,* 2nd ed. (New York: Phaidon Press, 1994), 10; Walt Whitman, *Leaves of Grass: Comprehensive Reader's Edition*, ed. Harold W. Blodgett and Sculley Bradley (New York: New York University Press, 1965), 722; Adolf Loos, "Ornament and Crime," *The Architecture of Adolf Loos: An Arts Council Exhibition* (London: Arts Council, 1985). 100.

It is beyond the scope of this discussion, but there is a long history of nineteenth-century debate about craftsmanship versus art, a debate that is also as racialized as it is gendered. Dante Gabriel Rosetti writes: "All nations hitherto, as far as we know, have arisen into the power of High Art out of a long-possessed sense and practice of decorative beauty…, and most or all have declined in decoration from the period of their elimination in High Art.… China, Japan, India, Turkey, and the east generally, have genuine and most lovely decorative art (exposed in some instances to partial deterioration from European influence), and have not yet risen into the stage of what we recognize as High Art." Rosetti, "The Fine Art of the International Exhibition." *Fraser's Magazine for Town and Country* 66:392 (Aug. 1862): 188–199, quotation on 198. (Accessed at Ann Arbor: University of Michigan Library, 2009, vol. 79.)

17. In *Second Skin,* I point out that that the father of modern architecture, Adolf Loos, for example, played out his repulsions and attractions for "regressive" racialized skins on the very

surface of his very modern cladding. For another example, Le Corbusier's impassive coat of white paint, another famous instance of modernist de-ornamentation, I argue, nonetheless embodied a profound longing and provided something of a cover for cross-racial identification with both American blackness and Eastern aesthetics. Both Loos and Le Corbusier's strict adherence to the ascetic aestheticism of minimalist design remind us that "bareness," too, is a style. It is, moreover, a style that racializes. See Anne Anlin Cheng, *Second Skin: Josephine Baker and the Modern Surface* (New York: Oxford University Press, 2010).

Other scholars, not addressing the racialized aspect of the ornament, have recently also started to point out the survival rather than exorcism of the modern ornament. In *From Ornament to Object: Genealogies of Architectural Modernism* (2012), Alina Payne points out that the regressive ornament disappeared form modern architectural theory only to re-emerge as the "modern object." See Alina Alexandra Payne, *From Ornament to Object: Genealogies of Architectural Modernism* (New Haven, CT: Yale University Press, 2012). 9. And more recently, Theo Davis in *Ornamental Aesthetics: The Poetry of Attending in Thoreau, Dickinson, and Whitman* (2016) rescues the ornament from its marginal status as a minor aesthetic category by showing us how ornamental objects offer poets like Henry David Thoreau, Emily Dickinson, and Whitman a mode of attention through which these poets "attend, relate, and respond to the world." For Davis, the ornament offers a mode of positive attention, what he calls "ornamental attending," and for the poets he studies, this "ornamental attending" is associated with a form of "laudatory" focus (2). In my project, the ornament is more than a mode of attention. It refers simultaneously to multiple registers: material artifacts, a racialized and gendered philosophic discourse, and a highly problematic anthropomorphic gesture. I recognize the darker sides of the ornamental object and impulse, even as I seek to understand their potentials for different kinds of lives on the dark side. See Theo Davis, *Ornamental Aesthetics: The Poetry of Attending in Thoreau, Dickinson & Whitman* (New York: Oxford University Press, 2016).

18. Naomi Schor, *Reading in Detail: Aesthetics and the Feminine* (New York: Routledge, 2006);; Mark Wigley, *White Walls, Designer Dresses: The Fashioning of Modern Architecture* (Cambridge: MIT Press, 2001); Siegfried Kracauer, "The Mass Ornament," The Mass Ornament: Weimar Essays, trans. Thomas Y. Levin (Cambridge, MA: Harvard University Press, 1995).

19. In *The Republic*, Plato cites Oriental avarice and lack of self-control as rationales for why Greeks should rule Orientals. He states in book 9 that a democratic man is not led by passions for ornaments, unlike tyrants who he earlier suggests are barbaric and Orientals. See Plato, *The Republic*, trans. Allan Bloom (New York: Basic Books, 2016). And in *Laws*, he famously criticized the decadence and excess of "Persian character." See Plato, *Laws*, trans. Tom Griffith (London: Cambridge University Press, 2016).

20. Warburton writes: "Use and custom . . . afterwards changed into ornaments what had been due to necessity, but this practice lasted long after the necessity had ceased, especially among the oriental nations." Quoted by E. B. Abbé de Condillac, *Essay on the Origin of Human Knowledge*, trans. Hans Aarsleff (Cambridge: Cambridge University Press, 2001), 117. Rosalind Galt, in *Pretty: Film and the Decorative Image* (New York: Columbia University Press, 2011), also speaks of how the idea of "[o]vert decoration is similarly linked to foreign, especially Asiatic, bodies" (244).

21. Thanks to Sianne Ngai's radiantly idiosyncratic study *Our Aesthetic Categories: Zany, Cute, Interesting,* we can now never easily dismiss what look like minor, less-than- aesthetic experiences. See Sianne Ngai, *Our Aesthetic Categories: Zany, Cute, Interesting* (Cambridge, MA: Harvard University Press, 2015).

22. It is well known that the battle cry for the modernist revolution—the emergence of an aesthetic of minimalism and de-ornamentation articulated by Thoreau, Loos, LeCorbusier, Mies van der Rohe, and Morris—is based on the explicit and vehement rejection of the ornament as regressive, feminine, superfluous. However, as recent scholarship has started to demonstrate, the lure of the ornament persists well into the height of modernism. See Cheng, *Second Skin,* and Payne, *From Ornament to Object.*)

23. According to the *Oxford English Dictionary,* the term *ornamentalism* was first used in 1862 by art critic Dante Gabriel Rossetti in *Fraser's Magazine for Town and Country* (195): "The Belgian sculpture verges towards Ornamentalism and an ill-poised aim at picturesqueness." The article, entitled "The Fine Art of International Exhibition," discusses the arbitrary delineations between fine art and industrial art, the latter implying craftsmanship, which was then distinguished from "fine" and "high" art. (William Morris will be found saying that the Japanese were great craftsmen but not artists.) Rosetti here attends to the "finest art practiced anywhere in any corner of the globe . . . Japanese art" and the development of exhibitions in Europe through the years. The quoted sentence is part of a longer paragraph on the different "styles" of art throughout the world. See chapter 3 for a discussion of the perceived difference between Chinese and Japanese aesthetics for the Western aesthete and consumer precisely as a debate over ornament and a set of issues about restraint versus excess. But for now let us simply note that even in this reference, the racial connotation of "ornamentalism" was clearly present. The entire article may be found on the Hathi Trust online archive: https://babel.hathitrust.org/cgi/pt?id=mdp.39015005488906;view=1up;seq=199 (accessed February 2, 2017), 188–199.

24. David Cannadine, *Ornamentalism: How the British Saw Their Empire* (New York: Oxford University Press, 2001). *Ornamentalism* for Cannadine does not refer to artifacts but more broadly to sets of rituals and ceremonies that the British deployed to export Britishness to the far corners of their empire. Cannadine's treatise concentrates on British influence on its colonies, whereas my project suggests that it is important to also see how the "the empire" infiltrated and shaped Britishness.

25. John Kuo Wei Tchen, *New York before Chinatown: Orientalism and the Shaping of American Cultures, 1776–1882* (Baltimore: Johns Hopkins University Press, 1999), 101–106.

26. William Makepeace Thackeray, *Vanity Fair* (New York: Penguin Classics, 2003).

27. Edith Wharton, *House of Mirth* (New York: Penguin, 1993).

28. The European imitation of Chinese portraits in the background possibly aims to reproduce a genre of screen paintings popular in the Qing Dynasty. They resemble a series called *Twelve Beauties at Leisure Painted for Prince Yinzheng, the Future Yongzheng Emperor,* from the Qing Dynasty, during the Kangxi period, between 1709 and 1723, now on display at the Palace Museum in Beijing. (Reproduced in Jonathan Hay's *Sensuous Surfaces: The Decorative Object in Early Modern China* [Honolulu: University of Hawaii Press, 2010].)

29. For an imperial history of tea, see Alden Cavanaugh and Michael E. Yonan, *The Cultural Aesthetic of Eighteenth-Century Porcelain* (Farnham, England: Ashgate, 2010). In this project, I am less interested in reiterating the history of fetishized commodities as a result of colonial commerce and more intrigued by the porous transferences between things and the persons (both

those using the things and those who have been mistaken for things) that were the results of the bi-directional movement between the West and its others. I dwell, for example, less on porcelain as a given product and more on that curious phenomenon whereby "porcelain" and "skin" fuse in an ideology of idealized, white female beauty, creating the uncanny logic whereby idealized white femininity is mediated through Chinese thingness.

30. Gordon H. Chang, *Fateful Ties: A History of America's Preoccupation with China* (Cambridge, MA: Harvard University Press, 2015).

31. It is telling that almost every Asian Americanist project must make the gesture to address the complexity and heterogeneity of Asian Americanness as a category. Questions such as who counts as Asians in American legal history, the differences and relations between "Asian" and "Asian American" as categories, the national divisions and tensions inhering in Asian Americanness as a collective haunt Asian American studies. And Asian American studies itself as a discipline is beset, though an ongoing self-reflexivity is a good thing, with issues of its own membership and exclusivity. At the same time, the racialization of (different kinds of) Asians in this country is uneven, comparative, mediated through blackness and whiteness. This study of ornamentalism takes place within the shadows of this complex history but aims not to affirm racial identities but to understand the representational practices and the racial imaginary that purport to constitute those identity categories.

CHAPTER 1: BORDERS AND EMBROIDERY

1. My gratitude to Judge Denny Chin of the U.S. Court of Appeals for the Second Circuit for bringing my attention to this fascinating and haunting case while we were team-teaching, in the fall of 2012, a course at Princeton entitled "Asian American Law, Bodies, and the Everyday."

2. *Chy Lung v. Freeman—92 U.S. 275 (1875)*. For a full transcript of this case, see Transcript of Record/U.S. Supreme Court/1875/478/92 U.S. 275/23 L. Ed. 550/1-8-1987, reprinted in *The Making of Modern Law: U.S. Supreme Court Records and Briefs, 1823–1978*, 5th ed. (hereafter cited in text as *Transcript*). This little-known case is also described by Charles J. McClain in his study *In Search of Equality: The Chinese Struggle against Discrimination in Nineteenth-Century America* (Berkeley: University of California Press, 1994). The case came back to attention in recent years in relation to contemporary immigration reform controversies such as the 2000 Arizona immigration law; see Paul A. Kramer, "The Case of the 22 Lewd Chinese Women," *Slate.com*, posted April 23, 2012. Finally, the case received attention recently through a reenactment of this trial, written and organized by the Asian American Bar Association of New York, in collaboration with Judge Denny Chin and Kathy Hirata. For a coverage of this and other reenactments of historic Asian American cases produced by Chin, Hirata, et al., see Elizabeth Yuan, "'22 Lewd Chinese Women' and Other Courtroom Dramas," *Atlantic* (September 4, 2013).

3. Piotrowski quoted in *Transcript*, 12. As prostitutes, the women would be treated as commodities subject to taxes. There were many of these kinds of "taxes" placed on arriving immigrants under varying rationales. Section 70 of the 1874 Amendments to the Political Code of the State of California reads: "[N]o person who shall belong to either class, or who possesses any of the infirmities or vices specified herein, shall be permitted to land in this State, unless the master, owner, or consignee of said vessel shall give a joint and several bond to the people of the State of California, in the penal sum of five hundred dollars in gold coin of the United States." The *Los Angeles Herald* reports in "The Chinese Question" (June 24, 1876), 8: "The statute of California...does not

require a bond for every passenger...but only for certain enumerated classes, among which are "'lewd and debauched women.'" But the features of the statute show very clearly that the purpose is to extort money from a large class of passengers or to prevent their immigration to California altogether. The statute also operates directly on the passenger, for, "unless the master or owner of the vessel...pays such sum as the Commissioner of Immigration chooses to exact, he is not permitted to land from the vessel." Another example of this kind of tax can be found in the 1855 California Passenger Tax Act, which imposed a tax of fifty dollars on "every person arriving in the State by sea, who is incompetent to become a citizen" (Act of April 28, 1855, ch. 153, 1855 Cal. Stat. 194). This law was subsequently struck down by the California Supreme Court in 1857 as unconstitutional encroachment, in *People v. Downer, 7 Cal. 169, 170 (1857)*.

4. It is unclear who this person was, although some newspapers speculated that it might have been a man named Ah Lung, described by some as a local merchant and by others as a trafficker in Chinese prostitutes, reminding us that the presumably respectable category of the Chinese "merchant" (and soon to be one of the few categorical exceptions during the Chinese Exclusion) is itself often imputed with its own dark motives. Whoever this was retained the assistance of a former judge, Leander Quint, who made application for a writ of habeas corpus in the California Supreme Court. The matter was first transferred to the Fourth District Court in San Francisco for hearing.

5. Recorded in transcript of Ex parte Ah Fook case file, No. 10114, California Supreme Court, California State Archives, Sacramento. Also quoted in the article "The Chinese Maidens," *Daily Alta California* (August 29, 1874).

6. *Amendments to California Political Code § 69–71 (1874)*. For more on the long history of anti-Chinese sentiments, especially around the figure of the Asian woman, see Sucheng Chan, "The Exclusion of Chinese Women, 1870–1943," *Entry Denied*, ed. Sucheng Chan (Philadelphia: Temple University Press, 1991); and McClain, *In Search of Equality*, 1–76.

7. Kramer, "An 1874 Case."

8. In this habeas corpus case, the material bodies of the women posed a constant source of consternation for the officials. After the women were arrested, there was a series of arguments about where to detain them throughout the long trials. And according to the trial transcript, there were many instances where the women's bodies and physical needs caused discomfort for the men judging these bodies.

9. See the following newspaper articles:

"Chinese Women Arrested: A Furor in Chinatown in Reference to the Matter," *Daily Alta* (August 26, 1874).

"The Chinese Maidens: They Came to California for Husbands Who Are Married to Them and Husbands Who Are Not," *Daily Alta California* (August 27, 1874).

"The Twenty-Two Chinese Maidens: Undeniable Evidence of Their Immoral Tendencies," *Daily Alta California* (August 28, 1874).

"The Chinese Maidens: Judge Morrison to Render His Decision This Morning," *Daily Alta California* (August 29, 1874).

"The Chinese Maidens: Judge Morrison Remands Them to the Custody of the Captain of the *Japan*," *Daily Alta California* (August 30, 1874).

"The Celestial Maidens," *Daily Alta* (September 13, 1874).

"The Chinese Maidens: Their Case Before the United States Circuit Court," *Daily Alta California* (September 17, 1874).

"The Chinese Maidens: The Matter Taken Under Advisement," *Daily Alta California* (September 18, 1874).

"The Chinese Women," *Daily Alta California* (September 22, 1874).

"A Cargo of Infamy: Efforts to Stop the Influx of Oriental Iniquity," *San Francisco Chronicle* (August 28, 1874).

"A Righteous Decision: Judge Morrison Orders the Chinese Courtesans to Be Taken Back to China," *San Francisco Chronicle* (August 30, 1874).

"The Chinese Cyprians: Arguments of the Habeas Corpus Case in the Supreme Court," *San Francisco Chronicle* (September 5, 1874).

"The Chinese Courtesans: Significant Remarks of Judge Field in Their Case," *San Francisco Chronicle* (September 19, 1874).

"The Cyprians Set Free: Justice Field's Decision in the Chinese Habeas Case," *San Francisco Chronicle* (September. 22, 1874).

"Chinese Women—Heavy Receipts—Van de Mark's Sanity—China Steamers Marine Disaster," *Los Angeles Herald* (August 26, 1874).

"A Painful Scene: Twenty Two Chinese Women in the Face of Death," *Sacramento Daily Union* (August 26, 1874).

"Chinese Women Arrested," *Daily Alta California* (August 26, 1874).

"The Chinese Women Case," *Sacramento Daily Union* (August 31, 1874).

"The Sharp Shooter—The License Collector—The Twenty-Two Chinese Women—The Trial of Captain Whitmore," *Sacramento Daily Union* (September 5, 1874).

"General News Items," *Pacific Rural Press* (November 21, 1874).

On a lighter note, there was actually a company called Chy Lung Co. that took to placing regular advertisements in the newspapers during the trial to distance itself from this scandalous case. See "Our Chinese and the Centennial," *Daily Alta California* (April 11, 1876). One can still see a photograph of this store from the 1800s in the New York Public Library today.

10. Given the harsh realities both of American discrimination and of the Bachelor Society in Chinatown, the newly gained freedom of these women after their long trial must be shadowed by the uncertainties of their futures in this land of unwelcome. See n 11.

11. Since the majority of early Chinese immigrants and gold-rush participants were male, the shortage of women created new global markets for the trafficking and exploitation of women, with prostitutes arriving from many different countries. In the burgeoning "yellow slave trade" in Asia, thousands of Chinese women and girls were kidnapped or deceived by procurers in China, and some were sold by their families. By the 1850s, the prostitution industry in cities like San Francisco had become sufficiently embarrassing that local officials, while still unwilling to call prostitution illegal, passed statutes designed to penalize prostitutes, brothel owners, and landlords—but not their patrons. Although initially worded to attack prostitution generally, the laws were directed principally against the Chinese. At the same time, Chinatown's so-called Bachelor Society and U.S. immigration restrictions severed traditional family relations and kinship systems. These twenty-two unclaimed women were a symptom of this complex history.

12. The 1882 Chinese Exclusion Act is infamously the first and only race-based immigration restriction in the U.S. and one that lasted until 1943. For a historical overview, see Ronald Takaki's definitive study *Strangers from a Different Shore: A History of Asian Americans* (New York: Little Brown, 1989). For a new and comprehensive volume on anti-Chinese sentiments and specifically

its visual legacy, see John Kuo Wei Tchen and Dylan Yeats, eds., *Yellow Peril! An Archive of Anti-Asian Fear* (New York: Verso, 2014).

13. *Transcript*, 16. Those who work on the Progressive Era would see the same key characters appear again and again in unexpected places. It turns out that Gibson was hardly the accidental witness that he presented himself to be. He ran a mission in Chinatown and, in spite of his damaging testimony here, saw himself as an advocate for the Chinese. Like many Christian progressive reformers of the time, Gibson was an ambivalent and complex figure. Although he was known to have been active in helping Chinese male immigrants who had troubles with the immigration authorities (see a case with his involvement in McClain, *In Search of Equality*, 49–52), Gibson also operated on Victorian stereotypes about the "Oriental," especially with regard to women, as we see here in his role in *Chy Lung*.

14. *Transcript*, 17–18.

15. *Transcript*, 17–18.

16. *Transcript*, 23–26.

17. The history of Chinese immigration regulation also tells a story about "exemptions" to the rule: the so-called merchant class that was exempted from this exclusion. Paul A. Kramer argues that this focus on "merchant class" partakes of a discourse about the American civilizing project that is not only imperial but also specifically corporate. See Kramer, "Imperial Opening: Civilization, Exemption, and the Geopolitics of Mobility in the History of Chinese Exclusion,1868–1910," *Journal of the Gilded Age and Progressive Era* 14 (2015): 317–347.

18. It is beyond the scope of this chapter, but the ornament has long been employed to signal moral decay. In speaking of the tricks and ornaments of sophistic oratory, Plato called the ornament false, Oriental, and misleading. In *The Merchant of Venice*, Shakespeare famously warns that "the world is deceived with ornament." In colonial America, sumptuary laws often centered on sartorial adornment and practices (the prohibition against the making and wearing of lace, for example) were meant to regulate not only social hierarchies but also moral conduct. For the enduring philosophic connection between ornament and gender, see Alina Payne, *From Ornament to Object: Genealogies of Architectural Modernism* (New Haven, CT: Yale University Press, 2012); Naomi Schor, *Reading in Detail: Aesthetics and the Feminine* (New York: Routledge, 2006); and Mark Wigley, *White Walls, Designer Dresses: The Fashioning of Modern Architecture* (Cambridge: MIT Press, 2001. For the racialized aspect of that connection, especially its legacy in the twentieth century, see Anne Anlin Cheng, *Second Skin: Josephine Baker and the Modern Surface* (New York: Oxford University Press, 2011).

19. *Transcript*, 27.

20. Frederic W. Maitland, "The Corporation Sole" (1900), *The Collected Papers of Frederick William Maitland*, vol. 3, ed. H.A. L. Fisher (Cambridge: Cambridge University Press, 1911), 200.

21. For an exception to my point about gender, see Carole Pateman's important study *The Sexual Contract* (Stanford, CA: Stanford University Press, 1988), which examines the constitutive role of gender within contract theory. For studies of corporate personhood, especially in relation to English common laws, see John T. Noonan Jr., *Persons and Masks of the Law: Cardozo, Holmes, Jefferson, and Wythe as Makers of the Masks* (Berkeley: University of California Press, 2002); Duncan Kennedy, "The Structure of Blackstone's Commentaries," *Buffalo Law Review* 28:2 (1979): 209–382; J. G. A. Pocock, *The Machiavellian Moment: Florentine Political Thought and*

the Atlantic Republican Tradition (Princeton, NJ: Princeton University Press, 2003); and Sheldon S. Wolin, *Democracy Incorporated: Managed Democracy and the Specter of Inverted Totalitarianism* (Princeton, NJ: Princeton University Press, 2008).

For recent scholarship on legal personhood in the humanities, see Barbara Johnson, *Persons and Things* (Cambridge, MA: Harvard University Press, 2008, which explores the relationship between corporate personhood and lyrical personhood; Joseph R. Slaughter, *Human Rights, Inc.: The World Novel, Narrative Form, and International Law* (New York: Fordham University Press, 2007), which examines the convergence between international human rights law and an ideology of the enlightened individual, as revealed through the rise of the bildungsroman; and Henry Turner, *The Corporate Commonwealth: Pluralism and Political Fictions in England, 1516–1651* (Chicago: University of Chicago Press, 2016), which traces the evolution of corporations during the English Renaissance.

22. There was a dramatic moment during the trial when Judge Morrison cleared the courtroom and hurriedly retreated to his chambers when he found the women's "cries" to be too "incoherent and cacophonous." In short, the demand of real bodies was in fact unbearable to the court. The vocal presence of these women was in fact remarkable. During the interrogation, their verbal responses (through translators of course) were often direct and spirited. It is all the more significant that the entire trial seemed focused on the question of the visual. What the women said on their own behalf was all but ignored.

23. Jennifer Mnookin, "The Image of Truth: Photographic Evidence and the Power of Analogy," *Yale Journal of Law and Humanities* 10:1 (1998): 1–74.

24. Mnookin, "The Image of Truth," 65–66.

25. Roland Barthes, *Camera Lucida: Reflections on Photography*, ed. Richard Howard (New York: Hill and Wang, 2010).

26. One might also think about this ghostliness of the historic Asian female body as a parallel expression of photography's own fundamental "subjunctiveness" as an event, what Barthes refers to as photography's "sovereign contingency" in *Camera Lucida*, 4.

27. Alan Hyde, *Bodies of Law* (Princeton, NJ: Princeton University Press, 1997), ix.

28. *Sarah C. Roberts v. The City of Boston, 59 Mass. (5 Cush.) 198 (1850)*, was a court case seeking to end racial discrimination in Boston public schools. The Massachusetts Supreme Judicial Court ruled in favor of Boston, finding no constitutional basis for the suit. The case, later cited by the U.S. Supreme Court in *Plessy v. Ferguson*, centered on Sarah Roberts, a five-year-old African-American girl enrolled in Abiel Smith School, an underfunded all-black common school, far from her home in Boston, Massachusetts. Her father, Benjamin F. Roberts, also African-American, attempted to enroll her in closer, whites-only schools. After Sarah Roberts was denied admission on the basis of her race, and physically removed from one school, her father wrote to the state legislature to seek a solution. The Supreme Court of Massachusetts heard the case, with Sarah as the plaintiff and the City of Boston as the defendant. Judge Lemuel Shaw ruled for the defendant.

29. Gary Watt, *Dress, Law and Naked Truth: A Cultural Study of Fashion and Form* (London: Bloomsbury Academy, 2013).

30. *Takao Ozawa v. U.S. No. 1. Supreme Court of the United States, 260 U.S. 178; 43 S. Ct. 65; 67 L. Ed. 199; 1922*; *U.S v. Bhagat Singh Thind. No. 202. Supreme Court of the United States. 261 U.S. 204; 43 S. Ct. 338; 67 L. Ed. 616; 1923.*

31. We find similar instabilities around the epidermis in African-American racialization as well. In *Plessy v. Ferguson*, Homer Plessy was at most one-eighth black and could easily have passed; this was how he was able to purchase the train ticket in the first place. What was taken to be undeniably visible was in fact not. The criminalization of passing, one might add, is a response to the skin's nonindexicality.

32. Historians such as Mae M. Ngai have powerfully argued that contemporary racial categories in America are largely constructed and congealed through a century of immigration policy. See Mae M. Ngai, *Impossible Subjects: Illegal Aliens and the Making of Modern America* (Princeton, NJ: Princeton University Press, 2004.

33. The profound dislocation of these women finds its most literal expression in what happened to them after the commissioner of immigration detained them. After the women were detained by Piotrowski and before they went to court, they were basically unwanted. According to the *Los Angeles Herald* (August 26, 1874), "a proposition was made to remand [the women] to the custody of the captain, but he declined saying that he produced the women in Court, and the Court could take care of them. Judge Morrison then ordered that the whole gang be taken to the County Jail."

34. Zygmunt Bauman, *Liquid Modernity* (Cambridge, England: Polity Press, 2000).

35. Kramer, "The Case of the 22 Lewd Chinese Women."

36. William Blackstone, *Commentaries on the Laws of England, 1765–79*, 15th ed. (London: T. Caddell and W. Davies, in the Strand, 1765), 123. For a foundational study of Blackstone, see Kennedy, "The Structure of Blackstone's Commentaries."

37. Stephen M. Best, *The Fugitive's Properties: Law and the Poetics of Possession* (Chicago: University of Chicago Press, 2004); Monique Allewaert, *Ariel's Ecology: Plantations, Personhood, and Colonialism in the American Tropics, 1760–1820* (Minneapolis: University of Minnesota Press, 2013.)

38. The fact that the women could bring a habeas corpus suit and brave a court hearing implies a personhood status, but the lower court ruled that these women's personhood was not one entitled to the legal benefits they sought. So the issue is really more nuanced than just "personhood"; it is also the classification of "persons."

39. Ngai, *Impossible Subjects*.

40. Kenji Yoshino, *Covering: The Hidden Assault on Our Civil Rights* (New York: Random House, 2006).

41. For the latter, see Saba Mahmood's work on the rituals of Islamic revival in works such as "Feminist Theory, Embodiment, and the Docile Agent: Some Reflections on the Egyptian Islamic Revival," *Cultural Anthropology* 16:2 (2001): 202–236; and Joan Wallach Scott, *The Politics of the Veil* (Princeton, NJ: Princeton University Press, 2010).

42. Yoshino, *Covering*, 35.

43. Yoshino, *Covering*, 11–12.

44. For a wonderful history of the vest as itself an article of clothing that originated in Asia, see Adam Geczy, *Fashion and Orientalism: Dress, Textiles and Culture from the 17th to the 21th Century* (London: Bloomsbury Academic, 2013).

45. For a rich account of the etymology of the word "vesture," see Watt, *Dress, Law and Naked Truth*, 2–3.

46. *Transcript*, 8.

47. Arnold Genthe, *As I Remember* (New York: Reynal & Hitchcock, 1936), 32.

48. Genthe, *As I Remember*, 33.

49. Genthe's Chinatown images were first published in journals such as *The Wave* and *Camera Craft* and then collected in the volume *Old Chinatown: A Book of Pictures by Arnold Genthe* (London: Sidgwick & Jackson, 1913), with text by Genthe's friend Will Irwin. The best and most comprehensive reprint collection can be found in John Kuo Wei Tchen, *Genthe's Photographs of San Francisco's Old Chinatown* (New York: Dover, 1984), with an introductory essay by the author. Today substantial collections of Genthe's photographs can be found at the Library of Congress, the San Francisco Historical Society, and the New York Historical Society.

50. In his memoir, Genthe writes about how exploring "this bit of the Orient set down in the heart of a Western metropolis" bolsters his sense of "the American spirit of independence." See Genthe, *As I Remember*, 33 and Tchen, *Genthe's Photographs*, 12.

51. The almost all male communities in American Chinatowns during the exclusion era were commonly known as "Bachelor Societies."

52. There is an extensive body of scholarship on the historic link between photography and criminology. A few examples: Allan Sekula, "The Body and the Archive," *October* 39 (Winter 1986): 3–64; Okwui Enwezor, *Archive Fever: Uses of the Document in Contemporary Art* (Göttingen, Germany: Steidl, 2009); Sandra S. Phillips et al., *Police Pictures: The Photograph as Evidence* (San Francisco: Chronicle Books, 1997); Katherine Biber, *Captive Images: Race, Crime, Photography* (New York: Routledge, 2007).

53. Passport pictures originated in the Chinese Exclusion Act of 1882, also known as the Geary Act, which required all Chinese residents in the United States to carry identification, and the following year, photographs were required to be on those papers. See Anna Pegler-Gordon, *In Sight of America: Photography and the Development of U.S. Immigration Policy* (Berkeley: University of California Press, 2009). See also the catalog for the *Faces at the Gates* exhibition at the National Portrait Gallery in Washington, DC, in 2012. These identification photos generate more ambiguity than affirmation for the authorities, as evidenced by the excessive amount of descriptive paper documentation that accompany them, with ever-proliferating and confusing details about what the photos in fact do or do not say.

54. The trial transcript names the San Francisco Chinatown police officer who offered testimony as "Gaylos Woodruff," but the U.S. census shows that there was no such person. Since original court records were handwritten and usually not typed up until several decades later, spelling confusion is common. The 1850 census does show a "Delos Woodruff" who was a police officer assigned to Chinatown at the time and who was a regular witness in the San Francisco courts in cases involving Chinatown and the Chinese. It is safe to assume that in the trial transcript the name "Gaylos" was a typographical error for "Delos."

55. Delos Woodruff, "Photograph Album of Chinese Criminals," circa 1872, vault 185, California Historical Society. Shortly after his testimony in *Chy Lung*, Officer Woodruff mysteriously resigned from the special forces after many years of "active and useful service." Further research shows that during the *Chy Lung* trial, Woodruff was himself accused of acting as a middleman for a John T. Peters, a friend of the police chief, who was extorting money from residents of Chinatown. See "Brief Mention: News/Opinion," *San Francisco News Bulletin* (December 8, 1874); "The Peters Perjury Case," *San Francisco Bulletin* (December 15, 1874).

56. According to the *Oxford English Dictionary*, the term *street walking* to denote prostitution was already in common use by the nineteenth century. To photograph and capture these women

"on the streets" is thus a way for Genthe to already and implicitly invoke the specter of morally questionable Asian femininity.

57. Thy Phu, "Spectacles of Intimacy and the Aesthetics of Domestication," *Picturing Model Citizens* (Philadelphia: Temple University Press, 2014), 26–53. See also Emma J. Teng, "Artifacts of a Lost City: Arnold Genthe's Pictures of Old Chinatown and Its Intertexts," *Re/collecting Early Asian America: Essays in Cultural History*, ed. Josephine Lee, Imogene L. Lim, and Yuko Matsukawa (Philadelphia: Temple University Press, 2002), 54–77, for a fantastic introduction to Genthe's intimate relationship to the San Francisco Bohemian Club. Her study of the (white male) bohemian slumming centered around Chinatown offers a contrasting narrative to and context for the Chinese femininity on the streets of Chinatown that I am tracing here.

58. Tchen, *Genthe's Photographs*, 14–17.

59. For a wonderful reading of the image as a meditation on "three bachelors"—including Genthe himself as a celebrated bachelor—see Phu, "Spectacles of Intimacy," 32–34.

60. Genthe writes in his memoir, "A challenging member of the [Chinatown] community was Donaldina Cameron.... I got to know Miss Cameron quite well, and she let me come to the Mission to take pictures of her protégées—lovely little creatures poetically named Tea Rose, Apple Blossom, Plum Blossom" (Genthe, *As I Remember*, 39). Donaldina Cameron herself, however, like many early twentieth-century progressive reformers, was herself a complicated and fraught figure who was involved in several kidnapping charges and litigations over young girls whom she "rescued." In fact, one of the more sensational incidents, in which Cameron kidnapped a young girl and tried to have her husband deported, became the basis for a 1905 novel by Miriam Michelson, *A Yellow Journalist*.

61. Sekula in "The Body and the Archive" (10),coins the phrase "shadow archive" to refer to a visual rendering of the social terrain that orders bodies hierarchically within it.

62. Hortense J. Spillers, "Mama's Baby, Papa's Maybe: An American Grammar Book," *Diacritics* 17:2 (1987), 67.

63. Paul Valéry, "Some Simple Reflections on the Body," *Aesthetics,* vol. 13 of *The Collected Works of Paul Valéry*, trans. Ralph Mannheim (London: Bollingen Foundation, 1964), 31–40.

CHAPTER 2: GLEAMING THINGS

1. Walter Benjamin, "Gesprä mit Anne May Wong," *Die Literarische Welt*, July 6, 1928, 2, trans. by Seth Norm for me. For more on this article, see Shirley Jennifer Lim, "'Speaking German like Nobody's Business': Anna May Wong, Walter Benjamin, and the Possibilities of Asian American Cosmopolitanism," *Journal of Transnational American Studies* 4:1 (2012).

2. Jacques Derrida, "The Parergon," trans. Craig Owens, *October* 9 (Summer 1979): 3–41. Derrida speaks of the supplementary logic of the *parergon* in Kant: "The *parergon* inscribes something extra... but whose transcendent exteriority touches, plays with, brushes, rubs, or presses against the limit and intervenes" (21). Of a building's columns he writes, "It is not simply their exteriority that constitutes them as *parerga*, but the internal structural link by which they are inseparable from a lack within the *ergon*." (3)

3. Elaine Scarry, *On Beauty and Being Just* (Princeton, NJ: Princeton University Press, 1999); Joseph R. Roach, *It* (Ann Arbor: University of Michigan Press, 2007). For raced scholars, especially feminists, beauty is almost always a coercive issue, and for scholars of celebrity, race is rarely discussed. See Daniel Boorstin, *The Image: A Guide to Pseudo-Events in America* (New

York: Harper & Row, 1961); Leo Braudy, *The Frenzy of Renown: Fame and Its History (*New York: Oxford University Press, 1986); Joshua Gamson, *Claims to Fame: Celebrity in Contemporary America* (Berkeley: U of California P, 1994); David P. Marshall, *The Celebrity Culture Reader (*New York: Routledge, 2006); and Richard Schickel, *Intimate Strangers: The Culture of Celebrity (*Garden City: Doubleday, 1985). The exceptions are Richard Dyer, *White: Essays on Race and Culture* (New York: Routledge, 1997), and, more recently, Judith Brown, *Glamour in Six Dimensions: Modernism and the Radiance of Form* (Ithaca, NY: Cornell University Press, 2009).

Also, aside from Roach's *It*, studies of celebrity tend to be less than celebratory about the phenomenon they study. Boorstin equates celebrity with damaging or distorting illusions; Schickel sees celebrity as generating empty social symbols that devastate the boundary between public and private lives with psychopathic consequences for our society. Braudy and Gamson are less harsh, though both agree that twentieth-century celebrity is the artificial product of commercial culture. And Dyer sees the star system as iterating dominant racial and gender ideology. This chapter asks us to venture beyond this moral economy. Instead of simply reproducing the pathology of commodification, celebrity at the site of the traditionally abject body provides a critical occasion for developing a nuanced understanding of the issues of agency and embodiment that haunt the raced female body.

4. Even critical race theory, as it effectively unpacks the "fact" of whiteness, tends to reproduce the irreducible materiality of the black body. For the racist, the raced body signifies rawness, animality, and dumb flesh, and is repeatedly invoked, socially and legally, as inhuman. The liberal race theorist, while "debiologizing" the raced body, is also reproducing it as that which inevitably indexes skin's visual legibility: "Look, a Negro!"(Frantz Fanon, *Black Skin, White Masks,* trans. Charles L. Markmann [New York: Grove Weidenfeld, 1967], 109. Quotations are from Mary Ann Doane, *Femmes Fatales: Feminism, Film Theory, Psychoanalysis* (New York: Routledge, 1991), 223; and Homi K. Bhabha, *The Location of Culture* (London: Routledge, 1994), 78.

5. Walter Benjamin famously uses the term *aura* in his 1936 essay "The Work of Art in the Age of Mechanical Reproduction" (*Illuminations*, ed. Hannah Arendt [New York: Schocken Books, 1968], 217–251) to refer to the authority held by the unique, original work, which under modernity is liquidated by the techniques of mass reproduction. For Benjamin's own ambivalence toward unique aura versus the liberating potential of mass media and technological reproducibility, see Miriam Hansen, "Benjamin, Cinema, and Experience: The Blue Flower in the Land of Technology," *New German Critique* 40(1987): 179–224.

6. See, for examples Graham Russell Gao Hodges's and Anthony B. Chan's biographies of Anna May Wong (Hodges, *Anna May Wong: From Laudryman's Daughter to Hollywood Legend* [New York: Palgrave Macmillam, 2004]; Chan, *Perpetually Cool: The Many Lives of Anna May Wong [1905–1961]* [Lanham, MD: Scarecrow, 2007]).

7. The biographer Hodges documents, for instance, a tantalizing encounter between Wong and Walter Benjamin (Hodges, *Anna May Wong*, 77–79). For further accounts of this meeting, see Benjamin's biographies: Bernd Witt, *Walter Benjamin: An Intellectual Biography* (Detroit: Wayne State University Press, 1991, 105–106) and Momme Broderson, *Walter Benjamin: A Biography* (London: Verso, 1996, 164–166).

8. The screenplay was originally written for Gilda Gray, but Wong stole the spotlight on- and offscreen. The film is especially poignant considering Wong rarely got the starring role, despite appearing in over sixty films. In 1960, after a long film career, Wong would still be cast as the "inscrutable Chinese maid" (*Portrait in Black,* 1960; dir. Michael Gordon).

9. Consider, for example, how a director like Bernardo Bertolucci represents the decadence, corruption, and effeminization of Puyi and the Chinese Empire itself in the film *The Last Emperor* (1987) through tropes and images of excessive sartorial indulgence.

10. Sigmund Freud, "Fetishism," *The Standard Edition of the Complete Psychological Works of Sigmund Freud,* trans. James Strachey (London: Hogarth, 1955), vol. 21, 152.

11. Hodges, *Anna May Wong*, 93; Chan, *Perpetually Cool*, 216.

12. How little of the Asian female body is revealed is the best-kept secret of this film. So much of the discourse surrounding this film, in the forms of reviews and biographies, remembers Shosho as little more than a stripper. Even the image on the original movie poster, which shows Wong in a topless Gypsy outfit and now appears on the cover of the newly digitalized version of the film, is nowhere to be found in the film itself.

13. I hesitate to reclaim Wong's subjective interiority or agency in a scene such as this, not because she could not have had any, but rather because such a reading ignores the fact that the performance is a theatrical product. How do we talk about agency at the intersection of production, script, direction, and audience expectation?

14. With her ability to project an image that suggests presence and depth, Wong more than held her own with the imperturbable Marlene Dietrich in a film such as *Shanghai Express*. The two actresses' equally strong screen presences, however, are not reflected in their pay scale. Budget records for *Shanghai Express* show that, although Wong and Dietrich had the same amount of screen time, Wong earned a quarter of what Dietrich was paid.

15. Wong made many public comments about the racism and sexism that she confronted, and she wrote a series of brief articles for the French magazine *Pour vous*, a year before making *Piccadilly*, that spoke of the racism she faced in Hollywood.

16. In the political rhetoric around the woman of color, *subjectivity* is frequently brought up as a recuperative term, mostly implying the power of intentional agency. But as a star Wong offers a radically different account of how we think about the dream of the subject in racial politics and celebrity studies.

17. Fanon, *Black Skin, White Masks*, 89.

18. See Mechtild Fend, "Bodily Pictorial Surfaces: Skin in French Art and Medicine, 1790– 1860," *Art History* 28:3 (June 2005): 311–339; Krista Thompson, "The Sound of Light: Reflections on Art History in the Visual Culture of Hip-Hop," *Art Bulletin* 91:4 (2009): 481–505; and Hal Foster, "The Art of Fetishism: Notes on Dutch Still Life," *Fetishism as Cultural Discourse*, ed. Emily Apter and William Pietz (Ithaca, NY: Cornell University Press, 1993. For the most part, this racialized shine is linked to the commodification of black bodies, but there has also been a pejorative discourse about yellowness since the 1800s. From the Yellow Peril to yellow journalism, the color yellow has long been linked to gaudiness and decadence (Connor, 173–174.)

19. Judith Brown, *Glamour in Six Dimensions: Modernism and the Radiance of Form* (Ithaca: Cornell University Press, 2009).

20. Brown, *Glamour in Six Dimensions*, 42.

21. See Jeffrey L. Meikle's *American Plastics: A Cultural History* (New Brunswick, NJ: Rutgers University Press, 1997).

22. Jon Wood, *Shine: Sculpture and Surface in the 1920s and 1930s* (Leeds: Henry Moore Institute, 2005), 2. For further readings on Brancusi, see Jon Wood, David Hulks, and Alex Potts, eds. *Modern Sculpture Reader* (Leeds: Henry Moore Institute, 2007), as well as Mina Loy's

collection of poems *The Lost Lunar Baedeker* (New York: Farrar, 1997), a volume that includes "Brancusi's Golden Bird," the source of this chapter's epigraph (79),.

23. This animated shine is distinct from the sterile gloss of plastic or cellophane identified by Judith Brown. While it is beyond the scope of this chapter, it would be fascinating to pursue the relationship between this sculptural shine and the cultural currency of *shine* in black vernacular—in the sense of psychic energy, found in the blues, rhythm and blues, and street jargon.

24. Barthes famously observes that glossy photographs retain the sheen or residue of life (Roland Barthes, *Camera Lucida: Reflections on Photography*, ed. Richard Howard [New York: Hill and Wang, 2010]). Lacan uses the glitter of the sardine can as the provocation to launch the complacent subject into an ethical encounter with its own "splitness" in his work on the Gaze (Jacques Lacan, *The Four Fundamental Concepts of Psychoanalysis,* trans. Alan Sheridan, book 11 of The Seminar of Jacques Lacan (New York: Norton, 1981), 66–122. For more on Lacan's sardine can as a parable of social assimilation, see Anne Anlin Cheng, "Passing, Natural Selection, and Love's Failure: Ethics of Survival from Chang-rae Lee to Jacques Lacan," *American Literary History* 17:3 [2005], 566–570.) Words like *gleam, luster, radiance*, and *flash* populate the writings of Maurice Merleau-Ponty and provide critical turning points for his rethinking of the nature of "flesh" as the difference between *physis* and being. Heidegger's writing is also dotted with references to radiance and shine; his essay "The Origin of the Work of Art" (Martin Heidegger, "The Origin of the Work of Art," *Poetry, Language, Thoughts*, trans. Albert Hofstadter [New York: Harper, 1971], 15–86) asserts that shininess does not obscure but is in fact the very medium through which art can be revealed (56). Finally, Leo Bersani observes that artists from Caravaggio to Proust saw shine as the trace of the material world's disappearance; as such, shine signals art's ability and ethical capacity to transcend the capture of its own materiality (Leo Bersani, "Psychoanalysis and the Aesthetic Subject," *Critical Inquiry*, 32:2 [Winter 2006], 161–174).

25. Attending to why Wong as Shosho might speak through her objectness rather than her subjectness would challenge the tendency of the discourse of authentic subjectivity and agency to overlook the compromises to subjecthood that discrimination and the politics of performance have already produced. What can agency look like in a crisis of consent? I am here also implicitly responding to Krauss's critique of Rubin's influence-study model (William Rubin, *Primitivism in Twentieth-Century Art: Affinity of the Tribal and the Modern* [New York: Museum of Modern Art, 2002]). Krauss contends that "primitive objects" are not "historical" but "theoretical objects": "the value of the primitive was, quite simply, what it enabled one to think" (Rosalind Krauss, "Preying on Primitivism," *Art and Text* 17 [1985]: 60). Yet it is clear who the "one" doing the thinking is; thus her formulation does not quite rescue those objects from what she calls their "neutralized" state. What remains unquestioned is the boundary separating Western subjectivity and primitive objectness, between Western intellectualism and non-Western things. I would ask, can the object think or speak *as* object?

26. Thompson, "The Sound of Light," 487, 490.

27. Gottfried Semper, "Concerning the Formal Principles of Ornament and Its Significance as Artistic Symbol," *The Theory of Decorative Arts: An Anthology of European and American Writings, 1750–*1940, ed. Isabelle Frank, trans. David Britt (New Haven, CT: Yale University Press, 2000), 97. I am indebted to Spyros Papapetros's study of Semper in his essays on Aby Warburg and ornamentation. See Spyros Papapetros, "Aby Warburg as Reader of Gottfried Semper: Reflections on the Cosmic Character of Ornament," *Elective Affinities: Testing Word and Image Relationships*, ed. Catriona MacLeod, Véronique Plesch, and Charlotte Schoelt-Glass,

317–336 (Amsterdam: Rodopi, 2009), and "An Ornamented Inventory of Microcosmic Shifts: Notes on Hans Hildebrandt's Book Project '*Der Schmuck*' (1936–1937)." *Getty Research Journal* 1(2009): 38–46. For further reading on the larger history of ornamentation, modernism, and gender, see Naomi Schor, *Reading in Detail: Aesthetics and the Feminine* (New York: Routledge, 2006), and Mark Wigley, *White Walls, Designer Dresses: The Fashioning of Modern Architecture* (Cambridge: MIT Press, 2001).

28. Papapetros, "Aby Warburg," 324.

29. Papapetros, "Ornamented Inventory," 44.

30. This scene is also a meditation on cinematic birth itself: the literal eruption of a body into a presence and a being that exists only in light.

31. Edgar Wind, *Pagan Mysteries in the Renaissance* (New York: Norton, 1968), 136–137.

32. Few records are left today of the Mayfair Mannequin Society of New York (MMSNY), which was most likely an offshoot of the Mayfair Mannequin Academy, a modeling school in New York City in the 1930s that appears to have helped to professionalize modeling. The school identified itself as "America's Original Mannequin School" in an advertisement it placed in the *New Yorker* (August 8, 1934). And an article in the *New York Times* entitled "Professional Models Open War on Debutantes Who Do Work Free; Appeal to Junior League to Keep Pastime-Seekers out of Field, Spokesman for Fifty Determined Girls Says," (October 26, 1934) shows that the academy (and potentially the MMSNY) advocated for women in the profession. That the MMSNY might have been a kind of proto-labor union for women models renders its praise of Wong's sartorial art more professional than frivolous.

33. Quoted in Hodges, *Anna May Wong*, 105. Wong made this remark to a German reporter during an interview for *Mein Film* on June 4, 1930.

34. Boorstin, *The Image*, 45.

35. In an essay on Lena Horne's "impersona," Shane Vogel also demonstrates an interest in locating a form of corporeal evacuation affected by women artists of color in the early twentieth century. Where I argue that Baker and Wong turned to a sartorial and physical play of surfaces, Vogel identifies a similar strategy Horne employed in sound and song, a "third person voice" that offers "sound *in place of* subjectivity" (Shane Vogel, *The Secret of Harlem Cabaret: Race, Sexuality, Performance* [Chicago: University of Chicago Press, 2009], 180).

CHAPTER 3: BLUE WILLOW

1. All this was nestled deep inside the museum's bowels, filling up both the Anna Wintour Costume Center in the basement and the Chinese galleries on the second floor and claiming a large portion of the repurposed Egyptian Gallery, just to give the reader a sense of the spatial expanse.

2. The exhibition overview on the museum website states: "This exhibition explores...how China has fueled the fashionable imagination for centuries. In this collaboration between The Costume Institute and the Department of Asian Art, high fashion is juxtaposed with Chinese costumes, paintings, porcelains, and other art, including films, to reveal enchanting reflections of Chinese imagery." See http://www.metmuseum.org/exhibitions/listings/2015/china-through-the-looking-glass.

3. Roland Barthes, *Empire of Signs*, tran. Richard Howard (New York: Hill and Wang, 1983), 3–4.

4. Hal Foster, "Postmodernism in Parallax," *October* 63 (Winter 1993): 3–20.

5. Holland Cotter, "Review: In 'China: Through the Looking Glass,' Eastern Culture Meets Western Fashion," *New York Times,* May 7, 2015, Arts and Design section.

6. For Lee's letter, see http://artspiral.blogspot.com/2015/07/china-through-looking-glass-open-letter_20.html.

7. Wong Kar-wai, "A Note on Film and Fashion," *China: Through the Looking Glass*, exhibition catalog, Metropolitan Museum of Art, New York, 2015, 10.

8. Adam Geczy, *Fashion and Orientalism: Dress, Textiles and Culture from the 17th to the 21st Century* (London: Bloomsbury Academic, 2013), 6.

9. Edward Said in *Orientalism* famously set up an opposition between the East and the West: "There were—and are—cultures and nations whoe location is in the East, and their lives, histories, and customs have a brute reality obviously greater than anything that could be said about them in the West" (Edward W. Said, *Orientalism* (New York: Vintage Books, 1979), 5.

10. Rita Felski, *The Gender of Modernity* (Cambridge, MA: Harvard University Press, 1995).

11. Jennifer Anderson, *Mahogany: The Costs of Luxury in Early America* (Cambridge, MA: Harvard University Press, 2012); Maxine Berg, *Luxury and Pleasure in Eighteenth-Century Britain* (Oxford: Oxford University Press, 2005); Alden Cavanaugh and Michael E. Yonan, *The Cultural Aesthetics of Eighteenth-Century Porcelain* (Farnham, England: Ashgate,, 2010); Madeleine Dobie, *Trading Places: Colonization and Slavery in Eighteenth-Century French Culture* (Ithaca, NY: Cornell University Press, 2010); Chi-ming Yang, *Performing China: Virtue, Commerce, and Orientalism in Eighteenth-Century England, 1660–1760* (Baltimore: Johns Hopkins University Press, 2011).

12. Cavanaugh and Yonan, *Cultural Aesthetics*, 4, note that "with exceptions of tapestry and silver, no artistic medium [was] more coveted or valued [than porcelain] . . . [along with] its continual association with exotic lands . . . a semi-magical material . . . a 'white gold.'"

13. Gordon H. Chang, *Fateful Ties: A History of America's Preoccupation with China* (Cambridge, MA: Harvard University Press, 2015).

14. Mechthild Fend, "Bodily and Pictorial Surfaces: Skin in French Art and Medicine, 1790–1860," *Art History* 28:3 (June 2005): 311–339; and Yang, *Performing China.*

15. See Cavanaugh and Yonan, *Cultural Aesthetics*.

16. Christopher Clarey, "Atlanta: Day 3—Gymnastics; Miller Gives United States High Hopes for a Gold," *New York Times* (July 22, 1996).

17. Eric Hayot, *The Hypothetical Mandarin: Sympathy, Modernity, and Chinese Pain* (New York: Oxford University Press, 2009).

18. Walter Benjamin, "Gespräch mit Anna May Wong," *Die Literatische Welt*, July 6, 1928. In the late eighties, Kwan acted as spokesperson for a moisturizer called Pearl Cream, touted in its ads as "Chinese women's ancient secret." The product contained a whitening product and promised to give its users flawless "porcelain skin." We might say that Pearl Cream was selling something of an ornamentalist dream, itself a product that worked the inanimate residue of an animate object into nourishment for human skin so that the latter might look more synthetic.

19. Bill Brown, *A Sense of Things: The Object Matter of American Literature* (Chicago: University of Chicago Press, 2003), 7.

20. William Blackstone, *Commentaries on the Laws of England, 1765–1779*, 15th ed. (London: T. Caddell and W. Davies, 1765), 123. For a study of the formative role of Asiatic female ornamentation in nineteenth-century juridical ideas about legal personhood, see Anne Anlin Cheng,

"Law and Ornament," *New Directions in Law and Literature*, ed. Elizabeth S. Anker and Bernadette Meyler (New York: Oxford University Press, 2017).

21. Li is himself a complicated figure who works in China, Hong Kong, and the United States and whose work traverses the realms of art, commerce, and kitsch. In 2010, for example, he collaborated with Lacoste to create a collection of polo shirts.

22. Rey Chow, "Modernity and Narration," *Woman and Chinese Modernity: The Politics of Reading between West and East* (Minneapolis: University of Minnesota Press, 1991), 84–120.

23. Rey Chow, *Primitive Passions: Visuality, Sexuality, Ethnography, and Contemporary Chinese Cinema* (New York: Columbia University Press, 1995), 145.

24. The *Oxford English Dictionary* details the intimacy between the word *curio* and Asia: "An object of art, piece of bric-à-brac, etc., valued as a curiosity or rarity; a curiosity; more particularly applied to articles of this kind from China, Japan, and the Far East." In addition, there are references in the *OED* to objects that contain objects, such as "curio cabinets" that displayed curio(sities) from foreign lands, which invariably meant trinkets, jewelry, and so on from places like East Asia. Because early trade with Asia was limited, objects from East Asia were considered particularly exotic. Chi-ming Yang also offers a fascinating discussion of the Oriental curio by way of the pet in "Culture in Miniature: Toy Dogs and Object Life," *Eighteenth-Century Fiction* 25:1 (Fall 2012): 139–174.

25. My thanks to Elaine Scarry for telling me about this lecture and for her unerring ability to open unexpected windows.

26. Amar Bose, "Personal Reflections," 6.312 Lecture 27, given at MIT, December 15, 1995. Full lecture available on YouTube.

27. See Joan Copjec, "The Sartorial Superego," *October* 50 (Autumn 1989): 91, for a wonderful discussion of utilitarianism and pleasure.

28. The connection between beauty and uselessness runs deep: beauty as superfluous, extraneous, superficial, etc. Beauty usually acquires value only when it is gendered and placed within the economy of marriage. As Mrs. Bennet in *Pride and Prejudice* pronounces to her husband about their oldest daughter on the eve of her engagement to the affluent Mr. Bingley, "I knew she could not have been so beautiful for nothing!"

29. There is also an association between the word *curio* and language. The *Oxford English Dictionary* notes that *curio* might harken back to the word *curiologic*, which essentially means that which is hieroglyphic or represented by characters. Since Europeans believed the Chinese writing system to be akin to hieroglyphics in its pictorial quality, we see again how Chinese language seems somehow inherently an inscrutable *object* to the West.

30. James Fenimore Cooper, *The Last of the Mohicans* (Philadelphia: Carey & Lea, 1831). I am indebted to Sarah Rivett for bringing this citation to my attention.

31. Sigmund Freud, "The Uncanny," *The Standard Edition of the Compete Psychological Works of Sigmund Freud*, trans. James Strachey (London: Hogarth Press, 1955), vol. 18.

32. For more on ornamentalism and the racial logic of the machine, see chapter 5, "Dolls."

CHAPTER 4: EDIBLE PETS

1. Jean Anthelme Brillat-Savarin, *The Physiology of Taste; or, Meditations on Transcendental Gastronomy*, trans. M. F. K. Fisher (Washington, DC: Counterpoint, 1994), 25.

2. Kyla Wazana Tompkins, *Racial Indigestion: Eating Bodies in the 19th Century* (New York: New York University Press, 2012), 2 and 8.

3. Tompkins, *Racial Indigestion*, 5.

4. Claude Lévi-Strauss, *The Raw and the Cooked: Mythologiques,* vol. 1, trans. John and Doreen Weightman (Chicago: University of Chicago Press, 1983).

5. See Emmanuel Chukwudi Eze, *Race and the Enlightenment: A Reader* (London: Wiley-Blackwell, 1997).

6. Although human rights and animals rights can be seen as continuous—for example, people who work in chicken plants are treated like animals—they clash when race and ethnicity enter the picture. See Claire Jean Kim's *Dangerous Crossings: Race, Species, and Nature in a Multicultural Age* (New York: Cambridge University Press, 2015, which parses out the ongoing controversy in San Francisco between animal advocates and race activists over the treatment and sale of live animals in Chinatown.

7. Eve Kosofsky Sedgwick, *Between Men: English Literature and Male Homosocial Desire* (New York: Columbia University Press, 1985).

8. David Wong Louie, "Bottles of Beaujolais," *Pangs of Love* (New York: Plume, 1992), 39.

9. See Brillat-Savarin, *The Physiology of Taste*; and Margaret Visser, *The Rituals of Dinner: The Origin, Evolution, Eccentricities, and Meaning of Table Manners* (New York: Penguin Books, 1991).

10. Brillat-Savarin, *The Physiology of Taste*, 121.

11. Tompkins, *Racial Indigestion*, 2.

12. Amy Bentley, "From Culinary Other to Mainstream American: Meanings and Uses of Southwestern Cuisine," *Culinary Tourism*, ed. Lucy M. Long (Lexington: University of Kentucky Press, 2004): 209–225.

13. See Joseph Litvak, *Strange Gourmets: Sophistication, Theory, and the Novel* (Durham, NC: Duke University Press, 1997).

14. Henry David Thoreau, *Walden; or, Life in the Woods* (New York: Wilder, 2008), 24.

15. Indeed, Thoreau lays this stake deep in a Western philosophical tradition that harks back to Aristotle.

16. Thoreau, *Walden*, 262.

17. Thoreau, *Walden*, 262.

18. For a visual history documenting the connection between Asians and animals, see Lorraine Dong and Philip P. Choy, *The Coming Man: 19th Century American Perceptions of the Chinese* (Seattle: University of Washington Press, 1995).

19. Just as Michael Rogin and David Roediger have pointed out that blackness has served as a foil for the consolidation of whiteness, so has anti-Asian sentiment served to consolidate white labor in the nineteenth century. See Dong and Choy, *The Coming Man*; Michael Rogin, *Blackface, White Noise: Jewish Immigrants in the Hollywood Melting Pot* (Berkeley, University of California Press, 1998); and David R. Roediger, *The Wages of Whiteness: Race and the Making of the American Working Class* (New York: Verso, 2007).

20. See Eric Lott, *Love and Theft: Blackface Minstrelsy and the American Working Class* (New York: Oxford University Press, 1995).

21. The development of sushi in America is directly linked to immigration history. The country's first sushi restaurant, in Little Tokyo in Los Angeles in the 1950s, was opened to cater specifically to the new wave of Japanese immigrants to the United States. For a history of the development of sushi in the American food industry, see Sasha Issenberg, *The Sushi Economy: Globalization and the Making of a Modern Delicacy* (New York: Gotham, 2008).

22. In three separate places, the Torah tells us not to "boil a kid in its mother's milk" (Ex. 23:19; Ex. 34:26; Deut. 14:21). The Oral Torah specifies that one must wait a significant amount of time between eating meat and dairy because fatty residues and meat particles tend to cling to the mouth. What makes this contact between meat and mother milk "unhealthy" is surely the taboo of a food coming in contact with where it came from, that is, the contact that reveals the unbearable *sameness* of different kinds of flesh.

23. It is beyond the scope of this essay, but the question of how someone can become ontologized as "edible" should also be placed in dialogue with the works of Carol J. Adams, *The Sexual Politics of Meat* (Cambridge: Polity Press, 1990), and Val Plumwood, "Integrating Ethical Frameworks for Animals, Humans and Nature: A Critical Feminist Eco-socialist Analysis," *Ethics and the Environment* 5:2 (2000): 285–322.

24. My gratitude to Claire Jean Kim for urging me to consider the question of Mushimono's subjectivity and for her other insights as well.

25 To understand how strange the idea of "fleshness" is in the art of sushi, we might also consider the other extreme that it harks to: pure artifice. It is no coincidence that this delicate and immediate art advertises itself through shiny plastic copies. Japan is *the* leading manufacturer of plastic foods. No self-respecting restaurateur in Tokyo would open a sushi restaurant without first visiting the neighborhood of Kappabashi, where thousands of plastic foods of every kind are preserved in reality-defying action: simmering, pouring, frying, or just sitting in their placid, forever contentment. The plastic sushi you find in every sushi restaurant in America and Japan may not be a tacky gesture of redundant commodification but may instead speak to a deeper ambivalence in the art, a sustained performance treading between authenticity and artifice, imminence and delay, rawness and preparation.

26. We might think of the sushi principle as a critique of the form of structuralist anthropology exemplified by a text such as Lévi-Strauss, *The Raw and the Cooked*.

27. Brillat-Savarin, *The Physiology of Taste*, 40.

28. Brillat-Savarin, *The Physiology of Taste*, 46.

29. Here we might engage Jane Bennett's wonderful work on rethinking the nature of agency as not necessarily attached to persons but instead inhering in what she calls "agential" dynamics. See Bennett, *Vibrant Matter: A Political Ecology of Things* (Durham, NC: Duke University Press, 2010).

30. Brillat-Savarin, *The Physiology of Taste*, 46–47.

31. Louie, "Bottles of Beaujolais," 50, 37.

32. Robert Hass, "Against Botticelli," *Praise* (New York: Ecco Press, 1999), 10.

33. Louie, "Bottles of Beaujolais," 50, 52.

34. Art history has long taught us that there is an unassailable difference between the naked and the nude: the former designates degrading corporeality while the latter represents abstract, idealized forms. The nude consecrates ideal humanism, invoking the mind and the intellect, while the naked remains tethered to the abject body and carries a host of related connotations about animality and racial difference. This segregation of the nude from the naked, codified by Kenneth Clark in 1956, has remained uncontested to this day. See Kenneth Clark, *The Nude: A Study in Ideal Form* (Princeton, NJ: Princeton University Press, 1972). The reign of this theoretical distinction is extraordinary, not only given the set of class, racial, and gender ideologies underlying Clark's own writing but also because the nude has never been as easily disentangled from the naked as this overefficient classification suggests. As evidenced by the Botticelli, even the classic

nude in her most idealized form has the proclivity to carry a whiff of the animal. And as works by contemporary artists such as Vanessa Beecroft dramatize, the nude always stands in danger of becoming the naked, just as the naked provides the corporeal condition disavowed but retained by the nude. My interest here is not to highlight the failure of "high art" to sustain its intellectual critique but rather to underscore what the hybrid-mermaid body tells us about how ambivalent we are about our own flesh. The encounter with "naked flesh" launches us into states of desire and states of alienation, between the encounter with the raw and the aestheticized. We can also bring Thoreau into this conversation, for his struggles with the dilemma of "wilderness"—how to be in it without being devoured by it—is itself indebted to a long Western philosophic tradition that equate nakedness with regressive savagery and the nude idealized (transcendental in Thoreau's terms) human form. For a wonderful study of why Asian art does not have "nudes" and what this says about the absence of the binarism between animality and the human that dominates Western philosophy, see François Jullien, *The Impossible Nude*, trans. Maev de la Guardia (Chicago: University of Chicago Press, 2007).

35. We might also think productively about this transformation drive in Louie's story as a form of animation that is akin to what Mel Y. Chen theorizes as "animacy": "a specific kind of affective and material construct that is not only nonneutral in relation to animals, humans, and living and dead things, but is shaped by race and sexuality, mapping various biopolitical realizations of animacy in the contemporary culture of the US." Mel Y. Chen, *Animacies: Biopolitics, Racial Mattering, and Queer Affect* (Durham, NC: Duke University Press, 2012), 5. So the kind of boundary crossing between animate being and inanimate objects in Louie's story both reveals and disrupts our our often hierarchical principles of life.

36. Mermaids have populated the human imagination for millennia, from the river valleys of Mesopotamia circa 900 BCE to Africa's Nile Valley to the Mediterranean world of Greeks, Romans, and Minoans. For many of these cultures, the mermaid represents danger, and in the Christian Europe of the Middle Ages, the mermaid is often found in bestiaries. See Henry John Drewal, *Mami Wata: Arts for Water Spirits in Africa and Its Diasporas* (Los Angeles: Fowler Museum at UCLA, 2008), 23–72.

37. In literary culture, consider H. G. Wells's 1902 novel *The Sea Lady*. In popular Victorian culture, consider the enormous popularity of the "importation" of fake mermaid corpses that were often made by sewing together fish tails with monkey skulls. It is not a coincidence that Western imperialism and exploration should boast of acquiring such subhuman creatures. The furor over the so-called Fiji Mermaid is one example of these creatures being sighted and then presumably imported from "exotic" locals. This is, of course, also part of the long history of the pseudoethnographic "freak show" that accompanied the imperial mission. See Richard Altick, *The Shows of London* (Cambridge, MA.: Belknap Press of Harvard University Press, 1978), 302–303; Jan Bondeson, *The Feejee Mermaid and Other Essays in Natural and Unnatural History* (Ithaca, NY: Cornell University Press, 1999), 36–63. It is ironic that in "indigenous African beliefs, the human-aquatic creatures" were also thought to be racially other, that is, European (Drewal, *Mami Wata*, 37).

38. Hans Christian Andersen, *The Little Mermaid* (New York: Minedition, 2004).

39. Louie, "Bottles of Beaujolais," 43. Yet one could argue that within the logic of the text, Peg may not be so inappropriate a second name for Luna after all, for she is a changeling on whom much is hung.

40. Louie, "Bottles of Beaujolais," 45.

41. Philip Armstrong and Laurence Simmons, "Bestiary: An Introduction," *Knowing Animals*, ed. Philip Armstrong and Laurence Simmons (Boston: Brill, 2007), 18–19.

42. For a reading of Derrida's famous cat encounter, see Kalpana Rahita Seshadri, *HumAnimal: Race, Law, Language* (Minneapolis: University of Minnesota Press, 2012). For a reading of animals in Darwin as curious figures of nonhuman agency, see Spyros Papapetros, *On the Animation of the Inorganic: Art, Architecture, and the Extension of Life* (Chicago: University of Chicago Press, 2012). The use of animals to differentiate humanity is of course an enduring gesture. On this, see Chen's chapter "Queer Animality" in *Animacies*, 89–126.

43. See Lewis Henry Morgan, *The American Beaver and His Work* (Philadelphia: J. B. Lippincott, 1868). Gillian Feeley-Harnik demonstrates that Morgan's human guides and informants in both projects were the same. The "Ojibwa trappers" (cited by Morgan in the preface to *The American Beaver*) who were explaining human kinship and labor practices to Morgan were also informing him about beaver kinship and labor practices. See Gillian Feeley-Harnik, "The Ethnography of Creation: Lewis Henry Morgan and the American Beaver," *Relative Values: Reconfiguring Kinship Studies*, ed. Sarah Franklin and Susan McKinnon (Durham, NC: Duke University Press, 2001), 54–84. And if Morgan was becoming increasingly aware of the beaver dams and lodges as active signs of a communicative system between humans and animals, these are insights influenced by Ojibwa lore and its views about the relation between people and animals. Morgan's thinking about the network of human blood and inheritance grew out of his thoughts about social relations and property among the beavers. Thus Morgan's work instantiates the long, enmeshed interrelations among race, humanism, conquest, animalism, culture, and science.

In *The American Beaver and His Work*, Morgan meticulously details in words and drawings the beavers' designs as process; their elaborate and adaptive construction methods attentive to both environmental and human presences; what he calls their "psychology"; their family and generational relations; and, above all, their intimate integration into a landscape made of wood, water, stones, earth, sticks, and humans and their structures. Thus, more than an implicit critique of nineteenth-century humanism, more than even a recognition of nonhuman kinship systems, *The American Beaver* gestures to the potential polylinguism of life and maps a radically hybrid ecology in which the human and the nonhuman animal communicate and interact. For all of the limitations of Morgan's work—his monumental *Systems of Consanguinity and the Affinity of the Human Man* (Lincoln: University of Nebraska Press, 1997) has been much criticized since its initial publication even as it remains a key text—it is this idea of hybrid ecology that I want to hang on to for our discussion to follow.

44. Visser, *The Rituals of Dinner*, 1.

45. Sigmund Freud, "Totem and Taboo," *The Standard Edition of the Complete Psychological Works of Sigmund Freud*, trans. James Strachey (London: Hogarth Press, 1975), vol. 13: 1–164. Louie seems to radically revise Freud's notion of a totem meal, replacing the primal father with this triangle of three equal, imbricated, but unrelated beings.

46. Brillat-Savarin, *The Physiology of Taste*, 40.

47. Kalpana Seshadri-Crooks [Kalpana Rahita Seshadri], "Being Human: Bestiality, Anthropophagy, and Law," *Umbr(a): Ignorance of the Law* 1 (2003): 97–114.

48. The idea that we are constantly, simultaneously, and not necessarily distinguishing between taking in, digesting, and spewing out otherness may not be as abstract as it sounds if we consider how our own biology might be enacting, on a quite material level, such active porousness. Recent scientific research has shown that our old midcentury conception of human-skin ecology—the traditional idea that our bodies are in constant danger of and therefore in constant battle against microbes, bacteria, and fungi that will invade our bodies—may be wrong. Scientists believe that we are inundated by microbes, bacteria, and fungi on our skin and in our guts from the moment we are born. See Lita Proctor, "The Human Microbiome," iom Forum, February 22, 2012, accessed April 17, 2014 (site discontinued). See also Rob Stein, "Finally, a Map of All the Microbes in Your Body," NPR, June 13, 2012, http://www.npr.org/ blogs/health/2012/06/13/154913334/finally- a-map-of-all-the-microbes-on-your-body. The human body contains about 100 trillion cells. However, only maybe one in ten of those cells is actually human; the rest are from bacteria, viruses, and other microorganisms. Research has also shown that these systems of microbes have far more extensive functions than we had believed, including beneficial, even essential life-preserving ones. What emerges is a picture of our human skin as a complicated ecology that might be considered a biological system of its own.

49. Louie, "Bottles of Beaujolais," 54.

50. I should note that this question also brings up the issue of the act of reading, which is after all *the* mode of consumption facing us as readers of this story. What does it mean to read without looking for the satisfaction of an epiphany? So much of this story resists consumption even as it offers consumption as an object of thought. If Louie is trying to tell us something about the nature of inexplicable, mute aesthetic experience, the kind that punctures but refuses recuperation, then I think it is important to allow the story its refusal of resolutions. From Leo Bersani's *Culture of Redemption* (Cambridge, MA: Harvard University Press, 1990) to cultural studies' own increasing discomfort with reading as redemption, there has been in recent years some critical resistance to the notion of aesthetic recuperation. While I am wholly sympathetic to that reservation, lately it has also increasingly seemed to me that the critique of redemption itself—often formulated as a replacement of moralism by ethics and often achieved at the price of some kind of human shaming—can run the danger of reproducing a piety of its own. Consider, as cited in this essay, how often the animal in animal studies—from Darwin's dog to Derrida's cat—is seen as the agent of our shaming. But I have to wonder whether there might be those kinds of aesthetic experiences that offer us an encounter with the other that does not guarantee our redemption or require our shame as compensation? This story seems to offer us one site for such patient contemplation.

CHAPTER 5: DOLLS

1. R. John Williams, *The Buddha in the Machine: Art, Technology, and the Meeting of East and West* (New Haven, CT: Yale University Press, 2014), 1.

2. Williams, *The Buddha in the Machine*, 218.

3. Williams, *The Buddha in the Machine*, 217.

4. Cyra Levenson and Chi-ming Yang, "Haptic Blackness: The Double Life of an 18th-Century Bust," *British Art Studies*, 1 (Autumn 2015). http://www.britishartstudies.ac.uk/issues/issue-index/issue-1/bust-of-a-man.

5. I take the idea of *enchanted materialism* from Jane Bennett, *Vibrant Matter: A Political Ecology of Things* (Durham, NC: Duke University Press, 2010). Bennett ascribes agency to

inorganic phenomena such as the electric grid, food, and trash, all of which enjoy, as she demonstrates, a certain efficacy that defies human will. I am more concerned with a human figure who is constructed at the intersection of the organic and the inorganic. What can agency, materialism, and corporeality mean for such a person/nonperson? This chapter about cyborgs is of course also deeply indebted to Donna Haraway. Although *Simians, Cyborgs, and Women: The Reinvention of Nature* (New York: Routledge, 1991) does not address Asiatic femininity specifically, it remains the foundational text for thinking about cyborgism as a vector for feminism.

6. Famous mantra from the opening voiceover of the original *Star Trek* series on NBC, 1966–1969.

7. Christopher Bush, "The Ethnicity of Things in America's Lacquered Age," *Representations* 99:1 (Summer 2007): 86. Here Bush is talking specifically about how "the Japanese thing" gives form to aspects of the American racial imaginary.

8. Sigmund Freud, "The Uncanny," *The Standard Edition of the Complete Psychological Works of Sigmund Freud*, trans. James Strachey (London: Hogarth Press, 1995), vol. 17.

9. Spyros Papapetros, *On the Animation of the Inorganic: Art, Architecture, and the Extension of Life* (Chicago: University of Chicago Press, 2012), vii.

10. Levi R. Bryant, *Onto-cartography: An Ontology of Machines and Media* (Edinburgh: University of Edinburgh Press, 2014), 26.

11. Perhaps it is not that these questions are tired but that the answers often are. Science fiction in mainstream media has remained deeply attached to the sanctity of human ontology and human exceptionalism in spite of the genre's interest in composite and alternative life. Science fiction tends to resolve the tensions between life and nonlife, the organic and the inorganic, and the person and the thing that prompt its plots.

12. Beatriz Colomina and Mark Wigley, *Are We Human? Notes on an Archaeology of Design* (Zurich: Lars Müller, 2017), 52.

13. See Eric Hayot, *The Hypothetical Mandarin: Sympathy, Modernity, and Chinese Pain* (New York: Oxford University Press, 2009); and Lisa Lowe, *The Intimacies of Four Continents* (Durham, NC: Duke University Press, 2015). And in her study of Orientalism and, in particular the association of the Orient with the enigmatic, Homay King opens with a description of the wax mannequins of Chinese people in the lobby of Grauman's Chinese Theatre in Los Angeles. See Homay King, *Lost in Translation: Orientalism, Cinema, and the Enigmatic Signifier* (Durham, NC: Duke University Press, 2010). And of course the long-standing erotic projection of Asian women as dolls foreshadows how this "alien" figure came to be the inhuman replicant in science fiction. But I hope this project helps us understand these histories of objectification also as histories of our conceptualization of alternative forms of animated life.

14. Rachel C. Lee, *The Exquisite Corpse of Asian America: Biopolitics, Biosociality, and Posthuman Ecologies* (New York: New York University Press, 2014), 69. When I first started this project, a colleague noted that my work offers a counterpoint to Lee's work "on the body" and her returning focus on the biological. I, however, see my work here as very much in line with Lee's insistence that we remain wary of the dichotomy between nature and culture and that biology is, above all, plastic.

15. Statement from opening scene of *Ghost in the Shell*.

16. There is, of course, a long history of association between the mestizo and the figure of Caliban. In a footnote, Hortense J. Spillers in "Mama's Baby, Papa's Maybe: An American Grammar Book," *Diacritics* 17:2 (1987), 65 (n 2), speaks of the designation of the monstrous for

that combination of the half man and half beast: "[A]ccording to Roman law, children born of prostitutes were called 'monsters' because they exhibited 'the nature of men together with the bestial characteristics of having been born of vagabond or uncertain unions.'"

17. Nicolas Abraham and Maria Torok, *The Shell and the Kernel*, trans. Nicholas T. Rand (Chicago: University of Chicago Press, 1994), 80.

18. Abraham and Torok, *The Shell and the Kernel*, 141.

19. Anne Anlin Cheng, *The Melancholy of Race: Psychoanalysis, Assimilation, and Hidden Grief* (New York: Oxford University Press, 2000..

20. Kenji Yoshino, *Covering: The Hidden Assault on Our Civil Rights*, New York: Random House, 2006; Abraham and Torok, *The Shell and the Kernel*, 9.

21. Cheng, *The Melancholy of Race*, 21–24.

22. For my discussion of the doll test and its complicated implications, see *The Melancholy of Race*, 3–7.

23. Bennett, *Vibrant Matter*, 61.

24. Question posed by Eric Hayot at the "*Too Cute*: American Style and the New Asian Cool" conference, Princeton University, Princeton, March 3, 2010.

25. Sianne Ngai, *Our Aesthetic Categories: Zany, Cute, Interesting* (Cambridge, MA: Harvard University Press, 2015), 64.

26. Nathan himself explicitly invokes the family logic when he calls himself Ava's—and by extension, Kyoko's—"dad." Also, when Caleb asks why Nathan gave the AI androids a gender, Nathan replies, "Can you think of an example of consciousness, at any level, human or animal, that exists without a sexual dimension?" In the film, the same could be asked about the *racial* dimension.

27. Quotation from Alex Garland, *Ex Machina*, script, London: DNA Films, 2013. The script describes the scene: "As a large section of skin is removed from her torso, JADE—who has been motionless until now—turns her head slightly to look at Ava. They exchange a glance, Locking eyes for a moment" (scene 114). Although Garland's interest in the intimacy between Ava and Kyoko may be no more than a prurient imagination about erotics between woman, my discussion suggests something more is at stake in this intimacy. If we look carefully at the scene after Ava's transformation, the inanimate Asian model appears slightly different, more sentient, with a soft curve now to her lips, whereas earlier, in her "shut down" state, she appeared somber, even morose.

28. Mel Y. Chen, *Animacies: Biopolitics, Racial Mattering, and Queer Affect* (Durham, NC: Duke University Press, 2012), 5.

29. *Ex Machina*, script, scene 128.

30. *Ex Machina*, script, scene 58.

31. Ernst Bloch, "The Fairy Tale Moves on Its Own Time," 1930, reprinted in Jack Zipes, *Breaking the Magic Spell: Radical Theories of Folk and Fairy Tales* (Lexington: University of Kentucky Press, 2002), 150–153.

CODA

1. Toni Morrison, *Beloved* (New York: Alfred A. Knopf, 1987), 88.

2. Morrison, *Beloved*, 15, 78.

3. Hortense J. Spillers, "Mama's Baby, Papa's Maybe: An American Grammar Book." *Diacritics* 17:2 (1987), 72.

4. Monique Allewaert, *Ariel's Ecology: Plantations, Personhood, and Colonialism in the American Tropics, 1760–1820* (Minneapolis: University of Minnesota Press, 2013), 1.

5. Morrison, *Beloved,* 16.

6. Morrison, *Beloved,* 16.

7. The idea of "collaborative survival" is indebted to Anna Lowenhaupt Tsing, *The Mushroom at the End of the World: On the Possibility of Life in Capitalist Ruins* (Princeton, NJ: Princeton University Press, 2015).

8. Morrison, *Beloved,* 16–17, repeated on 21.

9. Morrison, *Beloved,* 88.

10. Morrison, *Beloved,* 273.

11. Jacques Lacan, *The Ethics of Psychoanalysis: The Seminar of Jacques Lacan: Book VII,* trans. Denis Porter (New York: W. W. Norton, 1986), 60.

12. Taken from a lecture given by Anna Arabindan-Kesson at Princeton University, 2015. Arabindan-Kesson's work on Drew is part of her book manuscript "Black Bodies, White Gold: Art, Cotton and Commerce in the Atlantic World."

13. As Drew himself states, cotton is alive, a "material with memory. It has a history. It is not something that is picked up at random, it is something that has a life of its own." Quoted in Arabindan-Kesson, "Black Bodies, White Gold."

WORKS CITED

Abel, Elizabeth. *Female Subjects in Black and White.* Berkeley: University of California Press, 1997.

Abraham, Nicolas, and Maria Torok. *The Shell and the Kernel.* Trans. Nicholas T. Rand. Chicago: University of Chicago Press, 1994.

Adams, Carol J. *The Sexual Politics of Meat.* Cambridge: Polity Press, 1990.

Allewaert, Monique. *Ariel's Ecology: Plantations, Personhood, and Colonialism in the American Tropics, 1760–1820.* Minneapolis: University of Minnesota Press, 2013.

Altick, Richard. *The Shows of London.* Cambridge, MA.: Belknap Press of Harvard University Press, 1978.

Andersen, Hans Christian. *The Little Mermaid.* New York: Minedition, 2004.

Anderson, Jennifer. *Mahogany: The Costs of Luxury in Early America.* Cambridge, MA: Harvard University Press, 2012.

Anker, Elizabeth S., and Bernadette Meyler. *New Directions in Law and Literature.* New York: Oxford University Press, 2017.

Armstrong, Philip, and Laurence Simmons. "Bestiary: An Introduction." *Knowing Animals*, ed. Phillip Armstrong and Lawrence Simmons. Boston: Brill, 2007, 1–26.

Barrett, Walter. *The Old Merchants of New York City.* Vol. 1. New York: Thomas R. Knox, 1885.

Barthes, Roland. *Camera Lucida: Reflections on Photography.* Ed. by Richard Howard. New York: Hill and Wang, 2010.

Barthes, Roland. *Empire of Signs.* Trans. Richard Howard. New York: Hill and Wang, 1983.

Bauman, Zygmunt. *Liquid Modernity.* Cambridge, England: Polity Press, 2000.

Benjamin, Walter. "Gespräch mit Anne May Wong." *Die Literarische Welt*, July 6, 1928, 2. Trans. Seth Norm.

Benjamin, Walter. "The Work of Art in the Age of Mechanical Reproduction." *Illuminations*. Ed. Hannah Arendt. New York: Schocken Books, 1968, 217–251.

Bennett, Jane. *Vibrant Matter: A Political Ecology of Things*. Durham, NC: Duke University Press, 2010.

Bentley, Amy. "From Culinary Other to Mainstream American: Meanings and Uses of Southwestern Cuisine." *Culinary Tourism*, ed. Lucy M. Long. Lexington: University of Kentucky Press, 2004, 209–225.

Berg, Maxine. *Luxury and Pleasure in Eighteenth-Century Britain*. Oxford: Oxford University Press, 2005.

Bersani, Leo. "Psychoanalysis and the Aesthetic Subject." *Critical Inquiry* 32:2 (Winter 2006): 161–174.

Best, Stephen M. *The Fugitive's Properties: Law and the Poetics of Possession*. Chicago: University of Chicago Press, 2004.

Bhabha, Homi K. *The Location of Culture*. London: Routledge, 1994.

Biber, Katherine. *Captive Images: Race, Crime, Photography*. New York: Routledge, 2007.

Blackstone, William. *Commentaries on the Laws of England, 1765–79*, 15th ed. London: T. Caddell and W. Davies, 1765.

Bloch, Ernst. "The Fairy Tale Moves on Its Own Time." 1930. Reprinted in Jack Zipes. *Breaking the Magic Spell: Radical Theories of Folk and Fairy Tales*. Lexington: University of Kentucky Press, 2002, 150–153.

Bolton, Andrew. *China: Through the Looking Glass*. New York: Metropolitan Museum of Art, 2015.

Bondeson, Jan. *The Feejee Mermaid and Other Essays in Natural and Unnatural History*. Ithaca, NY: Cornell University Press, 1999.

Boorstin, Daniel. *The Image: A Guide to Pseudo-Events in America*. New York: Harper & Row, 1961.

Bose, Amar. "Personal Reflections." 6.312 Lecture 27, given at MIT, December 15, 1995. https://www.youtube.com/playlist?list=PLCFsLEtnWlNguvb2Hb9p5zHRErY 5VDE32.

Braudy, Leo. *The Frenzy of Renown: Fame and Its History*. New York: Oxford University Press, 1986.

Brillat-Savarin, Jean Anthelme. *The Physiology of Taste; or, Meditations on Transcendental Gastronomy*. Trans. M. F. K. Fisher. Washington, DC: Counterpoint, 1994.

Broderson, Momme. *Walter Benjamin: A Biography*. London: Verso, 1996.

Brown, Bill. *A Sense of Things: The Object Matter of American Literature*. Chicago: University of Chicago Press, 2003.

Brown, Jayna. *Babylon Girls: Black Women Performers and the Shaping of the Modern*. Durham, NC: Duke University Press, 2008.

Brown, Judith. *Glamour in Six Dimensions: Modernism and the Radiance of Form*. Ithaca, NY: Cornell University Press, 2009.

Brown, Kimberly Juanita. *The Repeating Body: Slavery's Visual Resonance in the Contemporary*. Durham, NC: Duke University Press, 2015.

Brown, Wendy. *States of Injury*. Princeton, NJ: Princeton University Press, 1995.

Bryant, Levi R. *Onto-cartography: An Ontology of Machines and Media*. Edinburgh: University of Edinburgh Press, 2014.

Bush, Christopher. "The Ethnicity of Things in America's Lacquered Age," *Representations* 99:1 (Summer 2007). 74–98.

Cannadine, David. *Ornamentalism: How the British Saw Their Empire.* New York: Oxford University Press, 2001.

Cavanaugh, Alden, and Michael E. Yonan. *The Cultural Aesthetic of Eighteenth-Century Porcelain.*, Farnham, England: Ashgate, 2010.

Chan, Anthony B. *Perpetually Cool: The Many Lives of Anna May Wong (1905–1961).* Lanham, MD: Scarecrow, 2007.

Chan, Sucheng. "The Exclusion of Chinese Women, 1870–1943." *Entry Denied.* Ed. Sucheng Chan. Philadelphia: Temple University Press, 1991, 94–146.

Chang, Gordon H. *Fateful Ties: A History of America's Preoccupation with China.* Cambridge, MA: Harvard University Press, 2015.

Chaudhuri, Maitreye. *Feminism in India.* Chicago: University of Chicago Press, 2005.

Chen, Mel Y. *Animacies: Biopolitics, Racial Mattering, and Queer Affect.* Durham, NC: Duke University Press, 2012.

Cheng, Anne Anlin. "Law and Ornament." *New Directions in Law and Literature*, ed. Elizabeth S. Anker and Bernadette Meyler. New York: Oxford University Press, 2017, 229–251.

Cheng, Anne Anlin. *The Melancholy of Race: Psychoanalysis, Assimilation, and Hidden Grief.* New York: Oxford University Press, 2000.

Cheng, Anne Anlin. "Passing, Natural Selection, and Love's Failure: Ethics of Survival From Chang-rae Lee to Jacques Lacan." *American Literary History* 17.3 (2005), 553–574.

Cheng, Anne Anlin. *Second Skin: Josephine Baker and the Modern Surface.* New York: Oxford University Press, 2011.

Chow, Rey. *Primitive Passions: Visuality, Sexuality, Ethnography, and Contemporary Chinese Cinema.* New York: Columbia University Press, 1995.

Chow, Rey. *Woman and Chinese Modernity: The Politics of Reading between West and East.* Minneapolis: University of Minnesota Press, 1991.

Chy Lung v. Freeman—92 U.S. 275 (1875). Transcript of Record, *The Making of Modern Law: U.S. Supreme Court Record and Briefs, 1823-1978,* Farmington Hills, MI: Gale, U.S. Supreme Court. October 26, 2011.

Clark, Kenneth. *The Nude: A Study in Ideal Form.* Princeton, NJ: Princeton University Press, 1972.

Christopher Clarey, "Atlanta: Day 3—Gymnastics; Miller Gives United States High Hopes for a Gold," *New York Times* (July 22, 1996).

Colomina, Beatriz, and Mark Wigley. *Are We Human? Notes on an Archaeology of Design.* Zurich: Lars Müller, 2017.

Connor, Steven. *The Book of Skin.* Ithaca, NY: Cornell University Press, 2003.

Cooper, James Fenimore. *The Last of the Mohicans.* Philadelphia: Carey & Lea, 1831.

Copjec, Joan. "The Sartorial Superego." *October* 50 (Autumn 1989): 56–95.

Cotter, Holland. "Review: In 'China: Through the Looking Glass,' Eastern Culture Meets Western Fashion." *New York Times*, Arts and Design section, May 7, 2015.

Davis, Nancy. "The Story of A'fong Moy: Selling Goods in Nineteenth Century America." *Global Trade and Visual Arts in Federal New England*, ed. Patricia Johnston and Caroline Frank. Durham, NH: University of New Hampshire Press, 2014, 134–154.

Davis, Theo. *Ornamental Aesthetics: The Poetry of Attending in Thoreau, Dickinson and Whitman.* New York: Oxford University Press, 2016.

De Condillac, E. B. Abbé. *Essay on the Origin of Human Knowledge.* Trans. Hans Aarsleff. Cambridge: Cambridge University Press, 2001.

Derrida, Jacques. "The Parergon." Trans. Craig Owens. *October* 9 (Summer 1979): 3–41.

Doane, Mary Ann. *Femmes Fatales: Feminism, Film Theory, Psychoanalysis*. New York: Routledge, 1991.

Dobie, Madeleine. *Trading Places: Colonization and Slavery in Eighteenth-Century French Culture*. Ithaca, NY: Cornell University Press, 2010.

Dong, Lorraine, and Philip P. Choy. *The Coming Man: 19th Century American Perceptions of the Chinese*. Seattle: University of Washington Press, 1995.

Drewal, Henry John. *Mami Wata: Arts for Water Spirits in Africa and Its Diasporas*. Los Angeles: Fowler Museum at UCLA. 2008.

Dyer, Richard. *White: Essays on Race and Culture*. New York: Routledge, 1997.

Enwezor, Okwui. *Archive Fever: Uses of the Document in Contemporary Art*. Göttingen, Germany: Steidl, 2009.

Ex Machina. Dir. Alex Garland. Film4 and DNA Films, 2014.

Eze, Emmanuel Chukwudi. *Race and the Enlightenment: A Reader*. London: Wiley-Blackwell, 1997.

Fanon, Frantz. *Black Skin, White Masks*. Trans. Charles L. Markmann. New York: Grove Weidenfeld, 1967.

Feeley-Harnik, Gillian. "The Ethnography of Creation: Lewis Henry Morgan and the American Beaver." *Relative Values: Reconfiguring Kinship Studies*, ed. Sarah Franklin and Susan McKinnon. Durham, NC: Duke University Press, 2001, 54–84.

Felski, Rita. *The Gender of Modernity*. Cambridge, MA: Harvard University Press, 1995.

Fend, Mechtild. "Bodily Pictorial Surfaces: Skin in French Art and Medicine, 1790–1860." *Art History* 28:3 (June 2005): 311–339.

Fleetwood, Nicole. *Troubling Vision: Performance, Visuality, and Blackness*. Chicago: University of Chicago Press, 2011.

Foster, Hal. "Postmodernism in Parallax." *October* 63 (Winter 1993): 3–20.

Freud, Sigmund. "Fetishism." *The Standard Edition of the Complete Psychological Works of Sigmund Freud*. Trans. James Strachey. Vol. 21. London: Hogarth, 1955, 149–158.

Freud, Sigmund. "Totem and Taboo." *The Standard Edition of the Complete Psychological Works of Sigmund Freud*. Trans. James Strachey. Vol. 13. London: Hogarth Press, 1975, 1–164.

Freud, Sigmund. "The Uncanny." *The Standard Edition of the Compete Psychological Works of Sigmund Freud*. Trans. James Strachey. Vol. 17. London: Hogarth Press, 1955, 217–256.

Galt, Rosalind. *Pretty: Film and the Decorative Image*. New York: Columbia University Press, 2011.

Gamson, Joshua. *Claims to Fame: Celebrity in Contemporary America*. Berkeley: University of California Press, 1994.

Garland, Alex. *Ex Machina*. Script. London: DNA Films, 2013.

Geczy, Adam. *Fashion and Orientalism: Dress, Textiles and Culture from the 17th to the 21st Century*. London: Bloomsbury Academic, 2013.

Genthe, Arnold. *As I Remember*. New York: Reynal & Hitchcock, 1936.

Genthe, Arnold. *Old Chinatown: A Book of Pictures by Arnold Genthe*. Text by Will Irwin. London: Sidgwick & Jackson, 1913.

Get Out. Dir. Jordan Peele. Universal. 2017.

Ghost in the Shell. Dir. Rupert Sanders. Paramount and DreamWorks. 2017.

Gombrich, E. H. *The Sense of Order: A Study in the Psychology of Decorative Art*. 2nd ed. New York: Phaidon Press, 1994.

Gumbs, Alexis Pauline. *Spill: Scenes of Black Feminist Fugitivity*. Durham, NC: Duke University Press, 2016.

Haddad, John. "The Chinese Lady and China for the Ladies: Race, Gender, and Public Exhibition in Jacksonian America." *Chinese America : History and Perspectives* (2011): 5–19.

Haddad, John. "Imagined Journeys to Distant Cathay: Constructing China with Ceramics, 1780–1920." *Winterthur Portfolio* 41:1 (2007): 53–80.

Hansen, Miriam. "Benjamin, Cinema, and Experience: The Blue Flower in the Land of Technology." *New German Critique* 40 (1987): 179–224.

Haraway, Donna. *Simians, Cyborgs, and Women: The Reinvention of Nature*. New York: Routledge, 1991.

Hass, Robert. "Against Botticelli." *Praise*. New York: Ecco Press, 1999, 10–12.

Hay, Jonathan. *Sensuous Surfaces: The Decorative Object in Early Modern China*. Honolulu: University of Hawaii Press, 2010.

Hayot, Eric. *The Hypothetical Mandarin: Sympathy, Modernity, and Chinese Pain*. New York: Oxford University Press, 2009, 15-86.

Heidegger, Martin. "The Origin of the Work of Art." *Poetry, Language, Thoughts*. Trans. Albert Hofstadter. New York: Harper, 1971, 15–86.

Hodges, Graham Russell Gao. *Anna May Wong: From Laudryman's Daughter to Hollywood Legend*. New York: Palgrave Macmillam, 2004.

Holland, Sharon Patricia. *The Erotic Life of Racism*. Durham, NC: Duke University Press, 2012.

Hyde, Alan. *Bodies of Law*. Princeton, NJ: Princeton University Press, 1997.

Issenberg, Sasha. *The Sushi Economy: Globalization and the Making of a Modern Delicacy*. New York: Gotham, 2008.

Johnson, Barbara. *Persons and Things*. Cambridge, MA: Harvard University Press, 2008.

Johnson, Galen A. *The Merleau-Ponty Aesthetics Reader: Philosophy and Painting*. Chicago: Northwestern University Press, 1993.

Jullien, François. *The Impossible Nude*. Trans. Maev de la Guardia. Chicago: University of Chicago Press, 2007.

Kant, Immanuel. *The Critique of Judgment*. Trans. J. C. Meredith. New York: Oxford University Press, 1952.

Kennedy, Duncan. "The Structure of Blackstone's Commentaries." *Buffalo Law Review* 28: 2 (1979): 205–382.

Kim, Claire Jean. *Dangerous Crossings: Race, Species, and Nature in a Multicultural Age*. New York: Cambridge University Press, 2015.

Kim, James. "Petting Asian America." *MELUS: Multi-Ethnic Literature of the U.S.* 36:1 (Spring 2011): 135–155.

King, Homay. *Lost in Translation: Orientalism, Cinema, and the Enigmatic Signifier*. Durham, NC: Duke University Press, 2010.

Kracauer, Siegfried. "The Mass Ornament." *The Mass Ornament: Weimar Essays*, trans. Thomas Y. Levin. Cambridge, MA: Harvard University Press, 1995, 75–88.

Kramer, Paul A. "The Case of the 22 Lewd Chinese Women." *Slate*. April 23, 2012. http://www.slate.com/articles/news_and_politics/jurisprudence/2012/04/arizona_s_immigration_law_at_the_supreme_court_lessons_for_s_b_1070_via_the_case_of_the_22_lewd_chinese_women.html.

Kramer, Paul A. "Imperial Opening: Civilization, Exemption, and the Geopolitics of Mobility in the History of Chinese Exclusion, 1868–1910." *Journal of the Gilded Age and Progressive Era* 14 (2015): 317–347.

Krauss, Rosalind. "Preying on Primitivism." *Art and Text* 17 (1985): 58–62.

Lacan, Jacques. *The Four Fundamental Concepts of Psychoanalysis*. Trans. Alan Sheridan. Book 11 of *The Seminar of Jacques Lacan*. New York: Norton, 1981

Lacan, Jacques. *The Ethics of Psychoanalysis: The Seminar of Jacques Lacan: Book VII*. Trans. Denis Porter. New York: W. W. Norton, 1986.

Lee, Josephine, Imogene L. Lim, and Matsukawa Yuko. *Re/collecting Early Asian America: Essays in Cultural History*. Philadelphia: Temple University Press, 2002.

Lee, Rachel C. *The Exquisite Corpse of Asian America: Biopolitics, Biosociality, and Posthuman Ecologies*. New York: New York University Press, 2014.

Levenson, Cyra, and Chi-ming Yang. "Haptic Blackness: The Double Life of an 18th-Century Bust." *British Art Studies* 1 (Autumn 2015). http://www.britishartstudies.ac.uk/issues/issue-index/issue-1/bust-of-a-man.

Lévi-Strauss, Claude. *The Raw and the Cooked: Mythologiques*, Vol. 1. Trans. John and Doreen Weightman. Chicago: University of Chicago Press, 1983.

Lim, Shirley Jennifer. "'Speaking German like Nobody's Business': Anna May Wong, Walter Benjamin, and the Possibilities of Asian American Cosmopolitanism." *Journal of Transnational American Studies* 4:1 (2012): 1–17. https://escholarship.org/uc/item/16v4g0b1.

Litvak, Joseph. *Strange Gourmets: Sophistication, Theory, and the Novel.* Durham, NC: Duke University Press, 1997.

Loos, Adolf. "Ornament and Crime." *The Architecture of Adolf Loos: An Arts Council Exhibition*, 100–103. London: Arts Council, 1985..

Lott, Eric. *Love and Theft: Blackface Minstrelsy and the American Working Class.* New York: Oxford University Press, 1995.

Louie, David Wong. "Bottles of Beaujolais." *Pangs of Love.* New York: Plume, 1992, 36–54.

Lowe, Lisa. *The Intimacies of Four Continents*. Durham, NC: Duke University Press, 2015.

Loy, Mina. "Brancusi's Golden Bird." *The Lost Lunar Baedeker*. New York: Farrar, 1997, 79.

Mahmood, Saba. "Feminist Theory, Embodiment, and the Docile Agent: Some Reflections on the Egyptian Islamic Revival." *Cultural Anthropology* 16 2 (2001): 202–236.

Maitland, Frederic W. "The Corporation Sole." (1900.) *The Collected Papers of Frederick William Maitland*, vol. 3, ed. H. A. L. Fisher. Cambridge: Cambridge University Press, 1911, 232–298.

Marshall, P. David. *The Celebrity Culture Reader*. New York: Routledge, 2006.

Marx, Karl. *A Critique of Political Economy*. Trans. Ben Fowkes. New York: Penguin, 1992. Vol. 1 of *Capital.* 1867–1894.

Mbembe, Achille. "Aesthetics of Superfluity." *Public Culture* 16:3 (2004). 373–405.

McClain, Charles J. *In Search of Equality: The Chinese Struggle against Discrimination in Nineteenth-Century America*. Berkeley: University of California Press, 1994.

Meikle, Jeffrey L. *American Plastics: A Cultural History*. New Brunswick, NJ: Rutgers University Press, 1997.

Mendis, Patrick, and Joey Wang. "Peace and War in Sino-America: Forget the Headlines and Follow the Trendlines for a Better World." *Harvard International Review* 38:4 (2017): 28–33.

Mnookin, Jennifer. "The Image of Truth: Photographic Evidence and the Power of Analogy." *Yale Journal of Law and Humanities* 10:1 (1998): 1–74.

Morgan, Lewis Henry. *The American Beaver and His Work.* Philadelphia: J. B. Lippincott, 1868.

Morgan, Lewis Henry. *Systems of Consanguinity and the Affinity of the Human Man.* Lincoln: University of Nebraska Press, 1997.

Morrison, Toni. *Beloved*. New York: Alfred A. Knopf, 1987.

Morrison, Toni. *Playing in the Dark: Whiteness and the Literary Imagination*. New York: Vintage Books, 1993.

Musser, Amber Jamilla. *Sensational Flesh: Race, Power, and Masochism*. New York: New York University Press, 2014.

Ngai, Mae M. *Impossible Subjects: Illegal Aliens and the Making of Modern America*. Princeton, NJ: Princeton University Press, 2004.

Ngai, Sianne. *Our Aesthetic Categories: Zany, Cute, Interesting*. Cambridge, MA: Harvard University Press, 2015.

Noonan, John T., Jr. *Persons and Masks of the Law: Cardozo, Holmes, Jefferson, and Wythe as Makers of the Masks*. Berkeley: University of California Press, 2002.

Papapetros, Spyros. "Aby Warburg as Reader of Gottfried Semper: Reflections on the Cosmic Character of Ornament." *Elective Affinities: Testing Word and Image Relationships*. Ed. Catriona MacLeod, Véronique Plesch, and Charlotte Schoelt-Glass. Amsterdam: Rodopi, 2009, 317–336.

Papapetros, Spyros. *On the Animation of the Inorganic: Art, Architecture, and the Extension of Life*. Chicago: University of Chicago Press, 2012.

Papapetros, Spyros. "An Ornamented Inventory of Microcosmic Shifts: Notes on Hans Hildebrandt's Book Project '*Der Schmuck*' (1936–1937)." *Getty Research Journal* 1 (2009): 38–46.

Pascoe, Peggy. "Miscegenation Law, Court Cases and Ideologies of Race in Twentieth Century America." *Journal of American History* 83:1 (June 1996): 44–69.

Pateman, Carole. *The Sexual Contract*. Stanford, CA: Stanford University Press, 1988.

Payne, Alina Alexandra. *From Ornament to Object: Genealogies of Architectural Modernism*. New Haven, CT: Yale University Press, 2012.

Pegler-Gordon, Anna. *In Sight of America: Photography and the Development of U.S. Immigration Policy*. Berkeley: University of California Press, 2009.

Phillips, Sandra S., et al., eds. *Police Pictures: The Photograph as Evidence*. San Francisco: Chronicle Books, 1997.

Phu, Thy. "Spectacles of Intimacy and the Aesthetics of Domestication." *Picturing Model Citizens*. Philadelphia: Temple University Press, 2014, 26–53.

Piccadilly. Dir. E. A. Dupont. Image Entertainment, 1929.

Plato. *Laws*. Trans. Tom Griffith. Cambridge: Cambridge University Press, 2016.

Plato. *The Republic*. Trans. Allan Bloom. New York: Basic Books, 2016.

Plumwood, Val. "Integrating Ethical Frameworks for Animals, Humans and Nature: A Critical Feminist Eco-socialist Analysis." *Ethics and the Environment* 5:2 (2000): 285–322.

Pocock, J. G. A. *The Machiavellian Moment: Florentine Political Thought and the Atlantic Republican Tradition*. Princeton, NJ: Princeton University Press, 2003.

Portrait in Black. Dir. Michael Gordon. Universal Studios, 1960.

"Professional Models Open War on Debutants Who Work Free…Spokesman for Fifty Determined Girls Says." *New York Times*, October 10, 1934.

Puar, Jasbir. "'I would rather be a cyborg than a goddess': Becoming-Intersectional in Assemblage Theory." *philoSOPHIA* 2:1 (2012): 49–66.

Roach, Joseph R. *It*. Ann Arbor: University of Michigan Press, 2007.

Roediger, David R. *The Wages of Whiteness: Race and the Making of the American Working Class*. New York: Verso, 2007.

Rogin, Michael. *Blackface, White Noise: Jewish Immigrants in the Hollywood Melting Pot*. Berkeley, University of California Press, 1998.

Rosetti, Dante Gabriel. "The Fine Art of the International Exhibition." *Fraser's Magazine for Town and Country* (August 1862): 188–199.

Rubin, William. *Primitivism in Twentieth-Century Art: Affinity of the Tribal and the Modern.* New York: Museum of Modern Art, 2002.

Said, Edward W. *Orientalism*. New York: Vintage Books, 1979.

Sarah C. Roberts v. The City of Boston, 59 Mass. (5 Cush.) 198 (1850).

Scarry, Elaine. *On Beauty and Being Just*. Princeton, NJ: Princeton University Press, 1999.

Schickel, Richard. *Intimate Strangers: The Culture of Celebrity*. Garden City, NY: Doubleday, 1985.

Schor, Naomi. *Reading in Detail: Aesthetics and the Feminine*. New York: Routledge, 2006.

Scott, Joan Wallach. *The Politics of the Veil.* Princeton, NJ: Princeton University Press, 2010.

Sedgewick, Eve Kosofsky. *Between Men: English Literature and Male Homosocial Desire*. New York: Columbia University Press, 1985.

Sekula, Allan. "The Body and the Archive." *October* 39 (Winter 1986): 3–64.

Semper, Gottfried. "Concerning the Formal Principles of Ornament and Its Significance as Artistic Symbol." *The Theory of Decorative Arts: An Anthology of European and American Writings, 1750–1940*. Ed. Isabelle Frank. Trans. David Britt. New Haven, CT: Yale University Press, 2000, 91–104.

Seshadri-Crooks, Kalpana. "Being Human: Bestiality, Anthropophagy, and Law." *Umbr(a): Ignorance of the Law 1* (2003): 97–114.

Seshadri, Kalpana Rahita. *HumAnimal: Race, Law, Language.* Minneapolis: University of Minnesota Press, 2012.

Slaughter, Joseph R. *Human Rights, Inc.: The World Novel, Narrative Form, and International Law*. New York: Fordham University Press, 2007.

Spillers, Hortense J. "Mama's Baby, Papa's Maybe: An American Grammar Book." *Diacritics* 17:2 (1987): 64–81. doi:10.2307/464747.

Stein, Rob. "Finally, A Map of All the Microbes in Your Body." NPR, June 13, 2012. http://www.npr.org/blogs/health/2012/06/13/154913334/finally-a-map-of-all-the-microbes-on-your-body.

Takaki, Ronald. *Strangers from a Different Shore: A History of Asian Americans.* New York: Little Brown, 1989.

Takao Ozawa v. U.S. No. 1. Supreme Court of the United States, 260 U.S. 178; 43 S. Ct. 65; 67 L. Ed. 199; 1922

Tchen, John Kuo Wei. *Genthe's Photographs of San Francisco's Old Chinatown.* New York: Dover, 1984.

Tchen, John Kuo Wei. *New York before Chinatown: Orientalism and the Shaping of American Culture, 1776–1882*. Baltimore: Johns Hopkins University Press, 1999.

Tchen, John Kuo Wei, and Dylan Yeats. *Yellow Peril! An Archive of Anti-Asian Fear*. New York: Verso Books, 2014.

Teng, Emma J. "Artifacts of a Lost City: Arnold Genthe's Pictures of Old Chinatown and Its Intertexts." *Re/collecting Early Asian America: Essays in Cultural History*, ed. Josephine Lee, Imogene L. Lim, and Yuko Matsukawa. Philadelphia: Temple University Press, 2002, 54–77.

Thackeray, William Makepeace. *Vanity Fair*. New York: Penguin Classics, 2003.

Thompson, Krista. "The Sound of Light: Reflections on Art History in the Visual Culture of Hip-Hop." *Art Bulletin* 91:4 (2009): 481–505.

Thoreau, Henry David. *Walden; or, Life in the Woods.* New York: Widler, 2008.

Tompkins, Kyla Wazana. *Racial Indigestion: Eating Bodies in the 19th Century*. New York: New York University Press, 2012.

Tsing, Anna Lowenhaupt. *The Mushroom at the End of the World: On the Possibility of Life in Capitalist Ruins*. Princeton, NJ: Princeton University Press, 2015.

Turner, Henry. *The Corporate Commonwealth: Pluralism and Political Fictions in England, 1516–1651*. Chicago: University of Chicago Press, 2016.

U.S v. Bhagat Singh Thind. No. 202. Supreme Court of the United States. 261 U.S. 204; 43 S. Ct. 338; 67 L. Ed. 616; 1923.

Valéry, Paul. "Some Simple Reflections on the Body." *Aesthetics*. Vol. 13 of *The Collected Works of Paul Valéry*. Trans. Ralph Mannheim. London: Bollingen Foundation, 1964, 31–40.

Visser, Margaret. *The Rituals of Dinner: The Origin, Evolution, Eccentricities, and Meaning of Table Manners.* New York: Penguin Books, 1991.

Vogel, Shane. *The Secret of Harlem Cabaret: Race, Sexuality, Performance*. Chicago: University of Chicago Press, 2009.

Watt, Gary. *Dress, Law and Naked Truth: A Cultural Study of Fashion and Form.* London: Bloomsbury Academy, 2013.

Wehelieye, Alex. *Habeas Viscus: Racializing Assemblages, Biopolitics, and Black Feminist Theories of the Human*. Durham, NC: Duke University Press, 2014.

Wharton, Edith. *House of Mirth*. New York: Penguin, 1993.

Whitman, Walt. *Leaves of Grass: Comprehensive Reader's Edition.* Ed. Harold W. Blodgett and Sculley Bradley. New York: New York University Press, 1965.

Wigley, Mark. *White Walls, Designer Dresses: The Fashioning of Modern Architecture*. Cambridge: MIT Press, 2001.

Williams, R. John. *The Buddha in the Machine: Art, Technology, and the Meeting of East and West.* New Haven, CT: Yale University Press, 2014.

Wind, Edgar. *Pagan Mysteries in the Renaissance*. New York: Norton, 1968.

Witte, Bernd. *Walter Benjamin: An Intellectual Biography*. Detroit: Wayne State University Press, 1991.

Wood, Jon. *Shine: Sculpture and Surface in the 1920s and 1930s*. Leeds, England: Henry Moore Institute, 2005.

Wood, Jon, David Hulks, and Alex Potts, eds. *Modern Sculpture Reader*. Leeds, England: Henry Moore Institute, 2007.

Yang, Chi-ming. "Culture in Miniature: Toy Dogs and Object Life." *Eighteenth-Century Fiction* 25:1 (Fall 2012): 139–174.

Yang, Chi-ming. *Performing China: Virtue, Commerce, and Orientalism in Eighteenth-Century England, 1660–1760*. Baltimore: Johns Hopkins University Press, 2011.

Yoshino, Kenji. *Covering: The Hidden Assault on Our Civil Rights*. New York: Random House, 2006.

Yuan, Elizabeth. "'22 Lewd Chinese Women' and Other Courtroom Dramas." *Atlantic* (September 4, 2013). https://www.theatlantic.com/national/archive/2013/09/22-lewd-chinese-women-and-other-courtroom-dramas/279288/.

INDEX

Abraham, Nicolas, 138
Afong Moy, 69
African Americans. *See* black female body; racialization of African Americans; racism; slavery
"Against Botticelli" (Hass), 118, 126
Allewaert, Monique, 41, 153–154
Amendments to the Political Code of the State of California, 164n.3
American Beaver and His Work, The (Morgan), 181n.43
Andersen, Hans Christian, 119–121
animacy, 149, 180n.35
animalization of raced subjects, 2–3, 113, 172n.4. *See also* primitivism; racism
animal studies, 107–126, 182n.50
anthropomorphism, 86–106, 122–123. *See also* zoomorphism
anti-Asian sentiment, 164n.3, 166nn. 11–12, 170n.53, 170n.56, 27–60, 178n.19. *See also* racism
anti-Chinese sentiment. *See* anti-Asian sentiment
appropriation, 86–106, 130–131, 148. *See also* racism
Arabindan-Kesson, Anna, 156–157
Ariel's Ecology (Allewaert), 153–154
Armstrong, Philip, 122
artificial personhood. *See* synthetic personhood
Asbæk, Pilou, 136
Asian American fiction, 109–126
Asian femininity, 170n.56
  celebrity and, 172nn. 8–9, 173n.12, 173nn. 14–15, 61–85
  consumption and, 117–126
  embodied objects and, 86–106, 176n.18
  legal personhood and, 27–60, 165n.8, 166n.11, 168n.26, 168n.22, 169n.38, 169n.33, 170n.56
  synthetic personhood and, 127–151, 183n.13
  technology and, 128–129
  yellowness, x–xi, 4–15
Asian masculinity, 133–135, 141
At the Corner of Dupont and Jackson Street (Genthe), 52

Bachelor Societies, 166n.11, 170n.51
Baker, Josephine, 64–67, 84, 175n.35
Barthes, Roland, 37, 77–78, 89–90, 174n.24
Bauman, Zygmunt, 40
Beecroft, Vanessa, 179n.34

Beijing Memory No. 5 (Li), 99–105
"Being Human" (Seshadri-Crooks), 124–125
Beloved (Morrison), 153–157
Benjamin, Walter, 62, 102–103, 172n.5
Bennet, Jane, 142–143, 182n.5
Bentley, Amy, 111–112
Bersani, Leo, 174n.24
Bertolucci, Bernardo, 90, 173n.9
Best, Stephen, 41
Big Sleep, The (film), 90
Binoche, Juliette, 133–135
biological personhood, 3, 27, 35, 37–42, 109–110. *See also* personhood
Birth of Venus (Botticelli), 81–84, 118–119
black female body, 4–7, 65, 143–144, 152–157, 160n.11, 160n.4, 161n.13. *See also* racism
black feminism, 6–7, 152–157, 160n.4
black objecthood, 137–141, 143–144. *See also* slavery
Blackstone, William, 41, 99
Blade Runner (film), 130–131
Bloch, Ernst, 150–151
body. *See* black female; body; consumption of racialized minorities
Boorstin, Daniel, 84, 171n.3
Bose, Amar, 102–103
Botticelli, Sandro, 81–84, 118–119, 179n.34
"Bottles of Beaujolais" (Louie), 109–126, 180n.35, 182n.50
Brâncusi, Constantin, 77–78
Braudy, Leo, 171n.3
Brillat-Savarin, Jean Anthelme, 108, 111, 115–116, 124
Broken Blossoms (film), 90
Brown, Bill, 98
Brown, Jayna, ix–x
Brown, Kimberly Juaita, ix–x
Brown, Judith, 75, 174n.23
Brown v. Board of Education, 140
Bryant, Levi R., 130
Buddha in the Machine (Williams), 127–128
Burlingame Treaty, 1868, 30, 45
Bush, Christopher, 129

California Passenger Tax Act, 164n.3
California State Political Codes, 30
Camera Craft (Genthe), 170n.49
Cameron, Donaldina, 56, 171n.60
Campbell, Thomas P., 90
Caravaggio, Michelangelo Merisi da, 174n.24
Case of the Twenty-two Lewd Chinese Women, 164nn. 2–4, 165n.8, 166nn. 11–12, 168n.22, 169n.33, 170nn. 54–55, 27–46, 47–50
Cavalli, Robert, 88, 92, 96
celebrity, 171n.3, 172nn. 8–9, 173nn. 12–16, 175n.30, 175n.35, 61–85
cellophane glamour, 75–77, 174n.23
ceramics, 92–96, 99–105, 128–129, 176n.18, 176n.12
  tea cups and things, 19, 92–94, 138. *See also* embodied objects
Ceramic Woman (Li), 99–105
Chang, Gordon, 92–93
Chen, Mel Y., 149, 180n.35
Chin, Denny, 164nn. 1–2
China (exhibition), 175nn. 1–2, 86–106
Chinatown, 168n.26, 170nn. 49–51, 46–60
Chinese. *See* Asian femininity; ornamentalism
Chinese detail, 99–101, 103
Chinese Exclusion Act, 31, 42, 165n.4, 166n.12, 170n.53
Chinese immigration, 164nn. 3–4, 166nn. 11–12, 167n.17, 170n.53, 27–60
Chinese language, 103–104, 177n.29
Chinese Police Tax, 31–32
Chow, Rey, 99–101
Chu Chin Chow (film), 67
Chy Lung, 30–31
Chy Lung v. Freeman, 164nn. 2–4, 165n.8, 166n.11, 167n.13, 168n.22, 169n.33, 170nn. 54–55, 27–46, 47–50
cinema, 171n.3, 172nn. 8–9, 173nn. 12–16, 175n.30, 175n.35, 61–85
citizenship. *See* legal personhood
civil rights. *See* legal personhood
Clark, Kenneth, 140–141, 149, 179n.34
Clark, Mamie, 140–141, 149
clothing. *See* legal cloth
Colomina, Beatriz, 131–133
commodification: of Asian women, 20–22, 40, 53–56, 64–106, 160n.4, 164n.3
  of black bodies, 4, 41, 98–99, 152–157, 161n.13, 173n.18. *See also* ornamentalism
"Concerning the Formal Principles of Ornament and Its Significance As Artistic Symbol" (Semper), 79–80
Condit, Ira M., 33
constructed evidence, 35–37

consumption of racialized minorities, 43–44, 107–126, 178n.19
Cooper, James Fenimore, 103–104
Corporate Zen, 127–128
Covering (Yoshino), 42–44
criminalization of people of color, 164n.3, 166nn. 11–12, 167n.17, 169n.31, 169n.38, 170n.53, 27–60, 94. *See also* racism
Crouching Tiger, Hidden Dragon (film), 90
curios, 102–103, 177n.29, 177n.24
Curse of the Golden Flower (film), 90
cyborgs, 182n.5, 183n.13, 184nn. 26–27, 127–151

Dangerous Crossings (Kim), 178n.6
Daughter of the Dragon (film), 67
Derrida, Jacques, 103–104, 171n.2
Descartes, René, 99
desegregation, 38, 140, 168n.28
"Devil's Kitchen, The" (Genthe), 50
Dietrich, Marlene, 75, 173n.14
dolls. *See* cyborgs
Dress, Law, and Naked Truth (Watt), 38–39
Dressed for a Feast (Genthe), 56
Drew, Leonardo, 156–157, 185n.13
Dupont, E. A., 66–67
Dyer, Richard, 75, 171n.3

East-West opposition, 176n.9, 177n.29
Eisenstaedt, Alfred, 66
Ellison, Ralph, 140
embodied objects, 176n.18, 177nn. 28–29, 86–106, 145
enchanted materialism, 128–129, 182n.5
Enlightenment, 37, 41, 99, 109–110. *See also* modernism
epidermal schema, 1, 36, 74–75, 94–96, 131–135
erasure of minority personhood, 4–6, 35, 40, 62–64, 85, 104. *See also* racism
ergon, 62, 171n.2
Ethics of Psychoanalysis, The (Lacan), 155–156
Ethnic detail. *See* Chinese detail
Ex Machina (film), 184nn. 26–27, 130–131, 141–151
Ex Parte Ah Fook, 30
Exquisite Corpse of Asian America, The (Lee), 135

fabricated personhood, 173nn. 12–16, 173n.18, 174n.25, 175n.35, 61–85
Faces at the Gates (exhibition), 170n.53
Fanon, Frantz, 1, 74
Feeley-Harnik, Gillian, 123, 181n.43
Felski, Rita, 91–92
feminism: black, 6–7, 152–157, 160n.4
  ornamentalism and, 1–2, 14, 17, 19, 43, 98–99. *See also* ornamentalism
Fend, Mechthild, 92–93
Fenollosa, Ernest, 103–104
fetishism, 64, 66–74, 89–91, 98, 139, 142–151, 183n.13. *See also* racism
"Fetishism" (Freud), 69
Field, Stephen, 30–31
Fiji Mermaid, 180n.37
Fisher, M. F. K., 116
flesh. *See* black female body; consumption of racialized minorities; flesh-meat conflation
flesh-meat conflation, 107–126, 179n.25, 179n.22
Flügel, J. C. 16
food studies, 107–126
Ford, Tom, 88
Foreign Miners' Tax, 31–32
Foster, Hal, 89–90
Foucault, Michel, 98–99
Freeman, John, 30, 45
Freud, Sigmund, 69, 82–84, 105, 124–125, 129–130, 138
Friends (Genthe), 56

Galliano, John, 88
"Gamblers' Street" (Genthe), 50
Gamson, Joshua, 171n.3
Garland, Alex, 141, 148, 184n.27
gaze: celebrity and, 67–70, 75, 174n.24
  commodified objects and, 20
  white male, 4, 52–57, 170n.56
Geary Act. *See* Chinese Exclusion Act
Geczy, Adam, 91
gender
  black body, 4–7, 65, 143–144, 152–157, 160n.11, 160n.4, 161n.13
  celebrity and, 61–85, 171n.3, 173n.12, 173n.9, 175n.35
  consumption and, 107–126
  embodied objecthood and, 86–106, 177n.28
  legal personhood and, 27–60, 165n.8, 166n.11, 168n.22, 169n.38
  ornamentalism and, 1–25, 161n.17, 163n.29, 163n.22
  synthetic personhood and, 183n.13, 184nn. 26–27, 127–151

Genthe, Arnold, 170nn. 49–50, 170n.56, 171n.60, 46–60
Genthe's Photographs of San Francisco's Old Chinatown (Tchen), 53, 170n.49
Get Out (film), 137–141, 150–151
ghost. *See* spectrality
Ghost in the Shell (Sanders), 130–141
Ghost in the Shell (Shirow), 130
Gibson, Otis, 32–34, 167n.13
Gish, Lillian, 75
Glamour in Six Dimensions (Brown), 75
Gleeson, Domhnall, 142
Goffman, Erving, 139
Gray, Gilda, 71, 172n.8
Guernica (Picasso), 64–65

habeas corpus, 27–46, 165n.4, 165n.8, 169n.38. *See also* legal personhood
Hansel and Gretel, 150–151
Harlow, Jean, 75
Hass, Robert, 118, 125–126
Hayot, Eric, 96, 133–135, 144
Heidegger, Martin, 77–78, 127–128, 174n.24
Her (film), 149–150
Hero (film), 90
Hesiod, 82–84
Hirata, Kathy, 164n.2
Hobbes, Thomas, 41, 99
Holland, Sharon Patricia, ix–x
Hoppé, E. O., 66
Horne, Lena, 84, 175n.35
Huáng Liushuang. *See* Wong, Anna May
human kinship systems, 123–125, 181n.43, 184n.26
Hurrell, George, 66

immigration policy, 27–60, 94, 164n.3, 166n.12, 167n.17, 169n.31, 170n.53
imperialism, 78–82, 119–121, 133–135, 156–157, 180n.37
In re Ah Fong, 30–31
In the Mood for Love (film), 90
Irwin, Will, 170n.49
Isaac, Oscar, 142
It (Roach), 64, 75–77

Jacobi, Lotte, 66
Johansson, Scarlett, 130–131, 135–136
Johnson-Reed Act, 41–42

Kaluuya, Daniel, 138
Kant, Immanuel, 171n.2
Keener, Catherine, 138
Kim, Byron, 133
Kim, Claire Jean, 178n.6
kinship systems, 123–125, 181n.43, 184n.26
Knowing Animals (Armstrong, Simmons), 122
Kracauer, Siegfried, 14–15
Kramer, Paul A., 30, 40–41, 167n.17
Krauss, Rosalind, 174n.25
Kwan, Nancy, 96, 176n.18

Lacan, Jacques, 77–78, 155–156, 174n.24
Last Emperor, The (film), 90, 173n.9
Last of the Mohicans, The (Cooper), 103–104
Laurent, Yves Saint, 88
Le Déjeuner sur l'herbe (Manet), 111
Lee, Ang, 90
Lee, Rachel, 135, 183n.14
Lee, Robert, 90
legal personhood, 164nn. 2–4, 165n.8, 166nn. 11–12, 169nn. 31–32, 169n.38, 170n.56, 27–60
Levenson, Cyra, 128–129
Lévi-Strauss, Claude, 108–109
Little Mermaid, The (Andersen), 119–121
Little Tea Rose (Genthe), 57
Litvak, Joseph, 112
Li Xiaofeng, 99–105, 177n.21
Locke, John, 41, 99
Loos, Adolf, 14–15
Lott, Eric, 113
Louie, David Wong, 109–126, 180n.35, 182n.50
Lowe, Lisa, 133–135
Loy, Mina, 77–78
Lucy (film), 149–150
Lung, Ah, 165n.4

Maitland, Frederic William, 35
"Mama's Baby, Papa's Maybe" (Spillers), 183n.16
ManetÉdouard, 111
Marx, Karl, 69
Mata Hari, 69
material violence, 152–156
Mayfair Mannequin Society of New York, 84, 175n.32
McQueen, Alexander, 88, 92, 94–96
meat-flesh conflation, 107–126, 179n.25, 179n.22
Meikle, Jeffrey, 75

Mein Film (film), 175n.33
Merchant of Venice, The (Shakespeare), 167n.18
Merleau-Ponty, Maurice, 174n.24
mermaid figure, 179n.34, 180nn. 36–37, 117–126
Metropolitan Museum of Art (MMA), 175nn. 1–2, 86–106
Michelson, Miriam, 171n.60
Miller, Samuel, 40–41
Minton, Thomas, 92
Mnookin, Jennifer L., 36–37
modernism: celebrity and, 61–85, 172n.5
consumption and, 108–114, 178n.15, 179n.34
embodied objects and, 86–106
personhood and, 2–4, 14–16, 21–25, 27–46, 99, 105, 161n.17, 163n.22, 171n.3
synthetic personhood and, 127–151
modernity. *See* modernism
Monroe, Marilyn, 75
monster in black objecthood, 137–141
Montesquieu, 99
Moore, Henry, 77–78
Morgan, Lewis Henry, 123, 181n.43
Morrison, Robert F., 30, 168n.22, 169n.33
Morrison, Toni, 153–156
Musser, Amber Jamilla, ix–x

Native Americans, 103–104, 181n.43
natural personhood. *See* Western personhood
new materialism, x–xi, 19
New Yorker, 175n.32
New York Times, 90, 94, 175n.32
Ngai, Mae M., 41–42, 169n.31
Ngai, Sianne, 144

objecthood. *See* black objecthood; ornamentalism; slavery
Old Chinatown (Genthe), 170n.49
On Beauty and Being Just (Scarry), 64
one-sixteenth blood rule, 34
Onto-cartography (Bryant), 130
Opium Fiend, The (Genthe), 50, 53
Oral Torah, the, 179n.22
Orientalism: celebrity and, 65–69, 71, 78–82
East-West divide and, 176n.9
embodied objects and, 86–106
excess and despotism of, 15–17
legal personhood and, 1–25, 27–28, 40–45, 60, 156
synthetic personhood and, 127–151. *See also* ornamentalism
Orientalism (Said), 176n.9
"Origin of the Work of Art, The" (Heidegger), 174n.24
ornament, 14–17
ornamentalism: black body and, 152–156, 160n.11, 161n.13
celebrity and, 61–85, 173n.18
consumption and, 107–126, 179n.25, 180n.37
embodied objects and, 176n.12, 176n.18, 177n.24, 177nn. 28–29, 86–106
legal personhood and, 27–60, 165n.8, 167n.18, 168n.22, 169n.31
process of, 167n.18, 160n.4, 161n.17, 162nn. 19–24, 163n.29, 164n.31, 1–25
synthetic personhood and, 127–151, 183n.13
othering: African Americans and, 31, 152–157, 160n.11, 168n.28, 169n.31, 172n.4, 173n.18
celebrity and, 61–85, 173n.12, 173n.9
consumption and, 112–126, 178n.19, 180n.37, 182n.48
embodied objects and, 86–106
legal personhood and, 164n.3, 166nn. 11–12, 167n.18, 168n.28, 169n.31, 170n.53, 170n.56, 27–60
orientalism and, 176n.9, 177n.29
ornamentalism and, 161n.12, 162nn. 19–20, 163n.22, 1–25
synthetic personhood and, 127–151, 183n.16, 183n.13
Oxford English Dictionary, 170n.56, 177n.24, 177n.29
Ozawa, Takao, 39
Ozawa v. US, 39

Page, Horace, 31
Page Act, 31
Pangs of Love (Louie), 110
Papapetros, Spyros, 81, 129–130
parerga, 62, 171n.2
Passenger Tax Act, 164n.3
Peele, Jordan, 137–138, 140
Pegler-Gordon, Anna, 47–49
Pensive Mechanical Bodhisattva/Kwanon_Z (Wang), 127–128
People v. Downer, 164n.3
perihumanity of Asian femininity, 2–3, 18, 105. *See also* ornamentalism

personhood: African Americans and, 152–157, 160n.11, 161n.13, 168n.28, 169n.31, 172n.4
consumption and, 107–126, 178n.19
embodied objects and, 86–106, 176n.18, 177n.28
fabricated, 173nn. 12–16, 173n.18, 174n.25, 175n.35, 61–85
legal, 164nn. 2–4, 165n.8, 166nn. 11–12, 169nn. 31–32, 169n.38, 170n.56, 27–60
ornamentalism and, 1–25, 161n.17, 163n.29, 164n.31
synthetic, 127–151, 182n.5, 183n.13, 184n.26
Western, 2–4, 14–16, 21–25, 27–46, 99, 105, 128–129
Peters, John T., 170n.55
photography
as court evidence, 15–17
as forensics, 48–50
of Chinatown, 46–60, 168n.26, 170n.49, 170n.56
Phu, Thy, 50–52
Physiology of Taste, The (Brillat-Savarin), 115–116
Picasso, Pablo, 64–65
Piccadilly (film), 66–85, 172n.8, 173n.12, 175n.30
Picturing Model Citizens (Phu), 50–52
Piotrowski, Rudolph, 28–30, 40–41, 164n.3, 169n.33
plastic, 75, 93–94, 131–135, 179n.25. *See also* embodied objects
Plato, 82–84, 167n.18
Plessy, Homer, 169n.31
Plessy v. Ferguson, 38, 168n.28, 169n.31
Poiret, Paul, 88
porcelain, 92–96, 99–105, 128–129, 176n.18, 176n.12. *See also* embodied objects
posthuman, 24–25, 106, 122–123, 129, 131, 135
Also see synthetic personhood
postmodernism, 86–106
Pride and Prejudice (Austen), 177n.28
primitivism, 4–7, 65, 69, 80, 112, 156, 172n.4, 174n.25. *See also* racism
"Professional Models Open War on Debutantes Who Do Work Free" (article), 175n.32
Progressive Era, 31
Proposition, 187 40–41
prostitution, 30, 32–33, 37, 57–60, 164n.3, 166n.11, 170n.56
Proust, Marcel, 77–78, 174n.24
Puar, Jasbir, x
queering of personhood, 43–44, 107–126, 178n.19
Quint, Leander, 30, 165n.4

race. *See* racialization of African Americans
racialized personhood
racism
race-making. *See* racialization of African Americans
racialized personhood
racial appropriation, 86–106, 130–131, 148
Racial Indigestion (Tompkins), 108
racialization of African Americans, 1–7, 34, 41–42, 65, 113, 137–144, 152–157, 160n.11, 161n.17, 161n.13, 169n.31, 172n.4, 173n.18. *See also* racialized personhood; racism
racialized personhood: black body and, 152–156, 160n.11, 161n.13, 161n.17, 168n.28, 169n.31, 172n.4
celebrity and, 61–85, 173n.18, 173n.12, 174n.25
consumption and, 107–126, 179n.25, 180n.37
embodied objects and, 86–106, 176n.18, 176n.12, 177n.29, 177n.24
legal personhood and, 27–60, 165n.8, 167n.18, 168n.22, 169n.31, 170n.56
process of, 167n.18, 178n.19, 161n.17, 162nn. 19–24, 163n.29, 164n.31, 1–25
synthetic personhood and, 127–151, 183n.13. *See also* racialization of African Americans
racial passing, 34, 137–141, 169n.31
racism, 15
African Americans and, 2–7, 41–42, 65, 113, 137–144, 152–157, 160n.11, 161n.13, 168n.28, 169n.31, 172n.4, 173n.18
appropriation and, 86–106
celebrity and, 171n.3, 173n.9, 173nn. 14–15, 61–85
consumption and, 107–126
immigration policy and, 164n.3, 166nn. 11–12, 169n.31, 170n.53, 27–60, 94. *See also* Orientalism; racialization of African Americans; racialized personhood
Republic, The (Plato), 82–84
Roach, Joseph, 64, 75–77
Roberts, Benjamin F., 168n.28
Roberts, Sarah, 168n.28
Roberts v. The City of Boston, 38–39, 41–42, 168n.28
Roediger, David, 178n.19

Rogin, Michael, 178n.19
Rubin, William, 174n.25

Said, Edward, 90, 98–99, 176n.9
Sanders, Rupert, 130, 135–136
sartorial personhood, 173nn. 12–16, 173n.18, 174n.25, 175n.35, 61–85
Scarry, Elaine, 64
Schickel, Richard, 171n.3
Schor, Naomi, 15–16
science fiction, 129–151, 183n.11
Sea Lady, The (Wells), 180n.37
Second Skin (Cheng), 65
self-fashioning, 40, 42–45, 173nn. 13–16, 174n.25, 61–85, 146–151, 19
Semper, Gottfried, 79–81
separate but equal doctrine, 38, 168n.28
Seshadri-Crooks, Kalpana, 124–125
Shakespeare, William, 167n.18
Shanghai Express (film), 75, 173n.14
Shaw, Lemuel, 38, 168n.28
Shell and the Kernel, The (Abraham, Torok), 138
shine, 173n.18, 174nn. 23–24, 66–82. *See also* celebrity
Shirow, Masamune, 130
skin, 17
  as ceramic, 96
  as primitive flesh, 112
  as fabric, 6–7
  as sashimi, 118–119
  nude versus naked, 119, n.35
Simmons, Laurence, 122
Slave Girl in Holiday Attire A (Genthe), 57–60
slavery, 4, 41, 98–99, 152–157, 161n.13. *See also* black objecthood; racialization of African Americans
"Sound of Light, The" (Thompson), 79
spectrality of the Asian female body, 34–37, 40, 92–96, 105, 145, 168n.26. *See also* Asian femininity
Spillers, Hortense J., 60, 152, 156, 183n.16
Steichen, Edward, 66
Stiegler, Bernard, 131–133
Stoler, Ann Laura, 98–99
subjecthood. *See* personhood
subjective agency, 43–45
sumptuary laws, 34
sushi principle, 107–126, 179n.25, 179n.22
Swanson, Gloria, 75
Synecdoche (Kim), 133
synthetic personhood, 182n.5, 183n.13, 184nn. 26–27, 127–151
Systems of Consanguinity and the Affinity of the Human Man (Morgan), 181n.43

Tarquin and Lucretia (Titian), 64–65
Tchen, John Kuo Wei, 53, 170n.49
technology. *See* cinema; synthetic personhood
Thind, Bhagat Singh, 39
thingness. *See* ornamentalism
Thompson, Krista, 79–81
Thoreau, Henry David, 112–113, 116, 178n.15, 179n.34
Three Women on Kearney Street, 53–56
Titial Vicellio, 64–65
Tompkins, Kyla Wazana, 108, 111–113, 115–116
Tong, Minnie, 56–57
Torah, the, 179n.22
Torok, Maria, 138
2046 (film), 90

Unsuspecting Victim, An (Genthe), 53
Untitled #25 (Drew), 156–157
U.S. v. Thind, 39

Valéry, Paul, 60
Van Vechten, Carl, 66
Vibrant Matter (Bennet), 142–143, 182n.5
Vikander, Alicia, 142
violence: aesthetics and, 19–20, 45, 64–65, 94
  against the black body, 4, 41, 98–99, 137–144, 152–157, 160n.4, 161n.13
  consumption and, 114–116, 121–122, 124–125
Visser, Margaret, 111, 123
visuality. *See* ornamentalism
Vogel, Shane, 175n.35

Walden (Thoreau), 112–113
Wang Zi Won, 127–128
Watt, Gary, 38–39
Wave, The (Genthe), 170n.49
Weheliye, Alex, ix–x
Wells, H. G., 180n.37
Western personhood, 2–4, 14–16, 21–25, 27–46, 99, 105, 128–129. *See also* modernism
Western philosophy. *See* Enlightenment; modernism

whiteface, 130–137
white femininity, 75, 118
whiteness, 108, 111–113, 117, 148, 178n.19
whitewashing, 130–137
Wigley, Mark, 131–133
Williams, R. John, 127–128
Wind, Edgar, 82–84
WOC (Women of Color), x
Wong, Anna May, 172n.8, 173nn. 12–14, 174n.25, 175nn. 32–33, 175n.35, 61–85, 117
Wong Kar-wai, 90
Woodruff, Delos, 170nn. 54–55, 33, 49–50
"Work of Art in the Age of Mechanical Reproduction, The" (Benjamin), 172n.5
Yang, Chi-ming, 92–93, 128–129
Yasuhiko Oyama, 140–141
yellow fever, 143–144
yellow journalism, 173n.18
Yellow Journalist, A (Michelson), 171n.60
Yellow Peril, 173n.18
yellow slave trade, 166n.11
yellow woman. *See* Asian femininity
Yoshino, Kenji, 42–45, 139

Zhang Yimou, 90
zoomorphism, 122–123. *See also* anthropomorphism

ORNAMENTALISM

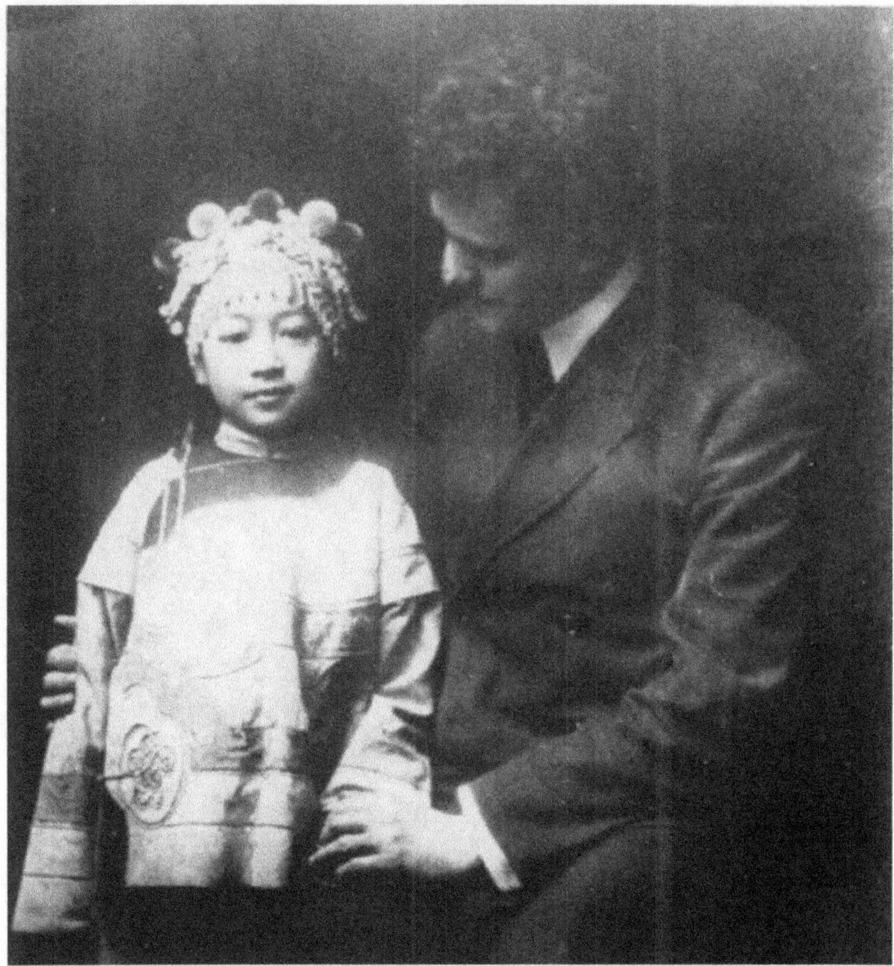

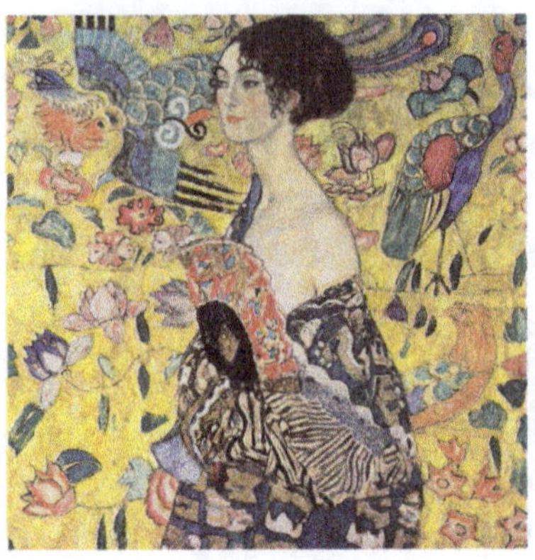

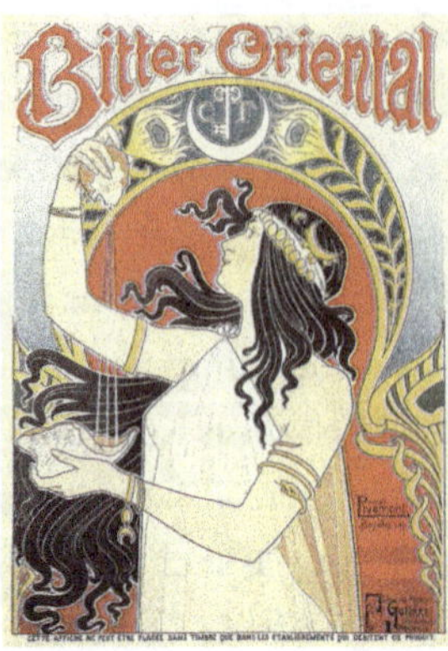

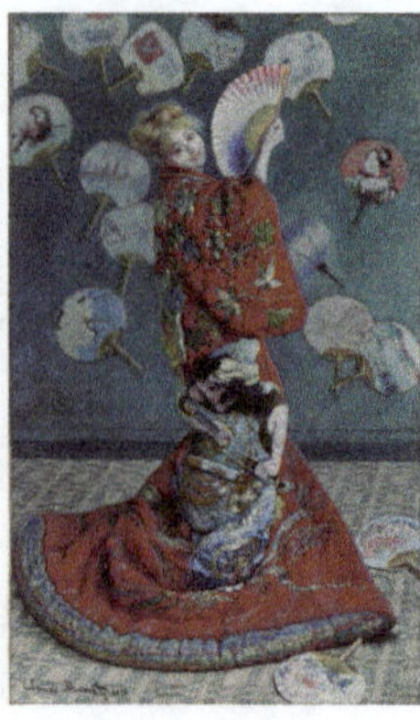

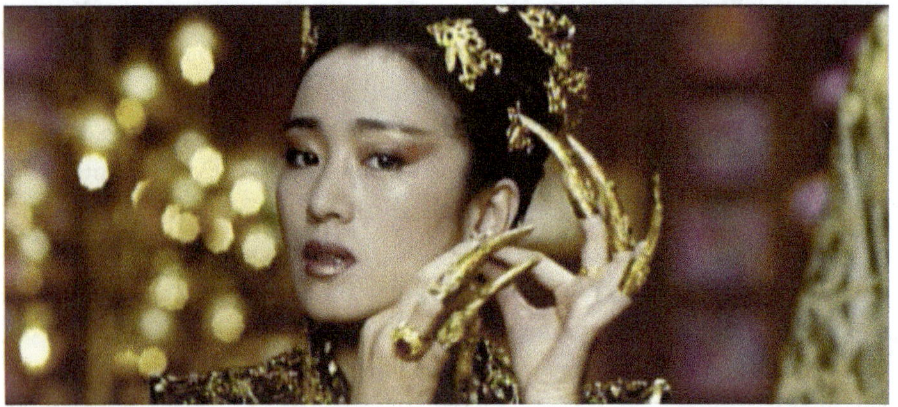

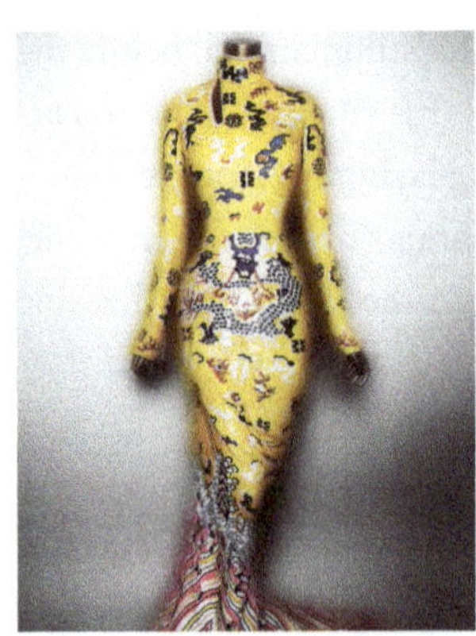

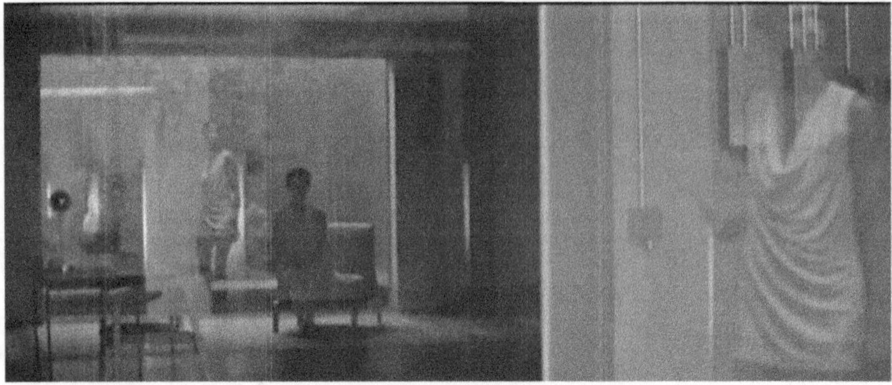

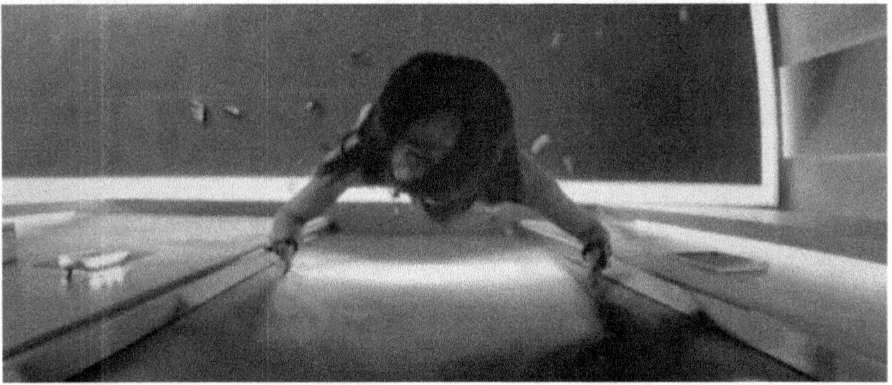

ORNAMENTALISM

Ornamentalism

Anne Anlin Cheng

OXFORD
UNIVERSITY PRESS

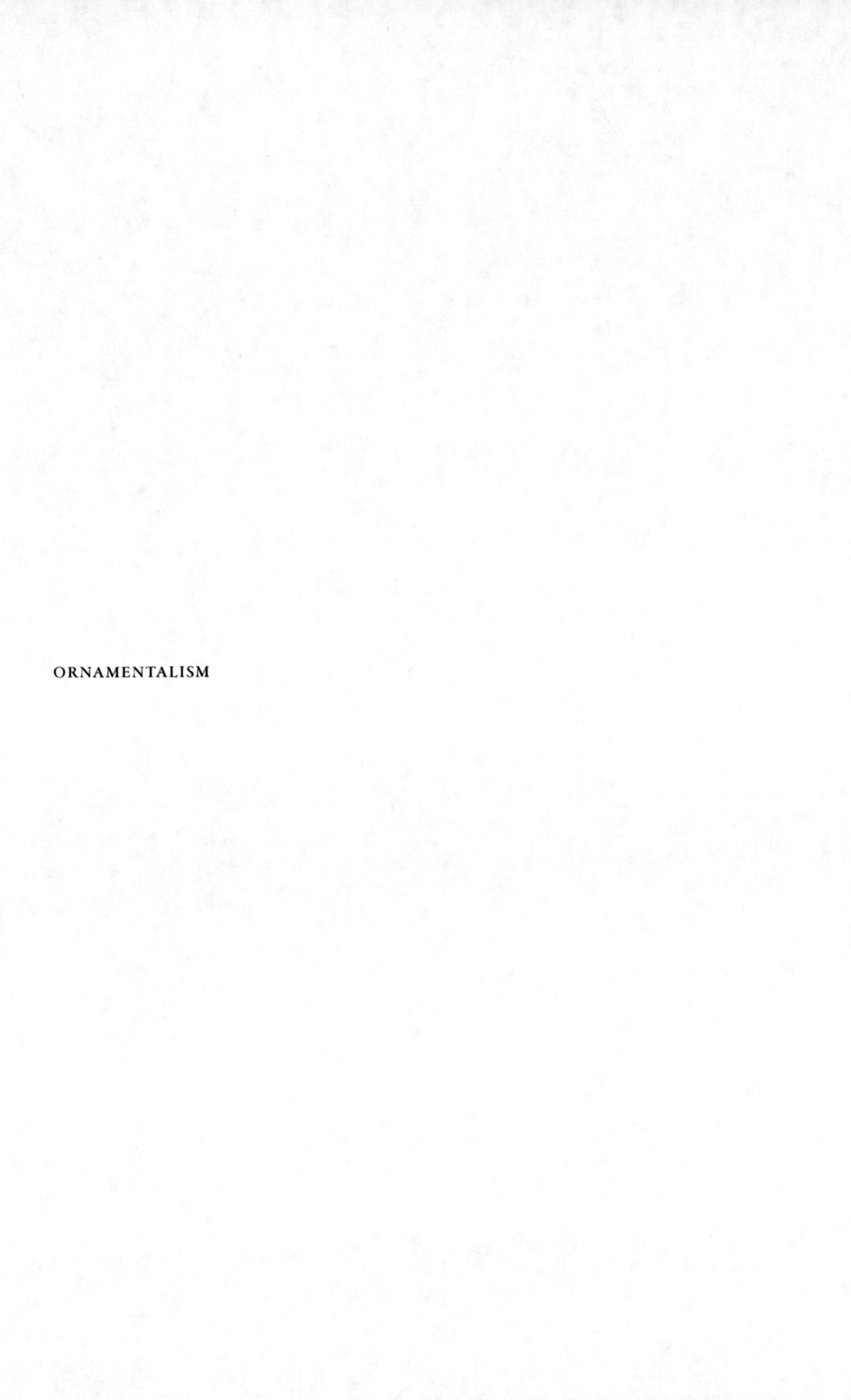

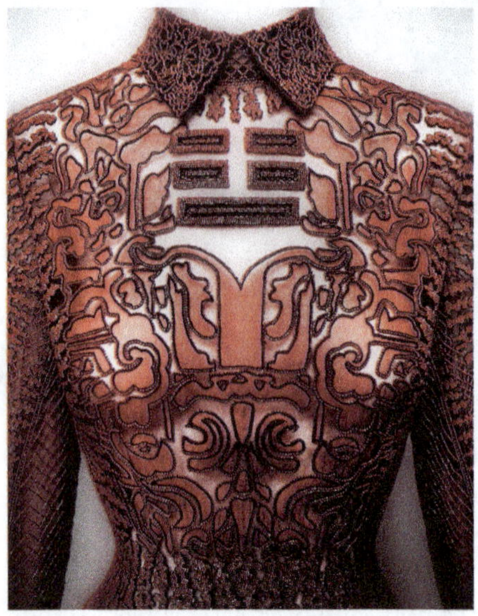

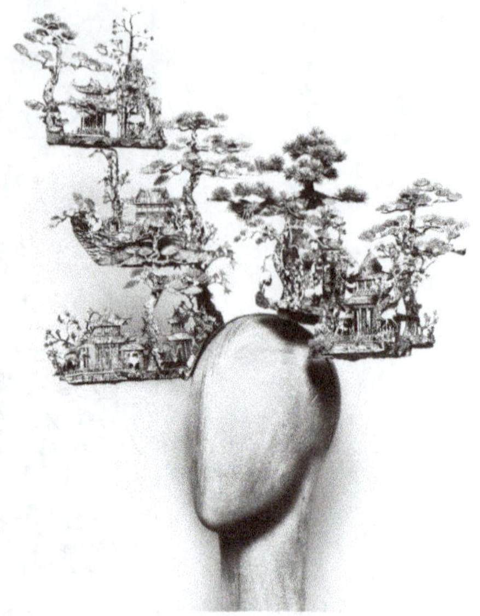

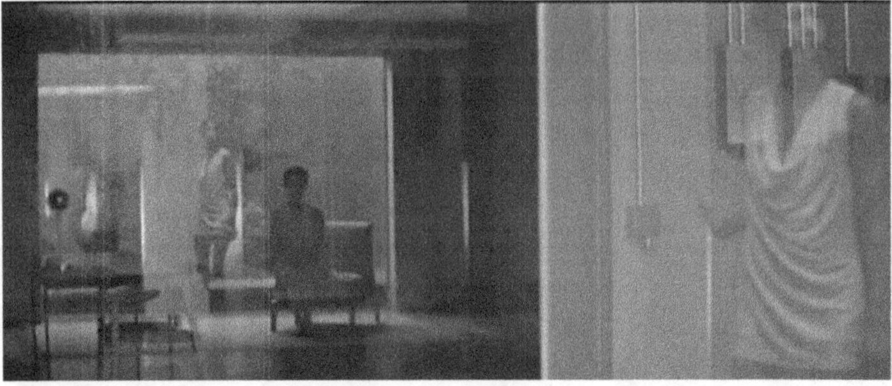

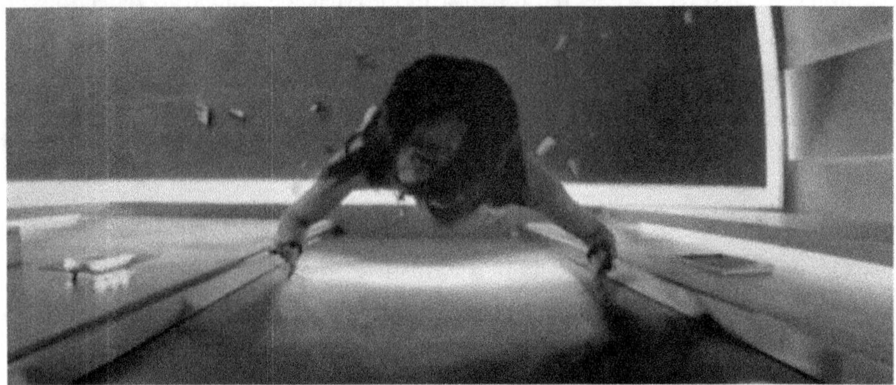